THE FATHER OF THE PROPHET

THE FATHER OF THE PROPHET

Stories and Insights from the Life of
Joseph Smith, Sr.

MARK L. McCONKIE

BOOKCRAFT
Salt Lake City, Utah

Library of Congress Catalog Card Number: 93–71117
ISBN 0–88494–887–0

First Printing, 1993

Printed in the United States of America

To
Amelia Smith McConkie,
one of Father Smith's own

Contents

Preface

Joseph Smith, Sr., fathered one of the greatest lineages of prophetic souls ever to minister among men. In this he is like Adam, Abraham, and Alma the Elder, penetrating the generations by the power of his teachings and example. He was foreordained to greatness, and like his prophetic sons he lived great and died great in the eyes of God and his people.

The greatness that is Father Smith is found only by placing him in *his* context, which is both prophetic and patriarchal. The historical, cultural, economic, political, and social conditions that surrounded him are important and will, I trust, one day be explored by others more competent in those fields than I. My intent, however, has been quite different. I have sought to understand Joseph Smith, Sr., as the father of the Prophet, as the first Patriarch to the Church in this dispensation, and as an example whose life is, in so many ways, worthy of emulation. We remember Father Smith because his very life is a sermon on humility, on overcoming affliction, on being true to the truth, on bearing testimony of the Restoration without fear of man, on living worthy of inspiration, and on the office and conduct of the Patriarch. If ever a man personified honesty, it was Father Smith; if ever a Patriarch pronounced inspired blessings, it was Father Smith; if ever a man was loved and trusted of heaven, it was Father Smith; and if ever a man consecrated his all to the upbuilding of Zion, it was the saintly Father Smith. His heart was pure, and his ministry, approved of God. He did all that the Lord required of him, and therein lay the essence of the man: he was true and faithful in all things.

We see him not as the world sees him, for the world has always focused on his poverty, on the simplicity of his life-style, on the fact that he was surrounded by a world of prejudice and superstition, or on some other irrelevancy—irrelevant because the issue at stake is so much greater than mortal eye can see; it is something the spirit of man must discern and feel. The archaeologist speaks of what the spade uncovers, the historian of what the diaries of the dead reveal, and the political scientist of what legislative assemblies intended. Our task is larger than any of these, for we cannot understand this man without understanding the gospel that he embraced, loving the men and the ideas that he loved, and feeling the power of that God to whom he prayed. There is an eternal law which stipulates that like embraces like, that it takes a prophet to understand a prophet, and that just as the ungodly cannot understand the things of God, neither can they comprehend the works and motives of those whom God chooses as his own.

To study the life of Joseph Smith, Sr., is to learn the lessons that his life teaches. And, somehow, to know Father Smith is to know more about the Prophet Joseph Smith, more about the restoration of the gospel, and more about the workings of the Great Almighty, who chose both the Prophet and his father in the premortal councils of eternity. Father Smith was, in many ways, the mold in which the Prophet Joseph Smith was formed. On this count alone his life is worthy of our consideration.

On a technical note, in the pages that follow I have often standardized spelling and punctuation in quotations from sources such as diaries, journals, and letters; this has been done to facilitate readability.

In the course of gathering the many pieces of information that fold together to paint a picture of the father of the Prophet, I incurred a debt of gratitude to Frederick (Rick) M. Huchel, who spent many hours in books and in libraries hunting down and sifting through the big and little of early Church history. His valuable cranium was an invaluable sounding board, and I am grateful for and bettered by both the spirit and content of his assistance. Finally, I express my appreciation to Garry Garff of Bookcraft for his careful attention to detail in the editing process.

Overview of the Life and Times
of Joseph Smith, Sr.

His Life	His Times
1771: Born of Asael and Mary Duty Smith at Topsfield, Mass.	**1771:** Benjamin Franklin begins work on his *Autobiography*
	1773: New England patriots/activists conduct Boston Tea Party
1775: Lucy Mack, future wife of Joseph Smith, Sr., born at Gilsum, N.H.	**1775:** Patrick Henry gives speech at Virginia Convention: "Give me liberty, or give me death!"
	1776: Thomas Paine publishes *Common Sense*; Declaration of Independence signed
	1782: American revolutionary war ends
	1789: U.S. Constitution ratified; first elections held, George Washington elected president
1796: On January 24, marries Lucy Mack in Tunbridge, Orange Co., Vt.	**1796:** George Washington gives "Farewell Address"
1798: Son Alvin born at Tunbridge, Orange Co., Vt.	**1799:** George Washington dies

His Life

His Times

1800:   Son Hyrum born at
        Tunbridge, Orange Co., Vt.

                                          1801:   House of Representatives
                                                  chooses Thomas Jefferson as
1802:   About this time Father   third U.S. president
        Smith enters ginseng
        business; is defrauded

1803:   Daughter Sophronia born at
        Tunbridge, Orange Co., Vt.

1805:   Joseph Smith, Jr., born at   1805:   Thomas Jefferson inaugurated
        Sharon, Windsor Co., Vt.   for second term as U.S.
                                                  president; Lewis and Clark
                                                  reach the Pacific

1808:   Son Samuel H. born at
        Tunbridge, Orange Co., Vt.   1809:   Abraham Lincoln born at
                                                  Hodgenville, Ky.

1810:   Son Ephraim born at
        Royalton, Windsor Co., Vt.;
        dies eleven days later

1811:   Son William born at
        Royalton, Windsor Co., Vt.

1812:   Daughter Catherine born at   1812:   U.S. declares war against
        West Lebanon, Grafton Co.,   Great Britain
        N.H.

1813:   About this time, Joseph, Jr.,   1813:   James Madison is
        contracts typhoid, infection   inaugurated for second term
        moves to leg, operation   as U.S. president
        follows
                                          1814:   British capture city of
                                                  Washington

1816:   Son Don Carlos born at   1816:   James Monroe elected
        Norwich, Windsor Co., Vt.;   president; inaugurated March
        Smith family moves from   1817
        Vermont, locates in Palmyra,
        N.Y.

His Life   # His Times

1820:   In spring, Prophet Joseph
        Smith receives First Vision

1821:   Daughter Lucy born at
        Palmyra, Ontario Co., N.Y.

1823:   In September, Moroni
        appears for first time to
        Prophet Joseph Smith;
        Father Smith weeps for joy;
        in November, son Alvin dies

1825:   Unable to make payments,
        Smiths lose home; forced to
        rent

1827:   In September, Prophet
        Joseph receives gold plates
        from Moroni

1829:   Book of Mormon translation
        completed; Palmyra *Reflector*
        begins to publish attacks
        against Book of Mormon and
        Smiths

1830:   Book of Mormon published;
        on April 6, Church is
        organized, and Father and
        Mother Smith are baptized;
        in June, Father Smith is
        ordained a priest and given
        first license to preach; takes
        missionary journey to his
        parents and family

1820:   Daniel Boone dies in
        Missouri, age eighty-five;
        James Monroe reelected
        president

1821:   Davy Crockett elected to
        Tennessee legislature

1823:   Daniel Webster again takes
        seat in U.S. House of
        Representatives, where Henry
        Clay presides as Speaker

1825:   John Quincy Adams
        inaugurated as sixth U.S.
        president

1826:   On July 4, John Adams dies
        at Quincy, Mass., and
        Thomas Jefferson dies at
        Monticello, Va.

1829:   Andrew Jackson inaugurated
        as seventh U.S. president

1830:   Andrew Jackson signs the
        Indian Removal Act, giving
        Indians perpetual title to
        lands in the West, financial
        assistance, and government
        guarantee of security;
        population of New York is
        about 200,000

His Life	His Times
1831: Smiths move to Kirtland, Ohio; Saints also established in Independence, Mo.; Father Smith ordained a high priest	1831: Charles Darwin sails in H.M.S. *Beagle* to S. America, New Zealand, and Australia
	1832: Andrew Jackson reelected for second term as U.S. president
1833: Ordained as Patriarch to the Church	
1834: Called to high council in Kirtland, Ohio; holds family blessing meeting, gives blessings to his children	1834: Abraham Lincoln (at twenty-five) enters politics as assemblyman in Illinois legislature
1836: Attends Kirtland Temple dedication; with his brother John goes on mission to eastern states	1836: Sam Houston sworn in as first president of Republic of Texas; Martin Van Buren elected eighth U.S. president
1837: Sustained as Assistant Counselor to the Prophet Joseph Smith	1837: Financial panic sweeps across United States; many banks close; unemployment mounts
1838: Leaves Kirtland for Far West, Mo., where, under weight of persecution, his health is broken	1838: Iowa Territory is established, and Robert Lucas is appointed governor; Oberlin College, in Ohio, becomes first American institution of higher learning to admit women on equal basis with men; in England, coronation of Queen Victoria takes place
1839: Leaves Far West and goes to Commerce (near Nauvoo), Ill.	
1840: On September 14, at age sixty-nine, dies at Nauvoo, "worn out with exposure and toil"; while on his deathbed, in vision sees Alvin; before dying, gives final father's blessings to his children and their spouses	1840: William Henry Harrison elected ninth U.S. president

His Life

His Times

1841: President William Henry
Harrison dies, and Vice
President John Tyler becomes
president; Horace Greeley
begins to publish *New York
Tribune*

1844: In June, Prophet Joseph
Smith and his brother
Hyrum are murdered by a
mob at Carthage, Ill.

1856: Mother Smith dies at
Nauvoo, Ill.

Joseph Smith, Sr., Family Tree

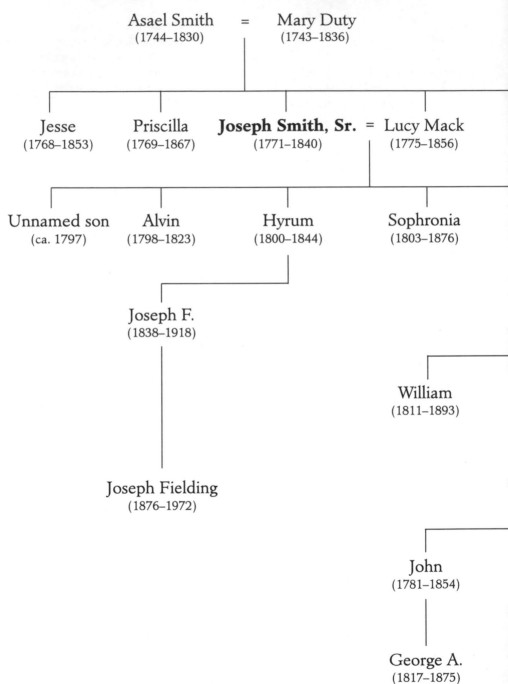

Asael Smith (1744–1830) = Mary Duty (1743–1836)

Jesse (1768–1853) — Priscilla (1769–1867) — **Joseph Smith, Sr.** (1771–1840) = Lucy Mack (1775–1856)

Unnamed son (ca. 1797) — Alvin (1798–1823) — Hyrum (1800–1844) — Sophronia (1803–1876)

Joseph F. (1838–1918)

William (1811–1893)

Joseph Fielding (1876–1972)

John (1781–1854)

George A. (1817–1875)

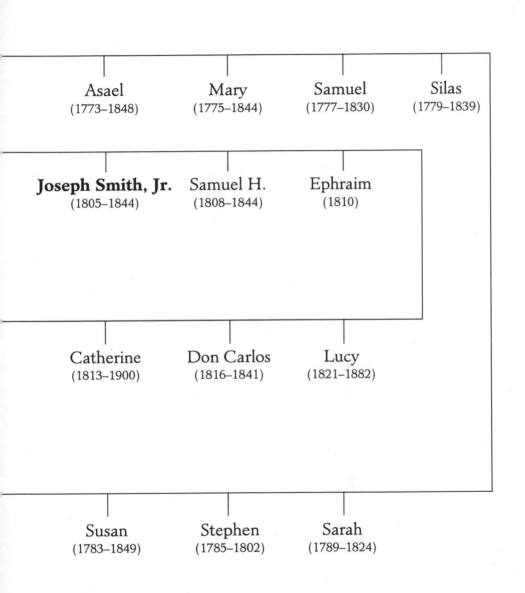

Asael
(1773–1848)

Mary
(1775–1844)

Samuel
(1777–1830)

Silas
(1779–1839)

Joseph Smith, Jr.
(1805–1844)

Samuel H.
(1808–1844)

Ephraim
(1810)

Catherine
(1813–1900)

Don Carlos
(1816–1841)

Lucy
(1821–1882)

Susan
(1783–1849)

Stephen
(1785–1802)

Sarah
(1789–1824)

CHAPTER 1

"After the Name of His Father"

In the person of Joseph Smith we have the greatest prophet since Jesus.[1] He was foreordained to the great mission he performed. All of the ancient prophets looked forward with gladness to the restoration of the gospel in these latter days[2] and to the role that Joseph Smith would play in that restoration. Indeed, except for the prophecies dealing with Christ and his mission, there is no subject that receives more prophetic attention by the ancient prophets than does the restoration of the gospel in the latter days.

In many instances these prophecies are remarkably specific, though much of what is contained in them is seen and heard, as is ever the case, only by those who have eyes to see and ears to hear. Nevertheless, we are told in holy writ of the First Vision and the climate surrounding it, as well as some of the very language Christ would utter to the young prophet.[3] The ancient Saints also knew that Joseph Smith was the Elias who was to come and "restore all things, as it is written by the prophets,"[4] and that this was to be done as a preparation for the coming of the Lord.[5] The Lord told Moses that Joseph Smith would be "like unto thee,"[6] and Isaiah referred to him as a "root of Jesse," whose mission would include gathering Israel "from the four corners of the earth."[7] Isaiah also wrote that Joseph Smith would give to the world sacred scriptures that would pull people

Portrait of Joseph Smith, Jr., by an unknown artist

out of apostasy, and even that portions of these writings would be delivered to and rejected by "one that is learned."[8] These writings would be contained on sacred metal plates, and so anxious were the ancient Saints that these writings come forth, that they exercised faith and prayed in behalf of Joseph Smith and the work he would do.[9] Ancients knew not only of the Lord's promise that he would bless Joseph Smith in his ministry[10] but also that he would be allowed to show the plates to three witnesses "as a testimony against the world at the last day."[11] The Savior himself announced that the Book of Mormon would come forth, in spite of the fact that wicked men would seek to "hurt" and "mar" Joseph Smith. All this was said with the dire warning that those who rejected the Lord's words, brought to light through the ministry of Joseph Smith, would be, in the Savior's words, "cut off from among my people who are of the covenant."[12] Clearly, it is the prophetic testimony of the ancient prophets that the measure of one's spiritual integrity in our day is determined by how he or she receives the message that Jesus is the Christ, as announced in the Book of Mormon and in the testimony of Joseph Smith.[13]

It becomes a self-evident truth that the testimony of the Book of Mormon's truthfulness and the testimony of Joseph Smith's prophetic calling are one and the same. When Joseph in ancient Egypt prophesied that one of his descendants—Joseph Smith—would be the means of restoring the lost sheep of Israel to the fold of Christ, he said he would do so through the words in the Book of Mormon.[14] So specific was Joseph's language that he not only called the Prophet Joseph Smith by name but also announced that his father would have the same name. "His [i.e., the Prophet Joseph Smith's] name shall be called after me," said the ancient Joseph; "and it shall be after the name of his father."[15]

Both Joseph Smith and his father were foreordained to be named Joseph. But was the foreordination limited to the names they bore? We have already observed that the ancient prophets knew Joseph Smith was foreordained to be the Elias through whom all things would be restored. But what can we say of his father?

The Prophet Joseph Smith taught that "every man who has a calling to minister to the inhabitants of the world was ordained to that very purpose in the Grand Council of heaven before this world was."[16] Could we expect anything less in the case of the man appointed to preside in the home in which the great prophet of the Restoration was to learn to pray, to love the Lord, to read the scriptures, to obey the commandments, and to love and serve his fellowmen? Could we even begin to imagine that the great God of heaven, who knows all things, and before whom all things are ever present, and before whom even a sparrow cannot fall without his notice—could we even begin to imagine that such a God would leave to chance the mortal homelife and training of the foreordained prophet of the Restoration?

Over the generations we seem to hear the Apostle Paul remind us that the same God who "is not the author of confusion"[17] no more rules his dominions by happenstance or accident than he does by chance, and that just as he appointed unto all Israel a time to be born, he also stretched forth his hand and foreordained Joseph Smith, Sr., to that great prophetic work which was his. And—let it be stated clearly!— Joseph Smith, Sr., was a majestic prophet in his own right. He dreamed inspired dreams and beheld inspired visions; he entertained angels, spoke prophetically of future events, healed the sick, taught and baptized many, constantly gave inspired insight and counsel to the Saints and others, and both blessed and cursed in the name of the Lord.

We are, then, led to ask: What better place to raise a prophet than in the home of a prophet? What better way to prepare Joseph Smith to confide in visions than to give him a father who first had visions? What better way to prepare Joseph Smith to think about the religious state of affairs in which he lived than to give him a father who would boldly subpoena the creeds of men before the court of his reason and reject all that was false? What better way to prepare the young prophet to confront sectarian piety than to give him a father who would first reject man-made dogma? And what better way to inspire the young and future prophet with a love of scripture than to give him a father who read and loved the scriptures? And, finally, what better way to reinforce and reteach every principle and truth that the father would teach the young prophet than to give him a mother who was the spiritual equal of the father?

We remind ourselves that the father of the Prophet won the trust and confidence of angels. Moroni, for example, instructed the Prophet to tell his father of the angel's visit, for Moroni knew that this particular father was prepared in the worlds afore to believe and accept the young prophet's testimony. Thus Moroni urged the Prophet Joseph forward, saying: "He will believe every word you say to him."[18] Moroni's promise proved correct, for the Prophet's father, upon hearing young Joseph's account, said: "My son, be not disobedient to this heavenly vision!"[19]

Just as Moroni trusted Joseph Smith, Sr., so also did the Prophet Joseph Smith, who throughout his entire life felt no reluctance either in seeking his counsel or in referring others to him for comfort, counsel, or blessings. The great issue, however, is that God trusted him, as is evidenced by the kinds of experiences that God gave him. These experiences shaped and molded the Prophet's father, who in turn played a central role in shaping and molding the Prophet himself.

But the mission of Father Smith—for so he was called by the Saints of his day—included more than teaching, preparing, and sustaining the Prophet Joseph Smith in his prophetic role. In addition, Father Smith is a role model for all Israel—a pattern all might emulate. When Robert B. Thompson spoke at the funeral services of Father Smith, he prophetically announced that "the whole Church will copy his examples, walk in his footsteps, and emulate his faith and virtuous actions."[20]

And so it should be. Salvation is a matter of doing what saved people before us have done. Jesus, of course, is the perfect exemplar, and we are commanded to follow his example.[21] Because Apostles and prophets are, to borrow a phrase, "imitators of God,"[22] we emulate their righteous examples as well—and therein lies much of the reason why we examine here the life of Father Smith: he is a study in gospel devotion and compliance, and as we watch his triumph over life's struggles, and as we see his unbending commitment to the cause of Christ, we not only see an example of what can be done but also feel an assurance that we can overcome the world and become pure, even as Christ is pure.[23] Moreover, because one life of faith is worth a thousand commentaries, the life of Father Smith should not be read but studied. In it there is an echo of the eternities, and, somehow, by coming to know him more fully we see eternity more clearly.

But great men speak to us only insofar as we have ears and souls to hear them. Inasmuch as the things of the Spirit are understood only by the power of the Spirit, the life of Father Smith is seen correctly only with the eye of faith. The carnal mind cannot comprehend communication with angels, seeing visions, predicting future events, healing the sick and enfeebled by the power of faith, enduring persecution and privation and thanking God for the very experience, or preferring to help the homeless rather than seek wealth or comfort. The carnal mind, then, cannot comprehend Father Smith, for it cannot comprehend that struggle is the law of growth, that persecution and opposition sanctify, and that obedience exalts.

The standard against which we judge Father Smith is the gospel standard. Let us, then, try to understand and judge him as God would judge him, for he is one of God's own. To watch him exercise faith, overcome oppression, preside in the family, speak prophetic patriarchal blessings, and counsel prophetic sons is to feast on a Christlike example; it is to taste of the good fruits of the gospel.

Come, then, let us dine.

CHAPTER 2

"Mine Aged Servant, Joseph Smith, Sen."

In the unimpaired vigor of youth Father Smith carried a powerful cast-iron frame and was built foursquare both in body and spirit. He stretched six feet two inches high and, said the Prophet Joseph Smith, "was very straight, and remarkably well proportioned. His ordinary weight was about two hundred pounds, and he was very strong and active. In his younger days he was famed as a wrestler, and, Jacob like, he never wrestled with but one man whom he could not throw."[1] He was a striking, handsome man, and his grandson recalled that "in stature he had no superior in the family. Not one of his sons excelled him in physical appearance."[2] William Henry Bigler remembered that "he was like his son the Prophet, large but not fat, rather tall and big-boned and heavy muscled."[3]

Like unto Abraham

Age and the mellowing effects of hardship and service conferred upon Father Smith a visible, patriarchal dignity that reflected the inner certainties of eternity. Those who knew him reached to describe his character, though they could never quite grasp it in full. "Of a fine physique," said Eliza R. Snow,

Topsfield, Massachusetts, home in which Joseph Smith, Sr.,
was born on July 12, 1771

"he was more than ordinarily prepossessing in personal appearance. His kind, affable, dignified and unassuming manner naturally inspired strangers with feelings of love and reverence. To me he was the veritable personification of my idea of the ancient Father Abraham." And, she said, peering into his soul, "in his decisions he was strictly just; what can be said of very few, may be truly said of him, in judging between man and man: his judgment could not be biased by either personal advantage, sympathy, or affection. Such a man was worthy of being the father of the first prophet of the last dispensation."[4]

When Father Smith and some others were accused by apostates of having caused a riot in the Kirtland Temple, Eliza could only smile. His very appearance, life, and character spoke against the charge: "The idea of such a man as Father Smith—so patriarchal in appearance—so circumspect in deportment and dignified in his manners, being guilty of riot, was at once ludicrous and farcical to all sane-minded persons."[5]

Eliza's brother Lorenzo, before joining the Church, came to a patriarchal blessing meeting at which Father Smith was giving blessings to the Saints. "Anyone seeing Father Smith as he then appeared," said Lorenzo of the sixty-four-year-old Patriarch, "and having read of old Father Abraham in the scriptures, would be apt to think that Father Smith looked a good deal like Abraham must have looked." Then, echoing both the heart and soul of all the Saints, Lorenzo continued: "I do not know that any man among the Saints was more loved than Father Smith." And, as if to explain why the Saints so loved "the venerable and venerated father of the Prophet,"[6] as Edward Stevenson called him, Lorenzo concluded: "When any one was seriously sick Father Smith would be called for, whether it was night or day. He was as noble and generous a man as I have ever known. . . .

"At the first sight, his presence impressed me with a feeling of love and reverence for him. I had never before seen age so prepossessing. Father Joseph Smith, the Patriarch, was indeed a noble specimen of aged manhood."[7]

Upon meeting her future husband and during those early moments of courtship when she decided to marry, Lucy Mack—the future "Mother Smith"—must have felt the peaceful confidence of this man whom one writer called "her gentle-voiced, blue-eyed lover."[8] Some fifty years after their marriage, Lucy referred to him as "my husband, an affectionate companion and tender father as ever blessed the confidence of a family."[9]

If we can judge greatness by a person's overcoming the world, by his subordinating personal ambition to the will of heaven, and by his hearing and heeding the promptings of the Holy Spirit, then Father Smith is incontestably one of the greatest of the great. The Prophet testified: "[My father] was a great and good man. The envy of knaves and fools was heaped upon him, and this was his lot and portion all the days of his life. He was of noble stature and possessed a high, and holy, and exalted, and virtuous mind. His soul soared above all those mean and groveling principles that are so congenial to the human heart." And, the Prophet adds, in a note which invites us all to be better, "he never did a mean act, that might be said was ungenerous in his life, to my knowledge. . . . The memory of his noble deeds rests with ponderous weight upon my mind, and many of his kind and parental words to me are written on the tablet of my heart."[10]

A Man of Prayer

A man's character is often better illustrated than described—and nothing reveals heart and character more fully than prayer. "My father's religious habits were strictly pious and moral," said William of his father, adding that the family met every morning and evening for family prayer. A hymn was "sung while upon the bending knees. My parents, father and mother, poured out their souls to God, the donor of all blessings, to keep and guard their children and keep them from sin and from all evil works."[11] William also said: "We always had family prayers since I can remember. I well remember father used to carry his spectacles in his vest pocket, . . . and when us boys saw him feel for his specks, we knew that was a signal to get ready for prayer, and if we did not notice it mother would say 'William,' or whoever was the negligent one, 'get ready for prayer.'"[12]

To hear Father Smith pray, we learn from Mosiah Hancock, was to hear honest, simple faith clothed with words. Brother Hancock tells of dining in the Prophet's home with both the Prophet and Father Smith. Gazing on the boiled corn on the Prophet's table, Brother Hancock thought it a princely meal: "The corn seemed to be of the King Phillip variety of yellow flint. Brother Joseph asked his father to return thanks on the food, and Father Smith took up an ear of corn in his right hand holding it between his thumb and forefinger, and said, 'Oh, God, the Eternal Father, we thank thee for this corn, and pray in the name of Jesus Christ to bless it to the strengthening of our bodies, and the strengthening of our stomachs till Thou can provide something better; which we ask of Thee in the name of Jesus Christ, Amen.'" Tears streamed down the cheeks of the grateful Patriarch, and, said Brother Hancock, "I thought it a repast of the most excellent type."[13]

Searching for Truth

The same unassuming honesty that characterized Father Smith's prayers also governed the instructions given in the Smith home. Father and Mother Smith earnestly taught their children about God. When the children were young, Father

Smith taught them in his own home school and used the Bible as a text.[14] Indeed, as early as 1797 the newly married Father Smith joined a Universalist Society, which was a group characterized by beliefs that the mainstream churches of the day erred in significant biblical understanding.[15] This strong-minded trust in the Bible was so thoroughly infused into the walk and thought of his children, that when young Joseph sought religious understanding he turned automatically to the scriptures, "believing," he said, "as I was taught, that they contained the word of God."[16]

It is, of course, hazardous to attempt to describe the spiritual stature of Father Smith in either a paragraph or a page, for spiritual growth is a process and not an event. It takes place over time. The patriarchal figure we see in the Kirtland, Missouri, and Nauvoo years is much more spiritually mature than the energetic young truth seeker living in Topsfield and Tunbridge. Yet even in these early years, up to and including the early years of marriage, Father Smith had strong instincts for right and wrong; he possessed a godly integrity that set him apart from the masses of mankind,[17] and he trusted, as has been noted, the Bible as the word of God. He attended church meetings of different sorts but was never so committed to any particular denomination that he would permit himself to be either baptized or named as a member, even though other members of the family did.[18]

It was in this early period of his marriage that his ever-sensitive wife received a comforting vision in which the Lord consoled her with the understanding that, though seemingly slow to mature, her husband was oak solid. "While we were living in the town of Tunbridge [,Vermont]," she said, "my mind became deeply impressed with the subject of religion." Consequently, she attended Methodist meetings, "and in order to oblige me," she explained, "my husband accompanied me; but when this came to the ears of his oldest brother"—the frenzied and recusant Jesse—"he was so displeased and said so much in regard to the matter that my husband thought it best to desist. He said that he considered it hardly worth our while to attend the meetings any longer as it would prove of but little advantage to us; besides this, it gave our friends such disagreeable feelings. I was considerably hurt by this, yet I made no reply." Rather, in characteristic Smith fashion, "I retired to a grove not far distant, where I prayed to the Lord in behalf of my husband—that the true gospel might be presented to him and that his heart might be softened so as to receive it, or, that he might become more religiously inclined. After praying some time in this manner," she returned home and, after having gone to bed, had a dream, or vision, in which she saw two trees stretching in a beautiful meadow. One was stern, stubborn, and unbending. The other wore a brilliant gold belt and gloried in the celestial breezes of heaven as they washed through its branches and leaves.

She was given to know that the interpretation of the dream was "that the stubborn and unyielding tree was like Jesse; that the other, more pliant and flexible, was like Joseph, my husband; that the breath of heaven, which passed over them, was the pure and undefiled gospel of the Son of God, which gospel Jesse would always resist, but which Joseph, when he was more advanced in life, would hear and receive with his whole heart, and rejoice therein; and unto him would be added intelligence, happiness, glory, and everlasting life."[19] Thus, wise enough to sense that by praying for her then less vigorous husband she would bind her heart to his, Lucy learned what history would later demonstrate: that the then budding Father Smith would one day blossom into the full bloom of gospel power.

Serving in the Temple

Father Smith's growth and development did come, step by step, and it included using the temple as a house of worship. After the dedication of the Kirtland Temple, the Prophet Joseph instructed that a schedule be made to govern its usage. On Thursday evenings a prayer meeting, generally conducted by Father Smith, was held in the lower part of the temple.[20] The first Thursday of each month was reserved for a fast meeting, and Father Smith developed the habit of going to the temple early on those fasting days, before the arrival of others, to pray. When the congregation of Saints arrived he would give counsel and instruction.[21] According to Eliza R. Snow, he "so strictly disciplined himself in the observance of fasting, as not even to wet his lips with water until after the dismissal of the meeting at four P.M."[22]

The spirit of these meetings was often pentecostal, and

Lorenzo Snow said that on occasions such as these the Saints "had the gift of prophecy—the gift of tongues—the interpretation of tongues—visions and marvelous dreams were related—the singing of heavenly choirs was heard, and wonderful manifestations of the healing power, through the administrations of the Elders, were witnessed. The sick were healed—the deaf made to hear—the blind to see and the lame to walk, in very many instances."[23] It was of such experiences that Robert B. Thompson spoke when he said that Father Smith's "daily delight" was to pray and meditate in the temple, and that there he "trod its sacred aisles, solitary and alone," long before the sun rose, and was rewarded by having the visions of heaven unfolded to his view.[24] And for our part, as we cast our gaze back upon those purifying moments, we are left to ask, What greater measure of a man is there than to be so trusted of heaven that God would open the rich treasures of eternity to his view?

Always Poor

While the treasures of eternity were Father Smith's, those of mortality never were. Our best records suggest that in the Topsfield home of his father, Asael, the Smith family was well provided for, and that the early Tunbridge years were also comfortable, if not prosperous. From the early seasons of marriage until his death, however, Father Smith and his family were constantly hounded by a wherreting indigency. Shortly after marrying, he was swindled by a business partner, losing his entire investment. The recovery from this loss required the sale of his farm and the expenditure of his wife's one-thousand-dollar marriage dowry.[25] The subsequent years were lean and eventually difficult. By 1816 the hard times, accompanied by three successive crop failures on the farm, pushed the Smiths out of Vermont and into Palmyra, New York. Upon leaving Vermont, family resources were further reduced by dishonest creditors, so that when they arrived in Palmyra their circumstances were, as Mother Smith described them, "destitute."[26] The Smiths lived on quarter-rations for some time thereafter, though Father Smith was able to provide "a scanty but honest living for himself and family."[27] If we can believe Pomeroy Tucker, the Smiths were so unmoneyed that "fresh meat was a rarity" at their dining table.[28] One local resident described Father Smith as "a poor man" who with his family "lived in squalid poverty";[29] Ezra Pierce remembered that "they were poor,"[30] and W. W. Phelps, not yet a member of the Church, wrote saying that, "the family of Smiths is poor."[31]

The Smiths were industrious, however, and therefore experienced economic ups as well as downs, though it is safe to conclude that they generally seemed about as poor as Job's turkey. It is clear that they lost their farm in Palmyra because of their inability to make the final purchase payment;[32] that when the Prophet went to secure the gold plates from Moroni neither he nor his parents owned so much as a chest with a lock and key in which the plates could be carried;[33] and that on the morning when the Prophet returned home after having gone to Cumorah to get the plates, there was "not a shilling in the house."[34] In the autumn of 1830, Father Smith spent a month in debtor's prison because he was unable to pay a fourteen-dollar debt,[35] and throughout his life indigence often compelled him and Mother Smith to live with their children, or compelled their children (and sometimes grandchildren) to live with them. While living in Kirtland, he was at least twice warned out of town because of his poverty,[36] and, to his dying moment, he never owned property in Nauvoo.

Consecration and Charity

While he lived most of his life with the wolf at his door, having an empty or near-empty purse, Father Smith was nevertheless ever willing to consecrate his all to the upbuilding of the kingdom. In October 1831—a mere four days before the formal writ of warning was issued by the Kirtland Overseers of the Poor—at a conference of the Church in Orange, Cuyahoga County, Ohio, Father Smith "said that he had nothing to consecrate to the Lord of the things of the Earth, yet he felt to consecrate himself and [his] family." He also said that he "was thankful that God had given him a place among his saints, [and] felt willing to labor for their good."[37]

And labor he did, seeming in those earlier days to sense what the Prophet expressed some years later: "When we consecrate our property to the Lord, it is to administer to the wants of the poor and needy according to the laws of God. . . . For a man to consecrate his property, his wife and children to the Lord is nothing more nor less than to feed the hungry, cloth the naked, visit the widows and fatherless, the sick and afflicted; and do all he can to administer to their relief in their afflictions, and for himself and his house to serve the Lord."[38]

Had the Prophet written this definition as an obituary for his father, he could not have more perfectly summarized the sixty-nine years that silvered Father Smith's hair. In a moment of candid reflection, Mother Smith, viewing the "trifling inconveniences" which the Saints experienced, some years after the martyrdom of the Prophet and his brother Hyrum recalled the storm she and her husband had weathered: "How often I have parted every bed in the house for the accommodation of the brethren, and then laid a single blanket on the floor for my husband and myself, while Joseph and Emma slept upon the same floor, with nothing but their cloaks for both bed and bedding."[39]

If anything, the kindly, charitable spirit that governed both Father and Mother Smith was too broad; they thought too much with their hearts. Their home had become "the hospitality house of the community."[40] Consequently, they received a great many visitors. With the coming of many visitors, however, came an attendant load of concerns and exhaustions. Thus, in March 1833 the Lord gave a revelation through the Prophet Joseph Smith that included counsel for Father Smith (whom the Lord affectionately referred to as "mine aged servant, Joseph Smith, Sen."[41]). "Let your families be small," the Lord said, in part, "especially mine aged servant Joseph Smith's, Sen., as pertaining to those who do not belong to your families; that those things that are provided for you, to bring to pass my work, be not taken from you and given to those that are not worthy—and thereby you be hindered in accomplishing those things which I have commanded you."[42] In this, Father Smith appears to have been like his son the Prophet Joseph, who the Lord said would not "have strength" in temporal labors but was commanded to magnify his office in the priesthood.[43]

In the case of Father Smith, the charitable virtue could easily grow into a burdensome vice. There was a limit. His heart notwithstanding, he could not care for all.[44]

But we are careful neither to condemn nor criticize, for his motives were right and his instincts pure, and if men are judged by their motives, Father Smith's crown is celestial. By making himself the friend of the needy and homeless, he became the friend of God, as well as of the Saints. In 1835 when the young Lydia Gates and Newel Knight joined hands and hearts in marriage, they did so under the blessing of the aged Patriarch. It was the first marriage performed by the Prophet Joseph Smith, as the elders had not previously been authorized by the state to perform marriages. Seymour Brunson had received a license to perform marriages while in southern Ohio, and thus the Saints generally went to him. The Prophet, however, chose to perform this one. According to the published account, on "the evening of the 23rd [of November, 1835,] about a dozen people gathered in Brother Hyrum's parlor, all of them intimate friends of the Patriarch and his family." Joseph performed the ceremony and then spoke prophetically, declaring that his enemies would never restrain him from performing marriages as they had hitherto sought to do. Father Smith then gave the happy yokemates "a hearty invitation to remain with his family during the Winter, and not attempt to set up housekeeping until they removed to their western home. They gladly accepted his offer, and spent several busy, happy months in this pleasant home."[45]

Loving and Helping the Saints

Father Smith's sensitivity to the needs of others was really nothing more than his love of the Saints, manifest in what he said and did. It was, we trust, the same sensitivity that enabled him to respond to spiritual promptings—and who is to doubt that many of his kind acts grew out of simple promptings that less sensitive souls would have either ignored or explained away? When the Kirtland Temple was dedicated, for example, the Saints were notified that infants in arms would not be admitted into the dedicatory services. According to Eliza R. Snow, one sister, apparently unaware of the ruling, traveled a long distance with her infant child, then but six weeks old. Upon arriving and learning of the restriction, the mother appealed to Father Smith for help. "The ever generous and kind-hearted father volunteered to take the responsibility on himself, and told her to take her child, at the same time giving the mother a promise that her babe should make no disturbance; and the promise was verified. But when the congregation shouted hosanna, that babe joined in the shout."[46]

When Cyrena Dustin, a faithful young convert who had no family but the Saints, needed assistance in obtaining employment, it was Father Smith who found her work.[47] Edward Stevenson was injured by an overturning wagon. He reported that "the first man who came to my relief after my arrival at home was Patriarch Joseph Smith." But for Father Smith it was not enough simply to come and visit the injured man. Rather, said Stevenson, "he helped me from the horse, for I was unable to stand alone without help. The Patriarch rubbed my legs which were swollen— for the chains, tightened by the weight of the horses, drew the flesh nearly to the bones. 'But,'" said the faithful Patriarch, "'you shall be healed and walk around tomorrow.'" His promise was prophetic, "and," testified Stevenson, "it proved true."[48]

When the young Prophet Joseph told his father about both the angel Moroni's visits and the existence of the gold plates, his father, sensitive to the eternal implications of what was unfolding, wept.[49] Years later, when Father and Mother Smith, by now bowed with age and hardship, watched their sons Joseph and Hyrum carried from the square at Far West toward a cruel and unjust imprisonment in Liberty Jail, they were, as Parley P. Pratt described the scene, "overwhelmed with tears, and took each of the prisoners by the hand with a silence of grief too great for utterance."[50] Parley shared the sons' languishing imprisonment, and he wrote of his reunion, which occurred the following year, with the Prophet's parents, neither of whom thought it ungracious to weep: they were "overwhelmed with tears of joy and congratulation; they wept like children," said Parley, "as they took me by the hand."[51]

In each of these instances the intensity of Father Smith's interest was magnified because of the power of a one-on-one interaction. While he worked well with groups, the most powerful and compelling memories of his presence and influence grow out of interactions with individuals—it was individualized, personalized attention that left a lasting impress. Caroline Crosby received her patriarchal blessing from Father Smith, and seemed to recall the conversations surrounding the blessing with almost as much affection as the blessing itself. She was encouraged when he told her that she and her husband "had come together right."[52]

Imbued with Missionary Zeal

Following a blessing meeting in 1836, a young truth seeker by the name of Lorenzo Snow was introduced to Father Smith, who told him: "You will become as great as you can possibly wish—even as great as God, and you cannot wish to be greater." This was a bold, daring doctrine, and Lorenzo stood dazed—"confounded," he wrote—wondering if the old gentleman could be a deceiver. Yet, wrote Lorenzo, "his every appearance answered in the negative. At first sight, his presence impressed me with feelings of love and reverence."[53] Then, eyeball-to-eyeball, the conversation continued: "Why, brother Snow," said the old Patriarch, "I discover that you are trying to understand the principles of Mormonism."

"Yes," replied Lorenzo, "that was the object I had in view."

"Well, do not worry but pray to the Lord and satisfy yourself; study the matter over, compare the scriptures with what we are teaching; talk with the brethren that you are acquainted with, and after a time you will be convinced that 'Mormonism' is of God, and you will be baptized."[54]

How could young Lorenzo resist the invitation of one who had such full-scale, guileless confidence in truth? Indeed, this very gift—the love of truth—authored multiple virtues in the life of Father Smith. The Prophet Joseph Smith took a good deal of satisfaction in the fact that his father was the first person to receive his testimony of Moroni and the Book of Mormon and that he immediately and ever thereafter remained true to that testimony.[55] Indeed, Father Smith learned of the Book of Mormon on the morning of September 22, 1823. That very evening he assembled his family together so that young Joseph might share with them what the angel had taught him. Family meetings such as this continued "every evening" for some time.[56] Initially, knowledge of the angelic visitation was confined to the family, but at appropriate moments Father Smith and others began to testify to a broader circle of inquirers, and we have a wide range of early records of both Father and Mother Smith stretching out in testimony to family,[57] friends,[58] and even strangers.[59]

Here, then, is a man always involved in sharing the gospel with others. He was a missionary to the marrow. The Church was organized in April 1830. By July of that same year Father and Mother Smith joined their son Samuel on what was already Samuel's second mission, visiting Livonia, New York.[60] One month later Father Smith took his son Don Carlos, then nearly fourteen and a half years of age, to visit relatives in St. Lawrence County, New York. It was on this mission that Father Smith's father, Asael Smith, and his brother John—"Uncle John," as the Prophet and the Saints knew him—and his nephew George A. all received his testimony.[61] Less than one year later, we find him staying at home tending to family chores so that his wife could visit her relatives in Michigan and tell them of the Restoration.[62] Months later he left with two other brethren for a missionary assignment in Northampton, Ohio.[63] About three years later, with his sons Joseph and Hyrum, he undertook a mission to Michigan.[64] He returned to Kirtland, labored with the Saints there for a time, and by May 1836 he and Uncle John left Kirtland for New Portage, Ohio, where in less than two weeks they baptized sixteen, gave ninety-five patriarchal blessings, and then had their mission cut short so that they could return to Kirtland to witness the death of their mother, Mary Duty Smith.[65] They stayed in Kirtland but a matter of weeks before they left for the eastern states, baptizing and giving patriarchal blessings wherever they went. On this journey, the Prophet says, they traveled twenty-four hundred miles,[66] sixteen hundred of which, according to George A. Smith, "they traveled in a one-horse wagon."[67]

The commandment to share the gospel, however, embodies more than simply traveling on missions. It includes standing as a witness of Christ at all times and in all places.[68] The Apostle Paul went "from house to house"[69] preaching, and while he was in Rome "there came many to him into his lodging; to whom he expounded and testified the kingdom of God, persuading them concerning Jesus . . . from morning till evening." Indeed, he "dwelt two whole years in his own hired house, and received all that came in unto him."[70] This system of preaching to one's neighbors from one's own porch and in one's own cottage reaches back to the ancient Saints and is recorded by them as an example for us. Whether Father Smith saw the power of their example or simply felt the power of doing what was right, he does not tell us. Our records, however, show that over the years he and Mother Smith constantly invited others into their home for gospel instruction. Edward Partridge, for example, had developed an interest in the gospel, attended a missionary meeting in the Smith home, and was baptized the next day.[71] Another early convert named John Smith (not the Prophet's uncle and apparently not a family relation) records in his diary that in January 1832 he convened two cottage meetings in, it appears, the home of Father and Mother Smith and that in the second he preached "to a large congregation."[72] As had been the Smith family experience in Palmyra, so also was it in Kirtland and Nauvoo: both Father and Mother Smith were always willing to bring people into their home to share the gospel.

Wisdom, of course, is born of experience, and missionary wisdom grows out of missionary experience. Thus it was that at a time when age and the debilitating effects of persecution and hardship would have forced lesser men into a grey harmlessness, Father Smith was someone to whom departing missionaries went for his blessing and counsel.[73] Heber C. Kimball, for example, received a call from the Prophet to open up missionary work in Great Britain at a time when trouble enveloped the Saints in Kirtland. John F. Boynton inveighed against Heber's going. "If you are such a fool as to go at the call of the fallen prophet, Joseph Smith," said Boynton, "I will not help you a dime, and if you are cast on Van Dieman's land, I will not make an effort to help you." Lyman E. Johnson also told Heber not to go. Still, above the din and clatter of apostate invective, Heber heard the sweet reassurance of the faithful: "Brothers Sidney Rigdon, Joseph Smith, Sen., Brigham Young, Newel K. Whitney and others said, 'Go and do as the Prophet has told you, and you shall prosper and be blessed with power to do a glorious work.'" The faith and devotion of Father Smith was reflected in that of his children. "Hyrum," Heber said, "seeing the condition of the Church, when he talked about my mission, wept like a little child; he was continually blessing and encouraging me, and pouring out his soul in prophecies upon my head; he said: 'Go, and you shall prosper as not many have prospered.'"[74] Following the voice of faith, Heber left and, fulfilling Hyrum's prediction to the letter, baptized hundreds.

By September 1839 Father Smith's iron frame had begun to totter; he lay beaten and worn, enfeebled by disease and the crushing effects of persecution. The seeds of death, sown in Kirtland and nourished in Missouri, had taken deep hold on his system. The light of truth still shone in his eyes, however, and

Artist's conception of Joseph Smith, Sr., by William Whitaker

when his nephew George A. Smith, also frail from the effects of sickness, came seeking his uncle's counsel and blessing, Father Smith "burst out laughing . . . and although bolstered up with pillows in a big chair," immediately saw an irony in the situation: "Who has been robbing the burying yard?" he demanded, implying that young George A. seemed as close to death as he himself was. George A. apparently ignored the inquiry and explained that he was on his way to preach the gospel in Great Britain. "The old gentleman blessed me and said I should go, should be restored to health, accomplish a great deal of good, and return safely home again."[75] Subsequent events proved the old man to be prophetic.

Some years before, when leaving for a mission to the eastern states, George A. had gone to Father Smith for the advice that would guide his missionary labor. Seeming to remember what the Lord had revealed some four years earlier—that "out of small things proceedeth that which is great"[76]—and knowing that out of modest beginnings come the giant rewards of faith, Father Smith clothed his counsel to be humble in the language of his New England upbringing: "Always go in at the little end of the horn and you are sure to come out at the big end, but if you go in at the big end of the horn you will be obliged to come out at the little end."[77]

Double blessed is the missionary who knows that in the service of the Master "whosoever shall exalt himself shall be abased; and he that shall humble himself shall be exalted."[78]

Were we to attempt to correctly summarize in a paragraph the missionary service of this faithful father in Israel, we would simply note the following: He was one of the Eight Witnesses of the Book of Mormon who saw the plates, and at every opportunity he bore witness of the Book of Mormon and the truths it teaches. In every regard he showed himself true to the commission he received when called upon to bear witness of the plates and the Restoration which they symbolized. With him it was a matter of integrity. He journeyed thousands of miles to preach the gospel, and when not traveling himself, he housed and fed missionaries passing through his neighborhood, opened up his house to the teaching of the gospel to his friends, sent his sons on missions, testified of his own missionary experiences, gave sage counsel to departing missionaries, and exercised faith on behalf of those in missionary service. Indeed, even while imprisoned for thirty days for his inability to pay a small debt, he put his time to good advantage, preached every Sunday he was confined, and upon his release baptized two of his former fellow inmates.[79] Truly, in Father Smith we have a man who sought to serve the Lord with all his "heart, might, mind and strength"— even as he had been commanded to do.[80]

Hardworking and Cheerful

To paint a picture of Father Smith's life in which everything worked out easily and well would be to miss the mark. One's commitment to eternal truths does not free him from the cares of mortality—or from its burdens. The gospel does not solve all the problems of life, and in some instances it makes them no easier to bear. This is a fallen world, and we came to be tried and tested. The gospel does, however, give comfort, hope, and perspective, and thus the continued confidence to press forward. In the instance of Joseph Smith, Sr., he worked hard and developed a number of different employment skills with which he provided for his family. His principal occupation was that of farmer, though he was a skilled cooper, apparently dug an occasional well for income, hired himself out for gardening work and harvesting, opened a general store while in Vermont, spent some time as an English and music teacher,[81] and, if Pomeroy Tucker can be trusted as a source of biographical information, when in Palmyra "opened a 'cake and beer shop,' as described by his signboard," thus earning "a scanty but honest living for himself and family." During summer months and when holidays arrived, Father Smith apparently did some street vending, and, according to Tucker, his "shop merchandise, consisting of gingerbread, pies, boiled eggs, root-beer, and other like notions of traffic, soon became popular . . . , commanding brisk sales, especially on Fourth of July anniversaries, and on military training days, as these prevailed at that period. Peddling was done in the streets on those occasions by the facility of a rude handcart of the proprietor's own construction."[82]

Just as he worked hard, we have some indication that he sometimes relaxed energetically. The older of the Jackaway boys, at least, told of Father Smith and the Prophet wrestling each other.[83] This is consistent with the Prophet's description of his father as a wrestler who never but once met a man he could not throw.

Mother Smith tells of evenings when the family would relax and reminisce in the warm evening air,[84] and others of the Saints, such as Wandle Mace,[85] tell of participating in such conversations. Some of these conversations held a serious, gospel focus. Others did not, for Father Smith knew that spirituality consists in a reverence for that which is sacred, and not in the forced and artificial piety of those who fear life's lighter side, or who think there is no smiling in heaven. "I know," said Heber C. Kimball, "that those Prophets who have lived in my day loved to tell stories and be cheerful: they delighted in a glad heart and a cheerful countenance. Father Smith was one of the most cheerful men I ever saw, and he was harmless as a child."[86]

While spirituality is not long-faced, neither is it overindulgent. When Jonathan and Caroline Crosby went to Father Smith to receive their patriarchal blessings, he conversed with them, perhaps to make them feel comfortable and at ease, and even asked their ages. "When we told him our ages," said Caroline, "and places of birth, he observed that he thought we were both born under one planet," but he spoke, she said, "merely by way of merriment."[87] He gave the couple inspired patriarchal blessings that undoubtedly were anchors to their faith for the rest of their lives.

Father Smith, with what must have been a reverent smile, shared a not too dissimilar experience with William W. Phelps when he came to receive his patriarchal blessing. Brother Phelps provides the details: "Says Father Smith, 'What shall I say unto you?'" Phelps answered, "What[ever] the Lord puts into your heart to say." Then the saintly Patriarch replied, "Well, the Lord has put it into my heart to say that you are a *strange man*." Phelps responded emphatically: "That I know."[88] When the mirth subsided, Father Smith conferred another inspired blessing upon another worthy Saint.

The Prophet and His Father

When dealing with one such as Father Smith, there is a danger of speaking too freely in superlatives. It is tempting to make him too much the hero, or to forget that it was his son the Prophet Joseph who was appointed to stand center stage, bear the greater burden, and do the greater good. This is a case in which the son was greater than the father. There was indeed a difference between the father and the son as respected some gifts—young Joseph was the more prophetic, the more insightful, the more discerning; he was also the greater teacher, the greater theologian, and the more resilient under persecution and pressure. But the groundwork of character was the same in both. To both were common the love of truth and the delight in testimony, the spiritual sensitivity to promptings both simple and great, the love of the Saints, and the consecration of all earthly possessions to the cause of Christ. To both was common a God-inspired inner strength that enabled each to overcome every obstacle and confrontation. And because they shared so much in common, from blood to purpose, there was a very real sense in which to know the father was to know the son, to love the one was to love the other.

Moreover, speaking of the great gifts and virtues of either of those two men without taking into account their backgrounds and the circumstances in which they lived can keep us from having a more balanced and discerning view of their lives. Father Smith was a New England Yankee, vigorously in love with life, skilled in multiple trades, and confident of overcoming when faced with hardship. He was, nonetheless, molded and humbled by the privations he endured. When his critics said he was simple, they were correct, though they missed the larger point that his simplicity was a virtue, for it signalled the fact that he was unpretentious and not a man of worldly affectations. By saying he was simple, critics and naysayers hoped to cast him as incompetent, bungling, and even unintelligent. But he was none of these. The list of his accomplishments could never have been written by bungling incompetence, and his mind saw through much of the error of his day; he embraced strong and powerful ideas, was ever ridiculed by the world for having done so, yet always saw through the prejudices directed against him.

It is true that he wore New England everywhere he went and that he was a product of the age and culture which helped shape him. His tongue shaped words differently than ours do, or even than did those of the wealthier class of his day. We smile and think it quaint that he or others with whom he associated would say that they visited friends who "used us civilly" or that "the subject of the Book of Mormon was aggitated."[89] He used the words *was* and *were, did, doesn't,* and *don't* somewhat differently than we would, but in his day, as in the Elizabethan era before that, it was common conversational English to say something like "You was hungry," or "They don't know nothing!"[90] Because of his upbringing we can only suppose that he spoke of things as being "onery" or "picayune," that a merchant with an eye for a bargain had "good horse sense," and that the wicked who conspired against the Saints were "in cahoots" with the devil and were often emboldened in their mobbery by different forms of alcohol: "rot-gut," "joy-water," or "phlegm cutter."[91] An unscrupulous politician was a "scalawag," or perhaps even "a monkey without a monkey's wit."[92]

Part of the greatness of the father of the Prophet, of course, is the fact that he overcame so much of his environment; his focus on heaven was so deliberate that it protected him from stepping from right paths, and because of this constancy and stability the Saints looked to him for guidance and comfort. He felt the full force of the lash of life, and we see him, perhaps impetuously, angered upon hearing that someone had chastised the young Prophet, and immediately humbled upon learning that that someone was the angel Moroni.[93] In April 1839, when the brethren determined to go to Far West—despite the danger of doing so—in order to fulfill the revelation that the Apostles would leave from the Far West Temple site to go on a European mission, Father Smith, knowing the danger of Missouri mobs, urged them not to go, suggesting the Lord would take "the will for the deed."[94] When in the fall of 1838 the mob imprisoned Joseph and Hyrum in the square at Far West, Father Smith was so overtaken with a bundle of emotions—fear, distress, anger, hurt—that he was driven to his sickbed, from which he never entirely recovered.[95] Yet through it all, he remained a pillar upon which the Saints leaned and in whom they trusted.

Committed to the Restoration

We are left, then, looking back some two hundred years, to ask the simple, summary question: What of Father Smith? What of this man whom God and angels trusted? Wherein lay his greatness, and why do we speak of him, when so many of his compeers—and particularly his critics and persecutors—have fallen into some forgotten oblivion? And why did the Saints so love this gentle greatness?

We answer with a voice that seems to read from the archives of heaven: It was the age of restoration, and the reach of the Restoration was broad, embracing angels and Gods and stretching from one end of eternity to the other; it was the age that God had promised "by the mouth of all his holy prophets since the world began,"[96] and the effects of this promised restoration were to be as extensive as eternity itself; it was the age when God raised up Apostles and prophets anew, and it was an age in which the faithful Saints realized that these apostolic and prophetic personalities were as great as any in history: to walk with the Smiths was to walk with some of the foreordained noble and great, those called and prepared from before the foundation of the world; to converse with them was to converse with those who stood with Adam and Abraham in the premortal sphere and who learned from them in this sphere; to touch the hands of the Prophet and his father was to touch hands prepared by the Great Almighty eons before this world came rolling into existence. And even without fully comprehending why—for which of us does?—the Saints knew and felt that they walked and worked with a humble but divine greatness.

For not since the Son of Man preached in the roadways of Judea and the Galilee had the gospel been preached with such force and clarity; not since Jesus was crucified and resurrected was the religious drama so intense and far reaching; and not since the meridian of time was the power of the gospel so forcefully manifest in angelic ministration, miracles, priesthood power, and the simple whisperings of the Holy Spirit—and Father Smith, when he was not at the center of these events, was but a hand stretch away. Because he was so close to the Prophet and so much a part of the Prophet's training, experiences, and affections, he became a symbol of all that the Prophet represented. The Prophet's difficulties were his difficulties, and the Prophet's triumphs and exultations were also his. The affections of the Saints for the events of the Restoration, the principles that inspired them, and the central figures of the great and divine drama could not help but reach out and embrace the father of the Prophet.

And so they did!

Father Smith was a Restoration man, and a Restoration man to the core; he drank its doctrines, lived its testimony, and rejoiced in its truths. Because he was so intimately associated with its foundational events, he became a symbol of them. When the golden plates were given to the Prophet, Father Smith wept for joy,[97] and later hid them under the hearthstone of his home and again under his old cooperage.[98] He stood in Grandin's print shop when portions of the Book of Mormon were printed,[99] and when the nefarious Abner Cole sought to illegally publish portions of the Book of Mormon manuscript in the Palmyra *Reflector*, it was Father Smith who went to Harmony to fetch the Prophet and put an end to the antagonistic publishing.[100] When the Church was organized, he was there, and with his wife was baptized that same day.[101] He was ordained a priest in the farmhouse where much of the Book of

Mormon had been translated,[102] and received the ordinance of washing of feet from the Prophet Joseph.[103] He was named in five of the revelations eventually placed in the Doctrine and Covenants,[104] was the recipient, through the Prophet, of yet another,[105] and was present when still others were given.[106] He was present during the pentecostal outpourings at the dedication of the Kirtland Temple, as the first Patriarch to the Church in this dispensation gave hundreds of patriarchal blessings, prophesied, healed the sick, and constantly gave comforting counsel to the Prophet.

How could a life more perfectly reflect the fact that the gospel had been restored in its full power than did the life of Father Smith? Moreover, he pronounced so many patriarchal blessings upon the heads of the Saints, and they therefore received so much inspiration from what he promised and predicted, that it is understandable that their memories of Father Smith were so closely tied to memories of having felt the Spirit of the Lord—and who could not love the man who facilitated such experiences?

He was a magnet for men's affections because he possessed the principle of love and because his very life was a sermon, spoken from his birth to his death and preached in flesh and bones, sweat, toil and tears—a sermon which repeatedly said that the faithful would overcome. Seldom had the Saints met a man so vivid, vital, and exuberant in the cause of truth, so full of the salt and tang of the human adventure, and yet so close to the heart and hand of heaven.

Seldom could the Saints meet such a man, and seldom can we, for a Father Smith comes but once in a generation, or perhaps even less frequently. We look to the day when we shall meet his like again.

CHAPTER 3

Seeing with the
Eye of Faith

Faith is a gift of the Spirit; it comes from the Holy Ghost.[1] The automatic and unavoidable consequence of having experiences with the Holy Spirit is that faith grows. Indeed, where there are no spiritual experiences, there is no faith; and where there is no faith, there will be no spiritual experiences. The answer, then, to the questions, "How does one exercise faith? and, What does one do to make faith grow? is relatively simple: exercising faith is a matter of doing the things that bring the Spirit of the Lord into one's life. Indeed, the Spirit of the Lord might rightly be called "the Spirit of faith," for faith is a fruit of the Spirit, and the greater the interaction with the Spirit of the Lord, the greater will be the faith of the individual involved. We repent, are baptized, and obey the commandments so that we can have the companionship of the Holy Ghost. One purifying consequence of having the companionship of the Holy Spirit is that our faith grows.

The commandment is that "the just shall live by faith,"[2] meaning, in part, that the righteous—those who are approved of God and who have claim upon the companionship of the Holy Spirit—become righteous through the process of exercising faith, or the process of having spiritual experiences. But when we speak of faith—saving faith!—what we really ought to have in mind is "faith in Christ." The seed, for example, that Alma taught we should all plant deep in the most fertile soils of our souls was not, as is so often supposed, the seed of faith; rather, it was the testimony that Jesus is the Son of God,[3] which is the seed out of which faith grows. When the revelations speak of faith they almost always mean "faith in the Lord Jesus Christ," or "faith in God," as it is sometimes expressed, and not faith in some general sense. This is best seen in the Book of Mormon, where phrases such as "faith in Christ,"[4] "faith in the Lamb,"[5] "faith in the Holy One,"[6] "faith in my Well Beloved,"[7] and "faith on the Lord"[8] abound. Because the Saints in ancient Israel taught the same gospel that was taught by the Nephite Saints, they too were given the command to "have faith in God"[9] and taught that they could become "the children of God by faith in Christ Jesus."[10]

While it was a contact with the Book of Mormon and the other revelations given through the Prophet Joseph Smith that refined and perfected the faith of Joseph Smith, Sr., it was from the biblical instructions of his parents that he first set his focus on Christ as the central object of his faith. "And now my dear children," wrote Father Smith's father Asael, to all of his children, "let me pour out my heart to you and speak first to you of immortality in your souls. Trifle not in this point; the soul is immortal; you have to deal with an infinite Majesty. . . . Do all to God in a serious manner; when you think of Him, speak of Him, pray to Him, or in any way make your addresses to His great Majesty, be in good earnest. Trifle not with His name nor with His attributes, nor call Him to witness anything but what is absolute truth. . . . If you find that you stand in need of a Savior, Christ saith: 'Look unto me and be ye saved all ye ends of the earth.'" Asael warned his children to look to Christ and counseled that they could find him through searching the scriptures and through sound reason; he said that they would find that God and Christ were both just and merciful and that Christ had the power to save all mankind from their fallen state. He pleaded with his children to honor the church of Christ, saying in addition that he was sure that "my Savior, Christ, is perfect, and never will fail in one circumstance."[11]

This conviction, nurtured from the crib, was the ancestral inheritance handed down through the generations to Joseph Smith, Sr. He was raised in a home where love was the motive

Last page of Asael Smith's address to his wife and children,
dated April 10, 1799

force and where his parents and grandparents, on both sides of
the family, spoke with reverence of Christ and his gospel.

Traditions of Faith

The family life of Joseph Smith, Sr., is important, because
family and ancestral traditions are the soils out of which faith
grows. Thus it was that the Apostle Paul gave thanks to God for
"the unfeigned faith" that was in Timothy but "which dwelt first
in [his] grandmother Lois, and [his] mother Eunice," and then
in Timothy also.[12] Generations earlier Abraham, the "father of
the faithful," had dramatized this principle for our instruction:
his great-grandson Joseph was faithful because Jacob, Isaac,
and Abraham had all been faithful before him. Faith was
Joseph's familial inheritance. Indeed, from the day of Adam to

the present, taught the Prophet Joseph Smith, "the knowledge of the existence of a God must have continued from father to son, as a matter of tradition."[13]

The traditions of the Lamanites and of the Nephites shaped their willingness to respond to the gospel message as well. As long as the Nephites honored and upheld the gospel traditions of their fathers, they had faith, while the Lamanites became a "wild, and ferocious, and a blood-thirsty people" because they adhered to the faithless traditions of their fathers.[14] Paul, in order to encourage the Jews to obtain and exercise saving faith, wrestled with them to get them to discard the traditions of their fathers,[15] and the Lord, in this dispensation, warned the Prophet Joseph Smith that false traditions were a tool of the devil[16] and the basis for the false creeds which led to the persecution of the Saints.[17]

And so it was in the life of Joseph Smith, Sr.: he inherited from his parents and grandparents, and from generations as far back as we can identify, the traditions out of which his faith was to grow. His grandfather Samuel Smith was, as Professor Richard Lloyd Anderson describes him, "a highly religious man who took his Congregational [church] covenant seriously, [and] . . . was active in public worship. His five children were all baptized in the Topsfield church, including youngest Asael four days after birth."[18] Samuel comfortably made public declarations of his faith, and the summary of his life, carried in his obituary, called him "a man of integrity and uprightness" and a "strenuous advocate for the doctrines of Christianity."[19]

This legacy of belief was passed from Samuel to his son Asael, father of Joseph Smith, Sr. Asael—in a way anticipating the Lord's plea that we acknowledge His hand in all things[20]— readily sighted the hand of the Almighty in the preserving of the colonists through the revolutionary war and in "the appointment of the Federal Constitution."[21] Both Asael and his wife, Mary Duty, who herself had been baptized as an infant, ensured that all their children were also baptized.[22]

But more than the spiritual discipline of seeking out the ordinances and rituals of salvation, Asael vigorously sought for an understanding of the laws of salvation. Indeed, as Richard Lloyd Anderson points out, "his records in the family Bible show that he honored it, and his quotations prove that he read and believed it." So serious were his Bible convictions, in fact, that

"Asael devoted about one-fifth of his 'will' to scriptural proof that no salvation comes through self-righteousness, but that 'sinners must be saved by the righteousness of Christ alone.' "[23]

When it came to the doctrines of the churches of his day, Asael was not so easily convinced, but his affection for biblical principles stands beyond question. His own heaven-inspired religious promptings amount to nothing short of revelation, and he knew and announced, to his family at least—and this is the recollection of his grandson George A. Smith—that "he always knew that God was going to raise up some branch of his family to be a great benefit to mankind" and "that something [religious] would turn up in his family that would revolutionize the world."[24] His study convinced him that an apostasy had occurred, and, George A. Smith wrote, "not long before his death he wrote many quires of paper on the doctrine of Universal Restoration."[25] As an old man standing at death's door, Asael heard of the Prophet Joseph's visions and, according to John Smith, received a copy of the Book of Mormon "with gladness" and "remarked that he had always expected that something would appear to make known the true gospel."[26] The overriding point, of course, is not only that Asael felt and acknowledged the divine power in the Book of Mormon but also that he had a deeply ingrained habit of reading and writing about gospel themes—the Restoration in particular—and that this tradition of study and reflection was part of the inheritance he bequeathed his children. In the instance of Asael and Joseph Smith, Sr., the religious character of the father became that of the son, who, well before the First Vision, embraced the doctrine that there was a universal apostasy which necessitated a universal restoration.[27]

Joseph Smith, Sr., then, freely received from his ancestors traditions of faith that were rooted in church attendance and worship, biblical study and gospel thought. Because of the convictions and conclusions of his fathers, it was automatic for him to anticipate a universal restoration and to respond to the spiritual promptings that planted those same convictions deep into his own soul. He believed in a personal God who would answer prayers, as did his fathers before him; he believed that dreams and visions could come to the faithful, as did his fathers before him; he believed (unlike those who espoused the doctrines of the churches of his day) in a God who would stretch out and make the message of salvation available to all of his children, as did his fathers before him.

In short, the faith and traditions of his fathers shaped and molded his own mind and thought, so that he himself was more receptive to the simple promptings of the Light of Christ and later to the promptings of the Holy Ghost. The fruits of his faith were planted in the ancestral soils that shaped and molded his own formative growth.

Rejecting False Teachings

Asael Smith understood that faith in Christ grows out of a study of the life, ministry, and doctrines of Christ, coupled with the effort to live in harmony with what Christ taught. It thus becomes just as important to reject false ideas as to embrace true ones. Joseph Smith, Sr., shared this understanding with his father, and his life was characterized by a bold stand against that which he understood to be wrong; he rejected much of the prevailing and popular theology of his day, for example, even before the Prophet Joseph's first vision occurred and the process of restoration began to unfold. He read and thought about what he was taught in the home and from the pulpit, and obviously conversed with his father on religious issues. Lucy recalled, for instance, that when as a young man Father Smith manifested interest in Methodism, Asael "came to the door one day and threw Tom Paine's *Age of Reason* into the house and angrily bade him read that until he believed it."[28]

We have no record telling us exactly how Father Smith reacted to *Age of Reason,* but we do know that Thomas Paine shows somewhat of a dual personality in this particular work. On the one hand, *Age of Reason* is an attack by an avowed anti-Christ on sectarian Christianity, and some of his reasoning is both excellent and answerable only by a knowledge of the gospel as restored through the Prophet Joseph Smith. Paine excoriates the churches of his day for enslaving the minds of men, for establishing themselves as institutions for financial gain, for being little more than paganism disguised in a new garment, for failing to follow the teachings of Christ or for announcing that they have power—for a price!—to forgive sins, and for thinking that by popular vote they could define the character and personality of God. "The most detestable wickedness," wrote Paine, "the most horrid cruelties, and the greatest miseries that have afflicted the human race have had their origin in this thing called revelation, or revealed religion," including what the world has called Christianity, and "no sooner were the professors of Christianity sufficiently powerful to employ the sword, than they did so, and the stake and fagot, too."[29] Sentiment of this kind appears consonant with what we know about the kindly father of the Prophet, who resisted the churches of his day both because of what they taught and what they failed to teach.

On the other hand, in his work Paine ridicules the divinity of Christ and the doctrines of virgin birth, atonement, and resurrection. He went to extended lengths to deride the biblical practice of prophesying, the doctrine that the Bible was a revelation, the teaching that miracles were a reality, and the concept that either the Old or New Testaments were inspired. On all of these issues, he crossed swords with Father Smith.

It seems clear that Father Smith was influenced both by his Father's rejection of much of the religious teachings of the day and by the kind of argumentation advanced by Thomas Paine. The issue, however, is much larger than mortal influences. Asael Smith had received heaven-inspired feelings that the true Church was not upon the earth, that a restoration was coming, and that it would come through one of his descendants.[30] It was his spiritual promptings that influenced his mortal walk and talk, and not his mortal experiences that dictated his religious views. No doubt it was because of premortal preparations that he felt as he did on religion, and these simple whisperings of the Spirit—which, like the promptings to others before him,[31] he may not even have recognized as such—caused him to interpret world events as he did. Asael felt, for example, that it was not his duty to counsel "the Supreme Ruler of universal nature" on His governing the affairs of men. Rather, he thanked the Lord for conducting the American people "through a glorious revolution" and conducting them to "the promised land of peace and liberty" as a prelude to restoring the gospel throughout the whole earth. So certain was he of his feelings that he wrote a friend on the matter, concluding that he believed that "the stone is now cut out of the mountain without hands, spoken of by Daniel, and has smitten the image upon his feet, by which the iron, the clay, the brass, the silver and the gold—viz., all monarchial and ecclesiastical tyranny—will be broken to pieces an[d] become as the chaff of the summer thrashing floor. The wind shall carry them all away that there shall be no place found for them."[32]

The prophecy to which Asael here refers promised that "the God of heaven" would "set up a kingdom, which shall never be destroyed" nor be given to another people, but which would "stand for ever."[33] Obviously, such a kingdom could not be restored if it already existed, and if it was to "stand for ever" it was equally obvious that it was the pre-millennial kingdom of Christ of which the prophet Daniel spoke. Because we do not have record of a conversation between Asael and Joseph, Sr., on this issue, we are left to speculate that the father influenced the son. How, we ask, could it have been otherwise? The father's premonitions were heaven inspired; the son was prepared from the eternities before for the very role he was fulfilling.[34] How could we fail to conclude that such a father, who was willing to share these feelings with a friend—Jacob Towne—would not at the same time earnestly share them with his own son? And, for that matter, is it not equally likely that he would have shared his feelings with all his sons and daughters, as well as with his wife? Again, the Prophet Joseph does not tell us how he knew of his grandfather's premonitions, but it seems a logical conclusion that he would have learned them from his father, who in turn undoubtedly heard them from Asael himself.

Even, however, if one ignored the likelihood that Asael's influence played a significant formative role in shaping Father Smith's thought, we know that Father Smith, long before the First Vision, had concluded that there was a universal apostasy and that therefore a universal restoration was needed. Mother Smith emphasized that "he would not subscribe to any particular system of faith, but contended for the ancient order, as established by our Lord and Savior Jesus Christ and His Apostles."[35] While he had earlier attended the Methodist meetings with his wife, he soon stopped attending, as it angered his brother Jesse. Moreover, Father Smith saw little profit in Methodism. "He said," recalled Lucy, "that he considered it hardly worth our while to attend the meetings any longer as it would prove of but little advantage to us; besides this, it gave our friends such disagreeable feelings." Lucy was considerably hurt by her husband's refusal to attend church but, in characteristic Smith fashion, retired to a grove not far from their house to pray in her husband's behalf. Her prayer was answered with a comforting vision in which the Lord showed her that her husband, in more advanced years, would receive the gospel with his whole heart.[36]

More significant, however, the Lord gave Father Smith himself a vision in which he was told that there had been a universal apostasy. Here is the account of that vision, according to his own report: "I seemed to be traveling in an open, barren field, and as I was traveling, I turned my eyes towards the east, the west, the north and the south, but could see nothing save dead, fallen timber. Not a vestige of life, either animal or vegetable, could be seen; besides, to render the scene still more dreary, the most death-like silence prevailed, no sound of anything animate could be heard in all the field. I was alone in this gloomy desert, with the exception of an attendant spirit, who kept constantly by my side. Of him I inquired the meaning of what I saw, and why I was thus traveling in such a dismal place. He answered thus: 'This field is the world, which now lieth inanimate and dumb, in regard to the true religion, or plan of salvation.' "

Thus, the conclusions Father Smith had drawn through his study and experience were later confirmed by the visionary voice of heaven. In short, Father Smith had a revealed knowledge that conclusions he had drawn about an erring and disfigured Christianity were correct. Yet the vision spoke hope, for he was at the same time assured that amid constant opposition, a restoration would be effected.[37] From this time forward, said Mother Smith, "my husband seemed more confirmed than ever in the opinion that there was no order or class of religionists that knew any more concerning the Kingdom of God than those of the world, or such as made no profession of religion whatever."[38] Additional revelations followed.[39]

The case of Father Smith is not just a case of God-inspired doubts. It is also a case of God-inspired certainties, for the Lord made it known to him that there had been a universal apostasy and that there would be a universal restoration. The process of rejecting false doctrine helped him develop a spiritual sensitivity for and recognition of true doctrine. Thus, twelve years before the revelation came announcing that the gospel would be preached in the world of the spirits to those who did not have the opportunity to receive it in this life, Father Smith instinctively recoiled against the strong intimations of Palmyra's Presbyterian minister that the recently deceased Alvin, the twenty-five-year-old son of Father and Mother Smith, had been damned because he was not a church member.[40] Father Smith's very soul screamed at the injustice of such a teaching: how could a just God everlastingly condemn one so good and so pure as Alvin simply because he did not receive that which he was never offered?

But God is just, and in the justice of God an opportunity has been provided for Alvin and all like him.[41] And in that same justice of God, we know that faith and doubt cannot exist in the same person at the same time,[42] just as truth and untruth cannot exist in the same mind at the same time. Hence the necessity of steering clear of false teachings, for faith is, by definition, not "a perfect knowledge of things; therefore if ye have faith ye hope for things which are not seen, *which are true.*"[43] Thus, in the case of Father Smith, as in the case of all, the purifying process of rejecting false teachings was also the purifying process of sanctifying the soul, making it the more receptive receptacle of the Holy Spirit. Plainly put, belief in false doctrine is a denial of faith. One cannot have faith in a false doctrine or principle and expect the Holy Spirit to testify of that particular falsehood. To repose confidence in falsehoods is to forfeit the companionship of the Spirit of truth, which is the Holy Ghost, and when the Spirit of the Lord withdraws, faith will not exist. The fact that Father Smith would struggle over doctrines, and reject that which did not harmonize with the scriptures available to him, molded his mind so that it was more responsive to true doctrines and thus to the Spirit of the Lord.

Thus it was that Father Smith was ever a student of the gospel. He read the scriptures with avidity. Even his enemies and critics knew that he "was a good deal of a smatterer in Scriptural knowledge,"[44] and just as he had been raised on scripture reading, so also did he raise his children in the same pattern. Rather than read many books, he read good books many times. He was the first to accept the Prophet Joseph's testimony of the coming of the angel Moroni; he wept when the Prophet could not obtain the plates, and rejoiced when they were finally secured;[45] and he read and preached from the Book of Mormon with eagerness. Throughout his life his mind became an ever increasingly strong magnet for scriptural knowledge. The corresponding consequence was that his faith grew, for faith grows out of a knowledge of truth. Moreover, where there is no intellectual growth, there can be no spiritual growth.

Faith: A Principle of Power

But faith, taught the Prophet Joseph Smith, is a principle of power,[46] and those who have faith are empowered to accomplish great good because of that faith. Thus men move mountains, raise the dead, heal the sick, preach great sermons, endure hardships, and overcome persecutions and sufferings, all because of faith. By definition, faith is the amount of influence one has with God; the greater the faith, the greater the capacity to join with God in working the works of righteousness. Where such faith exists, God cannot withhold his blessings.[47]

By the standard that faith is influence with God, Father Smith was one of the greats. When Father Smith prayed, the Lord listened. Mother Smith tells, for instance, of typhus fever striking Sophronia, who, after ninety days of enfeebling fever, seemed to knock on death's door. "As she thus lay," said Mother Smith, "I gazed upon her as a mother looks upon the last shade of life in a darling child. In this moment of distraction, my husband and myself clasped our hands, fell upon our knees by the bedside, and poured out our grief to God in prayer and supplication, beseeching him to spare our child yet a little longer.

"Did the Lord hear our petition? Yes, he most assuredly did, and before we rose to our feet he gave us a testimony that she would recover. . . .

"From this time forward Sophronia continued mending, until she entirely recovered."[48]

Some twenty years later, after Sophronia had married, she was again overcome with an illness that was so destructive that her husband, Calvin Stoddard, sent for a physician, who visited her for a short time before announcing that she was beyond the reach of medicine and that further visits would thus be pointless. Father Smith and his sons, with Jared Carter as voice, administered to her. Within half an hour she spoke and said she would get well, "not suddenly," she said, "but the Lord will heal me gradually"—and so it was.[49]

In both of these blessings Father Smith was not alone, but his faith was certainly contributive to the healings involved, as it was on other occasions.[50] There were, however, occasions when his faith seemed to stand alone in calling down the powers of heaven. Wilford Woodruff, in recalling the powers resident in the mind and soul of Father Smith the Patriarch, said that "when he put his hands on the head of a person to bless him, it seemed as though the heavens were opened, and he could reveal the whole life of that person."[51] Edward Stevenson experienced exactly what Wilford Woodruff described. He noted that in 1834 Father and Mother Smith, with Joseph and Hyrum, visited Pontiac, Michigan, where Stevenson resided. Father Smith gave some blessings, and Stevenson recalled: "The power of his priesthood rested mightily upon Father Smith. It appeared as though the veil which separated us from the eternal world became so thin that heaven itself was right in our midst. It was at one of these meetings held during this time when I received my patriarchal blessing under the hands of Father Smith. [By nature] Father Smith was not a man of many words, but sober-minded, firm, mild and impressive. The exception, however, was at those blessing meetings; for truly the Holy Ghost gave utterance. Many of his words, although not written, recur to my mind as I pen these lines, for so impressive and strikingly were they sealed upon our heads."[52] On another occasion Stevenson wrote that he "was one of many who, under [Father Smith's] hands, received choice and rare blessings, when the power of the Holy Ghost filled the house to such an extent that the tears flowed down the cheeks of even those who lived and died outside of the pale of the Church."[53]

Lorenzo Snow adds a corraborative testimony. "It was Sunday"—the Lord's Sabbath!—"June 5, (1836), about a week after I arrived in Kirtland, that I first saw Father Smith. He was holding a patriarchal blessing meeting, in the Kirtland Temple, at which there were twelve or fifteen persons present. I was then searching to know whether there was any truth in Mormonism. I had never experienced anything supernatural, with one slight exception, and I did not know that anything supernatural had ever occurred among the children of men. I had heard Methodists, Presbyterians, and others relate their experiences, but I thought I could attribute all they said to natural causes. It was hard for me to be convinced that there could be such extraordinary manifestations as I saw exhibited in visiting the temple and listening to the testimonies of persons and hearing the extraordinary accounts of what the Lord had manifested to them.

"It was at my sister's invitation that I attended this meeting conducted by Father Smith. I listened with astonishment to him telling the brethren and sisters their parentage, their lineage and other things which I could not help but believe he knew nothing about, save as the Spirit manifested them unto him. After listening to several patriarchal blessings pronounced upon the heads of different individuals with whose history I was acquainted, and of whom I knew the Patriarch was entirely ignorant, I was struck with astonishment to hear the peculiarities of those persons positively and plainly referred to in their blessings. I was convinced that an influence, superior to human prescience, dictated his words. . . ."

Lorenzo Snow was destined, however, to see yet greater power. He had heard Father Smith read, by the power of the Holy Ghost, from the lives of those whom he blessed, and he had also heard him make prophetic promises upon their heads. But after the meeting, Father Smith was to turn his inspired attentions to the young investigator. Lorenzo's sister Eliza introduced them. " 'Why, Brother Snow (he called me Brother Snow, although I had not been baptized, and I did not know that I ever would be), do not worry,' he said, 'I discover that you are trying to understand the principles of Mormonism,' 'Yes,' I replied, 'that was the object I had in view.' 'Well,' said he, 'do not worry, but pray to the Lord and satisfy yourself; study the matter over, compare the scriptures with what we are teaching; talk with the brethren that you are acquainted with, and after a time you will be convinced that "Mormonism" is of God, and you will be baptized.' "[54]

Father Smith's seeric sights saw further than Lorenzo's baptism, however, for in addition he announced: "You will become as great as you can possibly wish—even as great as God, and you cannot wish to be greater."[55] This announcement, that Lorenzo, not yet even a member of the Church, would one day become as great as God—which could only mean that he himself would therefore have to become a god!—is all the more dramatic when placed in its historical context: the Prophet

Kirtland Temple

Joseph Smith did not publicly announce this doctrine until the April conference of 1844,[56] nearly eight years after the conversation between Father Smith and Lorenzo Snow.

Just as one man's testimony often lights the fires of testimony in another, so also one man's faith often plants the seeds of faith in another. Thus it was in this exchange between the saintly Patriarch and the soon-to-be-baptized investigator, and in this instance Father Smith's inspired promise became the window through which Lorenzo received a great revelation himself. Brother Snow was baptized about two weeks after first meeting Father Smith, and within four years he was assigned to serve in the British Mission. Just prior to leaving for England, Brother Snow was in the home of Elder H. G. Sherwood in Nauvoo, listening to Brother Sherwood explain the parable of the laborers in the vineyard,[57] and, in Lorenzo Snow's own words, "while attentively listening to his (Elder Sherwood's) explanation, the Spirit of the Lord rested mightily upon me—the eyes of my understanding were opened, and I saw as clear as the sun at noon-day, with wonder and astonishment, the path-

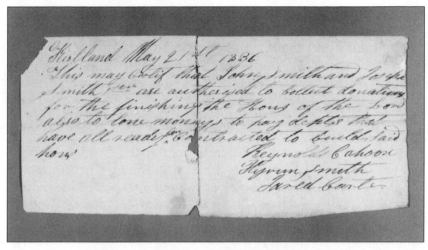

*Certificate, dated May 21, 1836, and signed by the
Kirtland Temple building committee (Reynolds Cahoon, Hyrum Smith,
and Jared Carter), authorizing John Smith and
Joseph Smith, Sr., to collect funds to pay for the temple*

way of God and man. I formed the following couplet which expresses the revelation, as it was shown to me, and explains Father Smith's dark saying to me at a blessing meeting in the Kirtland temple, prior to my baptism, as previously mentioned in my first interview with the Patriarch:

> *As man now is, God once was:*
> *As God now is, man may be."*

When Elder Snow returned from England, he shared his visionary experience with the Prophet Joseph Smith, who said: "Brother Snow, that is true gospel doctrine, and it is a revelation from God to you."[58] It was also a demonstration of the fact that one man's influence with the Almighty can also help magnify that of another.

Prescindia Huntington provides yet another illustration of the influence Father Smith had with heaven. The Saints in Kirtland had established a practice of fasting on the first Thursday of every month and meeting in the temple for worship. These "fast-meetings," as they were called, were, in the language of Eliza R. Snow, "hallowed and interesting beyond the power of language to describe. Many, many were the pentecostal seasons of the outpouring of the spirit of God on those days, manifesting the gifts of the gospel and the power of healing, prophesying, speaking in tongues, the interpretation of tongues, etc. I have there seen," Eliza added, "the lame man, on being administered to, throw aside his crutches and walk home perfectly healed; and not only were the lame made to walk, but the blind to see, the deaf to hear, the dumb to speak, and evil spirits to depart."[59]

Prescindia Huntington attended one such fast-meeting with her sister Zina. The established practice among the Saints was to drop curtains from the ceiling, dividing the large assembly room into quarters where, under the direction of a presiding officer, smaller groups of worshippers gathered for prayer, discoursing, and singing. At the end of the day the curtains were raised, and the four groups joined as one, and the season of prayer and prophesy, singing and speaking in tongues was continued with the larger body. At the particular meeting Sister Huntington describes, "the whole of the congregation were on their knees, praying vocally, for such was the custom at the close of these meetings when Father Smith presided; yet there was no confusion; the voice of the congregation mingled softly together. While the congregation was thus praying, we both heard, from one corner of the room above our heads, a choir of angels singing most beautifully. They were invisible to us, but myriads of angelic voices seemed to be united in singing some song of Zion, and their sweet harmony filled the temple of God."

The Huntington sisters, says Prescindia, "were also in the temple at the pentecost. In the morning Father Smith prayed for a pentecost, in opening the meeting." (Eliza R. Snow adds that Father Smith "very earnestly prayed that the Spirit of God might be poured out as on the day of Pentecost—that it might come 'as a rushing mighty wind.' "[60]) Prescindia continues: "That day the power of God rested mightily upon the saints. There was poured out upon us abundantly the spirit of revelation, prophesy and tongues. The Holy Ghost filled the house; and along in the afternoon a noise was heard. It was the sound of a mighty rushing wind. But at first the congregation was startled, not knowing what it was. To many it seemed as though the roof was all in flames. Father Smith exclaimed, 'Is the house on fire!'

" 'Do you not remember your prayer this morning, Father Smith?' inquired a brother.

"Then the patriarch, clasping his hands, exclaimed, 'The spirit of God, like a mighty rushing wind!' "[61]

One of the dramatic illustrations of the power of faith attending the ministry of Father Smith occurred in February 1839. By now, the hourglass had poured sixty-seven years of heavy sand into Father Smith's boots, which were embrowned by time and hardship. From the lurking places of Missouri the spirit of brooding darkness conspired, and armed mobs, sometimes dressed in the official military uniform of the state, pointed both bayonet and powdered ball at the Latter-day Saints. The official imprimatur of the state had decreed that "the Mormons must be treated as enemies and *must be exterminated* or driven from the state."[62] Liberty was guillotined. The disfiguring influence of blood-frenzied mobs hurried to drive the leaven from the Missouri loaf. Except among the Latter-day Saints, if the Bible was read it was hardly practiced in Missouri.

While we cannot recount the full catalog of miseries inflicted upon the Saints while in Missouri, we can justly note that every member of the Smith family was shadowed by the encroaching darkness. Father and Mother Smith shared the hunger of the Saints and saw their two sons, Joseph and Hyrum, violently wrenched from their own families and imprisoned. A court-martial, illegally convened and unlawfully conducted, condemned both men to be shot. In their absence, mobs entered their homes, stole their possessions, and threatened and harrassed their families. Around this time, Don Carlos's wife, Agnes, was first driven into exile, and then—while carrying her two helpless babes, "with the frost in the air and the earth frozen solid"—she left the "prints of her feet in blood upon the frozen soil of Missouri" as she fled "by the light of the flames that destroyed her little cabin home."[63] About a couple months before this, while Samuel was away a mob came to his home and assaulted his wife, Mary, and their children. One of her daughters later recalled, "They took her by picking up the featherbed, and carried her, with her babe, out into the sleet and rain. . . . Then they placed the two children, my sister Susan and myself, on the bed with her." They then burned the house to the ground.[64] These persecutions broke Mary's health and eventually led to her death. As for the Prophet's parents, during Joseph and Hyrum's imprisonment embittered apostates managed to purloin some property from the aged Father Smith.[65]

Still, Father and Mother Smith were determined to stay in Missouri as long as the Lord wanted them there. Finally, however, He spoke through the Prophet Joseph, who sent word that they should join the body of the Saints in Illinois. It was the depth of winter. The cold was severe, and the roads heavy with mire. They left Far West, leaving most of their furniture and provisions behind. Because their horses were wind-broken, they were compelled to walk much of the way.[66] Father Smith was sick. On the third day of the journey, a pouring rain began to fall, which continued throughout the following day. In the evening they sought shelter among the residents of northern Missouri but were continually refused.

It was at this point, if we have rightly pieced together the historical accounts, that they encountered a heavy snowstorm. "We halted," said Perrigrine Sessions, who was a member of the travelling party, "at a farm house to buy corn and to stay all night. Father Smith asked the owner if we could camp there and buy feed for our animals." The owner asked, "Are you Mormons?" Father Smith, with the forthrightness of Paul, said, "Yes, we are." In stone-cold anger the owner said, "Damn you, you can't stay on my property," and with insult and threat drove the travellers into the street. "Here we stopped and gathered together in the falling snow," recalled Brother Sessions. Then, Father Smith, who stood as silver purified seven times in the furnace, "removed his hat and with uplifted hands he prayed: 'In the name of the Lord whom we serve, let that man be cursed in his basket and in his store and let his name be cut off from under heaven.'" And, remembered Brother Sessions, "we all said, Amen."

Brother Sessions concluded: "When I came to travel this same road two years later, this incident was brought fresh to my mind. For behold, there was nothing to mark the spot but the ruins of his home, burned to ashes; his orchard [was] broken down; his farm [was] a picture of desolation; his wife and three children were burned to death in their home and he at this time was in close confinement for the insane. I saw the power of the priesthood manifested, for at the next farm we were received kindly and given all the comfort and assistance we needed and Father Smith left his blessing on this household as we departed.

Here my eyes beheld the fulfillment of his words to the letter as there I looked upon a picture of prosperity and happiness. All this passed and the two neighbors were ignorant of the curse or the blessing placed upon them as we passed on."[67]

Some may question the righteousness of calling down a curse on the wicked. We are quick to remember, however, that it was that God whose very name is Righteous[68] who honored the faithful prayer of his faithful son, and that, seeing all things at once, he makes neither error nor misjudgment. In the first instance, a man with great faith would not be prompted to petition inappropriately, and in the second, God himself would never honor an unrighteous petition, for he cannot look upon sin with the least degree of allowance.[69] The faithful have influence with God, but only upon righteous principles. Moreover, we remember that it was only the wicked who were cursed (first by their own actions!) while the righteous were blessed—again, by their own actions first. And, in the final analysis, both blessings and curses come from God, not man.

Faith: A Principle of Action

But if faith is power, how is that power obtained? And upon what principle does it come? In answer, the heavens thunder: "The powers of heaven cannot be controlled nor handled only [that is, *except*] upon the principles of righteousness."[70]

One such righteous principle is that of acting on inspired promptings. Nephi and his brothers, for example, were given a charge to return to Jerusalem to obtain the brass plates, which contained the word of God. At first they simply asked Laban for the plates[71]—but the word of God is not obtained simply by asking. It takes effort. Next they sought to purchase the plates[72] but learned that the word of God cannot be had by simple purchase. Finally, Nephi received a spiritual prompting: "I was led by the Spirit," he said, "not knowing beforehand the things which I should do."[73] Then it was that, by following the promptings of the Spirit of the Lord, they obtained the word of God.

And so it is with any desired blessing. Following spiritual promptings brings blessings. But it should be emphasized that following promptings means that we are moved to action. Faith, by definition, is a principle of action,[74] meaning, in part, that faithful people work to bring to pass the blessings they desire. Alma, for example, spoke of exercising faith as the ability to envision a righteous hope and then doing the things that would make that vision a reality. This process he called seeing with "an eye of faith."[75] Father Smith was another who understood this principle, and his life is dressed with illustrations of his seeing with the "eye of faith."

We have already mentioned some of the wondrous experiences that were a part of his temple worship, but we should place those experiences in their context. Father Smith worked to be worthy of the kinds of experiences he received. "On fast days," said Eliza R. Snow, "Father Smith's constant practice was to repair to the Temple very early, and offer up his prayers before sunrise, and there await the coming of the people; and so strictly did he discipline himself in the observance of fasting, as not even to wet his lips with water until after the dismissal of the meeting at four p.m."[76]

This sensitivity to spiritual preparedness evidenced itself in other ways as well. Caroline Crosby tells of falling sick and calling for Father Smith to administer to her. When he arrived he questioned her and her family about their faith and their feelings toward the First Presidency of the Church. In effect, he was probing to discern the level of her faith; he was also probing to ensure that she had not been influenced by the spirit of dissension then brooding over Kirtland. Having cultivated a spirit of faith by asking her about her faith—which means she was in a position to bear testimony of the gospel—Father Smith said "he would shut the door and keep the devil out," and then he, along with another elder, laid hands upon her head and gave her a blessing.[77]

Looking back, we can see that Father Smith did not simply walk in and give a blessing. Rather, he did things to create an environment into which the Spirit of the Lord might more freely enter: he asked questions about Sister Crosby's faith and about the gospel; he put her in a position to bear testimony; and he closed the door to banish distractions. Then, when he had created a climate in which the Spirit of the Lord was welcome, he lay his hands on her head and gave her a blessing.

Edward Stevenson reports that while he was quarrying stone to finish a stone chimney on his mother's house, the horse-drawn wagon he was using overturned. In the ensuing commotion the chains of the traces became wrapped around his legs and he could not free himself. The horses kicked and fought, and Stevenson thought he might at any moment be killed. Seeing two men in the distance, he shouted for assistance. He explained: "My shouts were answered . . . by one of the two men . . . who turned and beckoned [to the] other fellow, and lost no time in coming to my relief. To me it was an angel who hove in sight, and soon by my side a deliverer indeed, for so it proved to be. The hinder part of the horse was raised sufficient to loose the trace which I soon loosened by unhitching from the singletree hook. What on earth kept those horses so quiet I could only (and even now) account for as was predicted upon my head by Patriarch Joseph Smith, many years previously. . . . 'The devil,' he said, 'desires to sift you as wheat, but God shall set his angels and preserve you in the hour of need.' My angel deliverers helped me on my team which I safely brought back to Far West. And now, strange as it may appear, the first man who came to my relief after my arrival at home was Patriarch Joseph Smith. He helped me from the horse, for I was unable to stand alone without help. The Patriarch rubbed my legs which were swollen—for the chains, tightened by the weight of the horses, drew the flesh nearly to the bones. 'But,' said the Patriarch administering to me, 'you shall be healed and walk around tomorrow.' And indeed, it proved true."[78]

Again, not only was the kindly Patriarch prepared to give a blessing, but he administered temporally as well, massaging the injured legs and then prophetically promising that they would be healed on the morrow. But in this instance Father Smith's influence on the faith of Edward Stevenson was magnified by the patriarchal blessing he had given Stevenson, whose confidence in that blessing strengthened his faith that the Lord would preserve him.

After joining the Church, James and Drusilla Hendricks moved from Tennesee to Caldwell County, Missouri. Drusilla had had premonitions that her husband would be injured, and she had had a dream of something injurious befalling him. Her spiritual prescience was realized in the Battle of Crooked River, where her husband was shot in the neck. Drusilla said that she "rubbed and steamed him but could get no circulation. He was dead from his neck down." Left with naught but faith to lean

on, the Hendrickses looked to the priesthood. "About the mid-
dle of January [1839]," recalled Drusilla, "Father Joseph Smith
and Father [Isaac] Morely, with five or six others, came and
anointed and administered to my husband." It was, we note,
the administration of active faith: "They stood him on his feet
and he stood by them holding to each arm." James began to
work his shoulders, while Sister Hendricks "continued to rub
him with strong vinegar and salt and liniments."

The Hendrickses worried that, as the Saints were then in
the process of leaving Missouri, they would be left behind.
Armed with the assurances that they would not, however, they
pressed forward. "By this time," remembered Drusilla, "my husband had got so he could stand on his feet without helping him
to get on them." Then came time for the Hendrickses to leave:
"We started March 17, 1839, for Quincy, Illinois. On the first of
April as soon as the brethren found we were there, they secured
a bottle of oil, consecrated it, and came with Father Joseph
Smith at their head, (seven in number) while we were camped
out and got him [Brother Hendricks] on a chair and anointed
and administered to him again, then assisted him to his feet
and he walked, between two of them, some thirty yards and
back."[79]

Once again we see faith as a principle of action, and the
brethren were united not only in giving a blessing but also in
doing all that they could to see that blessing come to pass.
Again, they saw with the eye of faith.

Sarah DeArmon Pea Rich tells of yet another experience in
which Father Smith gave an inspired and life-saving blessing.
Sarah had recently arrived in Illinois, fresh from the Missouri
cauldron and newly reunited with her husband, Charles C.
Rich, after having been apart for three months. She took sick
following the birth of her firstborn, a daughter, born March 4,
1839. Her illness, she said, "came near proving fatal, for I grew
worse all the time, until my life was despaired for six weeks. No
one thought I would recover, except my husband, Mr. Rich. He
would not give up but said all the time that I could not die."
With death in the air, as it were, Sister Rich called for Father
Smith to make the five-mile trek from Quincy and give her a
patriarchal blessing, for she and those surrounding her were
emotionally preparing for her death.

The ailing and aged Patriarch came. He was advised of her

sickness and, looking at her frail form, said that he too thought she was about to die. Charles C. Rich, who would within a decade sit in the Quorum of the Twelve Apostles, had the faith to object, saying, "She won't die." Father Smith hung his head for a few moments in what we assume were moments of prayerful meditation, and then looked up and said: "Let us administer to her, and I will give her a patriarchal blessing."

Laying his hands upon her head, he blessed her, and as he did so, the Spirit of the Lord directed him to promise this dying woman not only that she would have a long life but also that she would "speedily recover"—oh, how the Spirit of the Lord changes how we think and feel!—leaving "all in the room . . . weeping for joy, for," wrote Sister Rich, "they had all been looking for me to die." But the Spirit of the Lord is the great change agent, which "knoweth all things"[80] and which "speaketh of things as they *really* are,"[81]—and Father Smith was the worthy receptacle. The Spirit of the Lord is also the author of faith, and when people have contact with that Holy Spirit, their faith grows; they get glimpses into eternity, which changes how they view mortality, as happened in this instance with Father Smith. "I did not have faith when I commenced blessing Sister Rich that she would get well," said this humble student of the Holy Ghost, "but the Lord poured out His Spirit upon me to give her the blessing, and promised her a long life, and many blessings"; and, he added by way of testimony and conviction, "every word will be fulfilled." Sister Rich reported that she "commenced to get better right away."

One experience with the Holy Ghost prepares the way for another; one prompting is often the platform from which a second prompting speaks. Thus it was in this instance. An inspired blessing was the preparation for another miracle. Before leaving the house the spiritually sensitive Patriarch gave Sister Rich a second blessing, and, she said, he "commanded me in the name of the Lord to arise and dress . . . and eat breakfast with him and the family, which I did, notwithstanding I had been confined to my bed for six weeks," during which time she was so enfeebled that she could not even sit up in the bed without assistance. Sister Rich rightly concludes her account—written some fifty years after the events—in the spirit of gratitude: "I gained slowly for a few weeks and all our friends were astonished at my being healed by the power of the Lord, for it was nothing else that had saved my life."[82] How contemporary truth is!

And how vital! For we paint an imperfect picture if we leave the impression that even the faithful receive every blessing they seek. There are moments when the Lord withholds his blessing, precisely to test the faith of those involved.[83] And there are moments when those with active faith prevail for the moment, only to see the agency of others unravel the good they have done. One such case, occurring "about the year 1835, in Kirtland," involved a man named Joseph Hunting, who was, said Zera Pulsipher, "possessed with the Devil, and was chained in a tight room." He was described as a maniac, and Father Smith is reported to have said that "the spirits that had possession of him were those that came out only through fasting and prayer." For sixteen years Hunting had been chained, wearing only a strong linen frock that stretched from his neck to his feet. He belonged to a family of Latter-day Saints, and so the brethren counseled "with old Father Smith," as Pulsipher gently identified the Prophet's father, who advised that they find seven brethren of good report, and fast and pray until Hunting was delivered. This was a case of actively seeking a blessing, of seeing with the eye of faith.

According to Ruth Tyler, it was under the direction of Father Smith that the Saints fasted. They met at the Hunting house every morning for five days, and those holding the priesthood administered to Brother Hunting. "When the Elders went in and administered to him the last time, his strength left him, as did also the evil Spirits, and he wept like a child. His chains were removed and because of his weakness it took two men to lead him into the house. . . .

"The man was shaved and dressed, although he had to rest several times while they were performing these duties for him." Over time, he developed the habit of frequently attending meetings in the Kirtland Temple with his mother.

"But, alas!" wrote Ruth Tyler. "After a time the family began to indulge in those things they had covenanted not to touch, thereby becoming covenant-breakers, and Satan took advantage of this and again entered the body of Joseph Hunting." When the devil entered him this second time, according to Zera Pulsipher, the elders were again called upon to administer to him. "The family had promised to keep the covenants, but we found they had returned to the old practice of breaking the Word of Wisdom. We therefore sent a message to Father Smith, and he said if they would not keep the covenants we might go about our business and let them all go to Hell together."

Oh, how could we not love such plainspoken honesty? And yet we are led to mourn, for, according to Ruth Tyler, "the family also, after a time became indifferent to their holy religion and apostatized, and the man who had been so miraculously healed, died a raving maniac."[84]

Faith that does not remain active dies.

Father Smith: A Faithful Example to the Saints

We cannot summarize in a paragraph the faith or ministry of Father Smith, but we can remember that he was not always "Father Smith." This tender appellation was conferred upon him by the affectionate Saints, probably during the Palmyra years. In the beginning he was Joseph, and it was in these early years of his life that his independence of mind and his vigor of spirit first showed themselves. He had the courage to stand against much of the popular religious thought of his day, and in his search for truth he rejected many of the teachings that centuries of apostasy had ingrained on the souls of men. The great issue, with Father Smith, however, is that he was foreordained to the mission that he fulfilled; he was the father of the Prophet of the Restoration by divine appointment, and was prepared in the eternities afore for that great role.

When the premortal preparation and the mortal need were joined in one moment, the Restoration began to unfold. Father Smith had faith while in mortality because he had had faith in the premortal world and with valiance there had defended the cause of Christ. He was one of the noble and great ones. Thus he came to this sphere schooled and prepared for the tutorial and supporting role he played. The same may be said of his wife, Lucy; she was his spiritual peer and, like him, was prepared in the premortal world for the stewardship she so valiantly fulfilled here. As part of the mortal schooling, he was born into a family where religious principle reigned, where the Bible was a principal teacher, and where his parents, like his grandparents before them, lived to the fullest degree in harmony with the light and knowledge available to them. We can only suppose that his parents were appointed to their preparatory mission in the same heavenly councils where he and Mother Smith were appointed to theirs.[85] To suggest otherwise is to envision a God who governs by accident, by chance, or who is not really in charge—an idea which in and of itself is unthinkable and which at the same time would imply a divine disinterest in one of the most important events in the history of this earth, the restoration of the gospel.

So in Father Smith we see the hand of the Almighty preparing and shaping him—first in the premortal world, then in the mortal family unit, later in his relationship with Lucy, again in his interaction with his family, particularly his sons Joseph and Hyrum, and later in his interactions with the Saints in general and with good men and women in the communities where he lived.

In a general sense, is it any different with the rest of us?

His faith grew because he did the things that brought him into contact with the Holy Spirit. His gospel study and meditation, for example, prepared his soul so that the Spirit of the Lord could instruct him with visions, of which he received many. Indeed, we justly observe that Father Smith learned more asleep than many men learn while awake—and this because his soul loved truth and hungered for it. Moreover, when he learned it he acted upon it and lived in harmony with it, and thus was endowed with power from on high.

Should it be any different with the rest of us?

For perspective, we recall that Edward Stevenson recorded from memory things that Father Smith had spoken, by the power of the Holy Ghost, some sixty years earlier.

Which of us has spoken with such force that our words will be recalled in sixty years?

Father Smith had such confidence in the gospel and its teachings that he promised Lorenzo Snow that with prayerful consideration of the truths of the Restoration, he would seek baptism.

Should we not all have such confidence in that same gospel?

He lived so closely to the promptings of the Holy Spirit that he felt the still small voice whisper that he should give a second blessing to Sarah Pea Rich, even though he had just given her a blessing within the hour. He then commanded her to arise and be made whole.

Should we not so live as to have claim on similar promptings and similar experiences?

He was so concerned with living the gospel that he dedicated all he had to the Lord, and he was so trusted of the Lord that God gave him visions and revelations, sent angels into his presence, poured out the spirit of prophesy onto him, and honored the promises which he made in the name of the Almighty.

Should we not all live as he did, and thereby share in the same blessings?

How could the Lord fail to pour out his Spirit on a man who tried so hard? Whether felling heresies, rejecting the error-filled inheritance of eighteen centuries of accummulated confusion, or embracing the sweet promptings of the eternal spirit of truth, the old lion of the faith, standing in his sunset years, could honestly acknowledge his imperfections, but could also offer a testimony that is a fitting summation of his life. He said: "I have never denied the Lord. . . . The Lord has often visited me in visions and dreams, and has brought me, with my family, through many afflictions, and I this day thank his holy name."[86]

Let us all so live that his faithful summation becomes our own.

CHAPTER 4

In the
Family Unit

In the instance of Father and Mother Smith, we have two
people who were rightly married and equally yoked; they were
two bodies animated by one soul. Their union, and the experiences and children it produced, is a rich weave of many colors,
set in a loom of love. They were drawn tightly together not only
by common affections and purposes but by common hardships
and privations as well. Such is the experience of many marriages. The fabric of the Smith weave, however, was drawn
more tightly together than most marriages by the power of the
Holy Ghost: they shared in spiritual experiences, and the Spirit
of the Lord, which is the author of the gift of love, wove their
hearts into one. In this they are a model for all.

Sharing Spiritual Experiences

When Lucy began attending a church, Joseph supportively
attended with her. Later, when he stopped attending church,
Lucy, rather than nagging and insisting that he return, retired
to a grove and pleaded with the Lord for and in behalf of her
husband. Later, after she had retired to bed, the Lord comforted her with a vision, in which she saw herself standing in a

Portrait of Lucy Mack Smith, by an unknown artist

large meadow near the house in which they then lived. Through the midst of the meadow flowed a stream of pure, clear water, on the edge of which she saw two trees. Each tree stood tall and beautiful with branches fully spread. One of the trees, said Lucy, "was surrounded with a bright belt, that shone like burnished gold, but far more brilliantly. Presently, a gentle breeze passed by, and the tree encircled with this golden zone, bent gracefully before the wind, and waved its beautiful branches in the light air. As the wind increased, this tree assumed the most lively and animated appearance, and seemed to express in its motions the utmost joy and happiness. If it had been an intelligent creature, it could not have conveyed, by the power of language, the idea of joy and gratitude so perfectly as it did; and even the stream that rolled beneath it, shared, apparently, every sensation felt by the tree, for, as the branches danced over the stream, it would swell gently, then recede again with a motion as soft as the breathing of an infant, but lively as the dancing of a sunbeam."

As the vision continued, Lucy focused her eye on the other tree, "which stood opposite; but it was not surrounded with the belt of light as the former, and it stood erect and fixed as a pillar of marble. No matter how strong the wind blew over it, not a leaf was stirred, not a bough was bent; but obstinately stiff it stood, scorning alike the zephyr's breath, or the power of the mighty storm.

"I wondered," she said, "at what I saw, and said in my heart, What can be the meaning of all this? And the interpretation given me was, that these personated my husband and his oldest brother, Jesse Smith; that the stubborn and unyielding tree was like Jesse; that the other, more pliant and flexible, was like Joseph, my husband; that the breath of heaven, which passed over them, was the pure and undefiled gospel of the Son of God, which gospel Jesse would always resist, but which Joseph, when he was more advanced in life, would hear and receive with his whole heart, and rejoice therein; and unto him would be added intelligence, happiness, glory, and everlasting life."[1]

This vision conferred a confidence and comfort that only the God of heaven can confer. The young Father Smith, for his part, also received of the confidence and comfort of heaven in the form of inspired dreams and visions, which he shared with his wife. She not only trusted but also recorded them. In one such vision, which confirmed the truths earlier revealed to Lucy, Father Smith found himself in an open, barren field in which he could see nothing but dead, fallen timber, surrounded by a death-like silence. With him in the vision was an "attendant spirit" of whom Father Smith asked the meaning of what he saw. Describing the apostasy which then enveloped the world, the spirit said: "This field is the world, which now lieth inanimate and dumb, in regard to the true religion, or plan of salvation; but travel on, and by the wayside you will find on a certain log a box, the contents of which, if you eat thereof, will make you wise, and give unto you wisdom and understanding." Obedient to this inspired instruction, Father Smith went to the box and picked it up. Then he lifted the lid of the box and began to eat—but, Father Smith said, as he did so, "all manner of beasts, horned cattle, and roaring animals, rose up on every side in the most threatening manner possible, tearing the earth, tossing their horns, and bellowing most terrifically all around me, and they finally came so close upon me, that I was compelled to drop the box and fly for my life. Yet, in the midst of all this I was perfectly happy, though I awoke trembling."

Thus it was that the Lord taught the father of the Prophet not only of the Apostasy and the coming Restoration but also of the persecution and opposition that eating the gospel fruit would bring. This same truth was reiterated in yet a second vision in which Father Smith saw, as did Lehi centuries earlier, the tree of life. Like Lehi, Father Smith partook of the fruit of the tree and shared it with his family, for which he was ridiculed and scorned by the world but embraced by the very God from whose fruit tree he had eaten.[2]

Joseph not only trusted his visions but also trusted his wife enough to share them with her. She recorded them, and they helped bind her heart to his—such is ever the effect of sharing in spiritual experiences among the worthy. So it was that throughout their marriage they prayed together and each trusted the answers to prayer received by the other. Shortly after Joseph and Hyrum were taken prisoner in the fall of 1838, for example, Mother Smith's inspired promptings concerning the assured well-being of her two sons comforted her children and no doubt her husband as well.[3] Father and Mother Smith went on missionary journeys together, and used their home for both missionary cottage meetings and Church services. She was lifted and inspired by the blessing meetings that she attended with her husband, and always showed great confidence in the blessings that he gave. This unity in spiritual purpose was reflected in temporal concerns as well, but the overarching influence binding them together was a recognition that they were children of the Almighty, and that while they felt like strangers and pilgrims on this earth, seeking for a heavenly country, they were charged with a mortal mission more important than they knew how to comprehend.

This sense of mission was breathed into the children as well, in part because the religious practices of the parents became those of the entire family. From the early moments of their marriage, they held daily family devotionals, which continued until their advanced years. These devotionals were held both in the mornings and in the evenings and included singing and prayer. After the Eight Witnesses—which included Hyrum,

Samuel H., and Father Smith—had seen the plates from which the Book of Mormon was translated, a group gathered at the Smith home for a testimony meeting in which the entire Smith family participated.[4] Gatherings similar to this meeting—gatherings of family or friends or both—continued throughout the years. The Prophet Joseph, for example, tells of one such meeting that he called together and which he began by telling his family of his love and affections for them. In the spirit of testimony, said the Prophet, "we sang the praise of God in animated strains, and the power of union and love was felt and enjoyed."[5]

One lesson to be learned from observing the Smith family is that the common affections of family ties were intensified and purified by the power of the Holy Spirit. They did things, as a family, to invite the Spirit of the Lord into their midst. In such a family, where family members were unafraid to show their affections for one another, the Spirit of the Lord found a more ready welcome. Thus we are not surprised to hear Father Smith say in a patriarchal blessing pronounced upon the head of his brother Asael, "Thou art my brother whom I love."[6] And when we read the words that the Prophet wrote to Emma about his family, we are left wishing his sentiments were more universal among humankind. "I am happy to find that you are still in the faith of Christ and at Father Smith's," wrote the Prophet to his wife, adding, "I hope you will comfort Father and Mother in their trials, and Hyrum and Jerusha and the rest of the family. Tell Sophronia I remember her and Calvin in my prayers. My respects to the rest [of the family]."[7]

Family Love

As we read from the journal of John Smith, one of Father Smith's brothers, we feel the tenderness that was a part of the Smith family from the infancy of these brothers. Six months before Father Smith died, Uncle John (as he was called) recorded in his journal the simple notation: "Visited my aged brother, Joseph, who has been sick all winter. Found him very low."[8] Three and a half months later he mournfully wrote to his son George A. about his brother Joseph: "Your Uncle Joseph is in a loose state of health and has been for a long time. [I] have not seen him for two weeks. Aunt Lucy is failing. They appear to be near the borders of the grave, preserved by the prayers of faith in life. Thus your fathers are fast going off the mortal stage to a place where we shall rest in peace, if faithful."[9] Then, just two weeks prior to the death of Father Smith, and in five melancholy sentences that seem to capture the whole rhetoric of tender family ties, Uncle John opened his heart again, unveiling an affectionate longing for the warmth of youth, and an irremediable disquietude over his brother Jesse, who did not accept the gospel: "[I] went over the river to see my brother [Joseph Smith, Sr.] . . . [who] to all human appearances is nigh unto death. But a few days have passed away since we were seven brothers—boys in the vigor of youth. Now three are not. One in unbelief in the state of New York. Three of us in the Church, but it seems that our days are few."[10]

These heart-embracing expressions of Uncle John are no accident but are the consequence of a family whose interactions were umbrellaed by love. What had happened among Father Smith and his brothers reoccurred among his children, and, Lehi-like, once having tasted of the fruit of the tree of life, each desired that the others eat as well. Mother Smith provides an illustration. In January 1833 all the male members of the Smith family were called home, and the Prophet "administered to them the ordinance of washing of feet; after which the Spirit fell upon them, and they spake in tongues, and prophesied. The brethren gathered together to witness the manifestations of the power of God. At that time I was on the farm a short distance from the place where the meeting was held, and my children being anxious that I should enjoy the meeting, sent a messenger in great haste for me. I went without delay, and shared with the rest, the most glorious out-pouring of the Spirit of God, that had ever before taken place in the Church." Indeed, so great was the joy of this moment—which Lucy shared in because her family sought her out and brought her to it!—that the Smith family thought that they should never grieve or feel sorrow again.[11]

Father and Mother Smith had nurtured close family unity since the beginnings of their marriage, though the knowledge of the gospel continually intensified their understanding of what a family is and how family ties stretch into the eternities. The human soul is eternal, and thus there is something about death that reveals life, and something about separation that reveals love. Perhaps it is the focus on what really matters that these two messengers bring. In any event, the circumstances surrounding the death of Alvin, the firstborn of Father and Mother Smith, reveal a great deal about the quality of love that cemented the Smiths together. In November 1823, Alvin was afflicted with what Mother Smith calls "the bilious colic." The attending physician, whom Mother Smith years later referred to as "a quack physician," administered a heavy dose of calomel,[12] which became lodged in his upper bowel and caused his death. In his painful and enfeebled state, and realizing that he was beyond the reach of medicine, Alvin called Hyrum, the second-born son, and worried out loud about his parents: "Hyrum, I must die. Now I want to say a few things, which I wish to have you remember. I have done all I could to make our dear parents comfortable. I want you to go on and finish the house"—which the family was then building—"and take care of them in their old age, and do not any more let them work hard, as they are now in old age."

He then called Sophronia to his deathbed and with selfless concern urged her to uphold the fifth commandment: "Do all you can for father and mother—never forsake them; they have worked hard, and they are now getting old. Be kind to them, and remember what they have done for us."

Knowing that life was slipping from his grasp, Alvin called for all the children, exhorting them as he had Hyrum and Sophronia. He spoke to Joseph in love and testimony: "I am now going to die, the distress which I suffer, and the feelings that I have, tell me my time is very short. I want you to be a good boy, and do everything that lies in your power to obtain the Record. Be faithful in receiving instruction, and in keeping every commandment that is given you. Your brother Alvin must leave you; but remember the example which he has set for you; and set the same example for the children that are younger than yourself, and always be kind to father and mother."

At last he called for little Lucy, the two-and-a-half-year-old child, for whom Alvin had a particular attachment, as she had for him. Awakened from her sleep, Lucy was taken to her dying brother. She embraced him, crying, "Oh, Amby," as she called him, and repeatedly kissed him. "Lucy," said Alvin, "you must be the best girl in the world, and take care of mother; you can't have your Amby any more. Amby is going away; he must leave little Lucy." At this, he kissed her, and then said to Mother Smith, "Take her away, I think my breath offends her." Lucy clung to Alvin with an iron grasp, and it was only with considerable difficulty that the others succeeded in disengaging her hands.

As Mother Smith, holding little Lucy, turned to leave, Alvin breathed his mortal end: "Father, mother, brothers, and sisters, farewell! I can now breathe out my life as calmly as a clock." And, adds Mother Smith, "saying this, he immediately closed his eyes in death." One member of the family, thinking, we suppose, to comfort little Lucy, said, "Alvin is gone; an angel has taken his spirit to heaven," which only seemed to intensify her anguish, for she cried in innocent despair until his body was removed from the house.[13]

Such love as that demonstrated at Alvin's death is the fruit of much cultivation; it is not found among the spiritually coarse. This love helps to assuage the anguish of the bereaved while holding out the hope of eternal reunion, and it is heightened by the nobility of a dying youth more concerned with the well-being of his parents than his own comfort. Almost twenty years later the Prophet Joseph Smith recalled these events and said that "the angel of the Lord visited [Alvin] in his last moments,"[14] which reminds us that at the death of the righteous Lazarus, in the story told by Jesus, Lazarus was carried by angels into the bosom of Abraham, while the wicked rich man was left to languish in hell.[15] By the Lord's standard, Alvin was a righteous man, and the Smiths a worthy family. For our part, we bow to the salutary influence of example.

Teaching the Gospel in the Home

What was it, we ask, that fostered such close ties in the Smith family? As usual, many causes worked together. The personalities and character of the parents set the pattern in all things; in addition to their natural affections for their children, they loved life. By nature Father Smith was a happy, cheerful soul, and, said the Prophet's son Joseph III with regard to Mother Smith, "there never was a more earnest and social body in the Smith family than Grandma Smith."[16] As is ever the case, parental example colored everything the Smith family did. At

*Artist's conception of Joseph Smith, Sr., and Lucy Mack Smith
with their children, by Dale Baxter*

the same time, their unique role in the events of the Restoration set them apart and made them the target of those who would unjustly accuse them of every range of vice and unholy tradition. The Prophet Joseph sat on the bull's-eye, but the entire family lived on the dart board, and, said the Prophet, "rumor with her thousand tongues was all the time employed in circulating falsehoods about my father's family, and about myself."[17] The hatred and violence mounted against the Prophet and his family continued through the duration of their lives, eventuating in the murder and death, said Mother Smith, of "no less than six" members of her family.[18] The hand of persecution, however, only enclosed the Smiths in tighter union, and even their critics and enemies saw it. One typical account, for example, said: "Among the earliest and most persevering disciples of Joseph Smith, Jr., were his father and brothers.

Through weal and through wo they clung to him with the utmost pertinacity. . . . They figured more or less conspicuously
during his career in the various arrangements and adventures
that characterized him."[19] At the same time, we must assume
that the hand of heaven steadied the Smith cradle with particular watchfulness. Our revelations tell us that both Father Smith
and the Prophet were foreordained to the labors they performed,[20] and it seems consistent with everything we know to
assume that Mother Smith similarly was set apart in the premortal life for her calling in mortality.[21] Who could suppose less
of Hyrum, Samuel, or of Don Carlos—or, for that matter, of
Alvin, whom the Prophet described as "the noblest of my
father's family"?[22] We seem compelled to the conclusion that
when the noble and great come to earth as father and mother,
brother and sister, their mortal instinct would be to create a
homelife enveloped in love.

There is, however, yet another clear certainty regarding the
Smiths and the close bonds they formed. They were taught
gospel principles from their infancy, and those principles unavoidably led them to greater love and unity. As mentioned previously, our records show that the Smiths raised their children
on daily devotionals,[23] in which they prayed and sang, sometimes even upon bended knee.[24] William reports that this practice stretched back as far as he could remember.[25] The family
even designated a special spot in the neighboring groves where
the family would retire for "offering up their secret devotions to
God."[26]

In what we might call the precursor to the family home
evening, they met as a family to teach and discuss the gospel.
When perplexed over which church to join and concerned for
his soul's welfare, the Prophet instinctively went to the scriptures for answers, "believing," he said, "as I was taught, that
they contained the word of God."[27] After the coming of Moroni, and in sessions where "the whole family were melted to
tears,"[28] the family gathered and listened as the young Prophet
rehearsed his experiences. "Joseph would occasionally give us
some of the most amusing recitals that could be imagined," said
Mother Smith. In scenes which tempt the envy of all, "he would
describe the ancient inhabitants of this continent, their dress,
mode of traveling, and the animals upon which they rode; their
cities, their buildings, with every particular; their mode of war-

fare; and also their religious worship. This he would do with as much ease, seemingly, as if he had spent his whole life among them."[29] The Lord, we trust, will forgive our jealousy at not having been able to be there!

On occasion these family gatherings (which sometimes might include friends) became testimony meetings, as occurred in the summer of 1829 when the Prophet and the Three Witnesses returned to the Whitmer home after having seen Moroni and the gold plates,[30] and again in the Smith home after the Eight Witnesses—who included three members of the Smith family—were shown the plates.[31] The Prophet frequently convened Church meetings in the home of Father and Mother Smith—surely the entire family would have been there!—to which member and nonmember alike were invited.[32] These family teaching moments were continued even while family members traveled, and they were extended to others who were not members of the family. When some of the Smith family (in company with other Saints) moved together from Waterloo, New York, to Kirtland, Ohio, in 1831, they preached to one another and sang hymns, even on the flatboat in transit. Some of the Saints feared that such public worship would incite mob reaction, but Mother Smith, with characteristic determination said, "Mob it is, then," and the worship services continued.[33] Such family teaching meetings appear to have continued through the Kirtland years and were well enough known that when Reynolds Cahoon spent a night with the Smiths in their home, he exhorted them to "silence and good order" in their family devotions.[34]

Mary Elizabeth Rollins Lightner illustrates how, for the Smiths, teaching the family and teaching the Saints became one and the same process. "The Smith family," said Sister Lightner, "came to Kirtland early in the spring of 1831. After they were settled in their house, mother and I went to see them. We had heard so much about the Golden Bible, as it was then called, that we were very anxious to hear more. The whole Smith family, excepting Joseph, was there. As we stood talking to them, Brother Joseph and Martin Harris came in with two or three others. When the greetings were over, Brother Joseph looked around very solemnly (it was the first time some of them had seen him) and said, 'There are enough here to hold a little meeting.'"[35]

Not surprisingly, the home of Father and Mother Smith became a center of gospel learning in the community. Prayer meetings with the Saints were often held in the Smith barn, as was the case in the summer of 1832 when Sidney Rigdon, in a moment of confusion and spiritual recusancy, announced that the keys of the kingdom were "rent from the Church."[36] Missionaries passing through Kirtland often stayed at the Smith home; and the diary of John Smith (not the Prophet's uncle) speaks of cottage meetings being held in what appears to be the home of Father Smith. We have clues that point to the fact that Father Smith encouraged gospel conversation and inquiry among those who came to his home, but none more delightfully illustrative than the account of the debating school established at his home in 1835. The Prophet Joseph tells the story: "At evening Bishop Whitney, his wife, father and mother, and sister-in-law came in and invited me and my wife to go with them and visit Father Smith and family. My wife was unwell and could not go; however, I and my scribe went. When we got there we found that some of the young elders were about engaging in a debate upon the subject of miracles. The question was this: Was or was it not the design of Christ to establish his gospel by miracles?" The question is wonderfully contemporary, for there were those, in the days of the Prophet as in our own day, who sought to establish the divinity of their claims by showing themselves possessed of miracles.

"After an interesting debate of three hours or more," the Prophet continues, "during which time much talent was displayed, it was decided by the presidents of the debate in the negative, which was a righteous decision." Then he adds this prophetic postscript: "I discovered in this debate much warmth displayed, too much zeal for mastery, too much of that enthusiasm that characterizes a lawyer at the bar who is determined to defend his cause, right or wrong. I therefore availed myself of this favorable opportunity to drop a few words upon this subject by way of advice that they might improve their minds and cultivate their powers of intellect in a proper manner, that they might not incur the displeasure of heaven, [and] that they should handle sacred things very sacredly and with due deference to the opinions of others and with an eye single to the glory of God."[37]

Thus it was by precept and example that Father Smith, ever

with Lucy's hand in his, taught the gospel in the home. When he was not home, she spoke in his stead. What they knew, they shared. More important, however, is that in following the parental example the children were able to feel and experience much that the parents before them had felt and experienced. The history of the family is filled with spiritual experiences of biblical proportions: visions, dreams, revelations, angels, healings, speaking and interpreting tongues, preaching convincing sermons, performing missionary service, and baptizing hundreds—these are all part of the family legacy. Father and Mother Smith knowingly placed the family on the right path, and placed the hand of each child with firm grasp on the iron rod. Any fingers that let go of the rod did so above and beyond the impress of parental influence.

Dealing with Discord

We long for families where love, peace, and unity so prevail that never a moment passes when we could not smile at heaven with the perfect assurance of the Lord's constant approval. And when discord rears its ugly head, we seek selfish solace in the knowledge that an Adam, a Lehi, an Eli, or an Isaac had difficult and sometimes wayward children, and that if the Lord approved of those parents—as he did—then perhaps there is hope that he will approve of us as well. There is, however, something disquieting in such thought, for we know and sense that this is a fallen world, that we are fallen creatures, subject to all the passions and pathos of a fallen condition, and that, like the brother of Jared, "because of the fall our natures have become evil continually."[38] Torn between good and evil, we feel, like Paul, sometimes at war with ourselves.[39] Still, through it all, we recognize that in this imperfect world, imperfection will sometimes reign as king—even in the family unit.

And so it is that even in the homes of the most perfect-minded and right-spirited of Saints, discord comes. It was ever thus. From the family of Father Smith, where discord on occasion found its mark, we have an illustration of how to deal, by gospel standards, with contention. The case has to do with a difference between the Prophet Joseph and his brother William. Father Smith is cast in the mediator's role and in this instance is our teacher. We are left to guess that the spirit of contention between these two brothers existed as far back as October 1835, when, during a disciplinary consideration of the Kirtland high council, Mother Smith introduced testimony dealing with materials that had previously been settled. In his capacity as the presiding officer, the Prophet Joseph objected, at which William took offense, accusing the Prophet of seeking to invalidate Mother Smith's testimony. William arose in anger—"enraged," said the Prophet, who ordered him to be seated in order to restore order to the proceedings. Governed by the fire of hot blood, William said he would not be seated unless Joseph "knocked him down." At this point Joseph desired to leave, but Father Smith, also a member of the council, persuaded him to stay. Eventually order was restored, and the business of the meeting continued.[40]

Whatever cooling occurred was only temporary, for less than two months later, when the Prophet visited a debating school at the home jointly occupied by the families of Father Smith and William Smith, William physically assaulted the Prophet at a moment when the Prophet was removing his outer coat. The Prophet's side, having already been wounded previously when Joseph was attacked by a mob, was further injured in this episode. Others present separated the two, and order was restored. Later, William wrote a letter of apology and Joseph responded with a letter whose spirit we can only admire. "In your letter you ask my forgiveness, which I readily grant," wrote the Prophet, later repeating, "I freely forgive you." He then closes with a word of admonition: "If at any time you should consider me to be an imposter, for heaven's sake leave me in the hands of God, and not think to take vengeance on me yourself." In a pattern worthy of emulation, the Prophet closed his letter with a prayer, knowing that with celestial assistance telestial turmoils could be overcome: "And now may God have mercy upon my father's house; may God take away enmity from between me and thee; and may all blessings be restored, and the past be forgotten forever." Then, with a recognition that families can be eternal only with the help of the Almighty, Joseph concluded: "May humble repentance bring us both to Thee, O God, and to Thy power and protection, and a crown, to enjoy the society of father, mother, Alvin, Hyrum, Sophronia, Samuel, Catherine, Carlos, Lucy, the Saints, and all the sanctified in peace, forever, is the prayer of your brother, Joseph Smith, Jun."[41]

Father Smith had been present during the altercation; we are not told if he saw either the Prophet's letter or the one written by William. We do know, however, that he felt very uneasy over the dynamite-and-fire relationship between the two brothers, and the explosion which it precipitated. At this point, therefore, he donned the full clothing of fatherhood and intervened to do more than restore order—he sought to turn an unpleasant experience into an opportunity by binding the brothers together under a bond that the Spirit of the Lord alone can provide. We go to the Prophet Joseph for the details: "Brothers William and Hyrum, and Uncle John Smith, came to my house, and we went into a room by ourselves, in company with father and Elder Martin Harris. Father Smith then opened our interview by prayer." Imagine! Solving family differences in a spirit of prayer! No such thought ever occurred to a Napoleon; but then, here we deal with men much greater than Napoleon. According to the Prophet's account, after the prayer Father Smith "expressed himself on the occasion in a very feeling and pathetic manner, even with all the sympathy of a father, whose feelings were deeply wounded on account of the difficulty that was existing in the family."

Here, then, is the pattern: If mountains can be moved by the power of faith, and the waters of the Red Sea parted, and if the dead can be raised and the lame made to walk, why not heal hurt feelings by the power of the Holy Ghost? Where there is discomfort, let the Comforter speak! And so it was in this instance: while Father Smith addressed those assembled, reported the Prophet, "the Spirit of God rested down upon us in mighty power, and our hearts were melted."

The Comforter comforts; the Sanctifier sanctifies. And it would not even have occurred to lesser men to use such an approach. Its effects were immediate. "Brother William made a humble confession," said the Prophet, "and asked my forgiveness for the abuse he had offered me. And wherein I had been out of the way, I asked his forgiveness. And the spirit of confession and forgiveness was mutual among us all, and we covenanted with each other, in the sight of God, and the holy angels, and the brethren, to strive thenceforward to build each other up in righteousness in all things, and not listen to evil reports concerning each other; but, like brothers indeed"—and here we gain a glimpse of an eternal view of brotherhood—"go to each other, with our grievances, in the spirit of meekness, and be reconciled, and thereby promote our happiness, and the happiness of the family, and, in short, the happiness and well-being of all."

The circle of gospel goodwill was then enlarged. "My wife and mother and my scribe were then called in," said the Prophet, "and we repeated the covenant to them that we had entered into; and while gratitude swelled our bosoms, tears flowed from our eyes. I was then requested to close our interview, which I did, with prayer; and it was truly a jubilee and time of rejoicing." As is so often the case, however, one spiritual experience simply becomes the foundation upon which another is built. Thus it was that the brethren present "all unitedly administered, by laying on of hands, to . . . George A. Smith, who was immediately healed of a severe rheumatic affection all over the body, which caused excruciating pain."[42]

The Prophet rejoiced in the entire experience, not just because a wound had been healed, but because the wound would not now be permitted to fester and canker the work to which he had been called, and because his family was once again the family it should have been. He thrilled that two days later, a Sunday, "William . . . preached a fine discourse; and," the Prophet said, "this day has been a day of rejoicing to me. The cloud that has been hanging over us has burst with blessings on our heads, and Satan has been foiled in his attempts to destroy me and the Church, by causing jealousies to arise in the hearts of some of the brethren; and I thank my heavenly Father," he concluded, "for the union and harmony which now prevail in the Church."[43] And, we add, he might well have said the same thing of his father's family.

What, then, have we seen? Several things, with a gospel spirit at the core of it all. In the first instance, Father and Mother Smith sought out the opportunity to heal the family breach, and Father Smith and the Prophet joined with a group of faithful Saints, some of whom were members of their own family, to join in a collective exertion of faith in order to solve an ugly problem. Father Smith began the meeting with prayer—nay, with mighty, faith-filled prayer—which he followed with his own testimony-filled expressions of love, counsel, and pleading. In consequence of what he said, and the power of the Spirit by which he spoke, the hearts of those assembled "were melted," which, we note, brings us to the central theme of the entire experience: the changes wrought were wrought by the power of the Holy Ghost. The covenants they made were made and remade in the presence of witnesses, who ever thereafter could offer gentle reminders to encourage these covenanters to uphold their sacred commitments. One compelling evidence that they operated by the power of the Holy Spirit is that that same Spirit inspired them in the healing of George A. Smith. Truly it was the collective faith of all assembled that generated the treasured experience, but it was the faith-filled prayer of Father Smith, with its accompanying testimony and pleadings, that laid the foundation upon which the rest of the spiritual outpouring was based.

The day after this family reconciliation, in a meeting of the Kirtland high council, William humbly confessed to charges that had been brought against him and asked forgiveness; those present voted to accept his confession and extend the hand of fellowship.[44] Such experiences as this drew the family closer together, and Mother Smith was later to comment, in an obvious reference to William and in an equally obvious reference to a good many other experiences like this one, "He has endeared himself to me by the trouble he has made me."[45]

This practice of finding comfort in the whisperings of the Holy Spirit was a characteristic part of the ministry of the Smith family from the beginning. Mother Smith, for example, tells of an 1829 trial in which she feared for the well-being of her son the Prophet Joseph, and in which the Spirit of the Lord spoke a promise to her that "not one hair of his head shall be harmed," leaving her with feelings of joy unspeakable.[46] Years later, when the Prophet and Hyrum were illegally abducted and displayed in the public square at Far West amid the howling of blood-witted mobsters, the Spirit of the Lord again spoke comfort to Mother Smith, promising that they would be delivered from the power of their enemies.[47] And, to bring the practice full circle, during the months preceding his death, Father Smith at times became very ill and weak. On one such occasion he expressed the fear that he would die without his family near. Again, the sweet whisperings of the Holy Spirit to Lucy, which she in turn shared with her husband, brought certain comfort.[48]

Thus, we once more bow in gratitude for the example of a family that so ably demonstrated the powers that the gospel brings into the lives of its adherents.

A Natural Patriarch

There are in the Church both ordained and natural patriarchs. An ordained patriarch holds the office of patriarch—called an "evangelical minister" in the revelation[49]—and gives patriarchal blessings to worthy members of the Church. By definition, a natural patriarch is one who has entered into the patriarchal order of celestial marriage in the house of the Lord, receiving for himself the blessings of Abraham, Isaac, and Jacob, and thereby becoming a natural patriarch to his posterity. Father Smith was ordained as the Patriarch to the Church by the Prophet Joseph Smith on December 18, 1833.[50] In that capacity he gave hundreds of blessings and much good counsel to the Saints.

Our understanding of the office and calling of the Patriarch has grown incrementally—line upon line and precept upon precept. So it is also with our understanding of the prerogatives of a natural patriarch; it too has grown incrementally. Still, there is much that Father Smith did that our current understanding permits us to see would fall under the natural embrace of the office of the natural patriarch, and in this we are both instructed and bettered.

To enlarge our view, we gaze in at a meeting of the Smith family (and some others), encircled in the home of the Prophet Joseph and Emma, in Kirtland, Ohio, on December 9, 1834. A feast has been prepared, and patriarchal blessings are to be given; they will feed both body and soul. It is but a few short months since the brethren have returned from Zion's Camp, and but two months since Eber D. Howe and Philastus Hurlburt joined to publish the venomous *Mormonism Unvailed*, attacking both the character of the Prophet Joseph Smith and the Book of Mormon. Still, it is a time when the persecutors of the Saints seem to sleep for a moment, and a spirit of worship and unity draws the Smiths together.

At the center of this serenity stands the head of the family, Joseph Smith, Sr., a man foreordained, it seems, for moments such as this. Humility is a gift of the Holy Ghost that enables us to know and feel our dependence upon God—and if it could be molded into arms and legs and sinew and features, one such molding would be Father Smith. He speaks without pretense, and voices a melting softness that binds every heart present to his own; with sometimes rainy eyes and always with immortal longings, he begins: "My children, I am now old—in my sixty-third year, and my head is white. I have seen many years, compared to those enjoyed by many . . . , and my frame is feeble because of the many trials and fatigues which I have endured in this life. I have not attained to the age of my fathers"—his father died at eighty-six, his grandfather at seventy-one, and his great-grandfather at seventy-two—"neither do I now know as I shall; but I desire, and for a long time have, to bless my children before I go hence."

What will you leave your children? Your lands and estate? The accumulated earnings of a lifetime? The assembled wealth of years of investments? In the spirit of his fathers before him, Father Smith chose to leave a priesthood blessing on each of his children and upon their spouses as well.

"It is a source of grief to me," he continues, "that I have not been more fruitful to the Lord in days which are passed than I have," reminding us of the humble expressions and feelings of seeming inadequacy voiced by such as John the Baptist,[51] the Apostle Paul,[52] and Nephi,[53] who were nonetheless entirely approved by the Lord. "I have not always set that example before my family that I ought; I have not been diligent in teaching them the commandments of the Lord, but have rather manifested a light and trifling mind." This is a harsh self-judgment, and in it we recognize the earnest yearnings of a humble soul, anxious only to purify every weakness and overcome every fault. His children testified that he taught them both deliberately and diligently, and others, such as Heber C. Kimball, saw what he calls a "light and trifling mind" as a love of life and of a good story.[54] Moreover, it is the righteous and not the slothful steward who humbly asks: "What could I have done more for my vineyard?"[55]

The overarching test, of course, is in the spirit of the man, and the spirit of Father Smith comes forward as he continues, noting that, in spite of weaknesses, "I have never denied the Lord. Notwithstanding all this, my folly, . . . the Lord has often visited me in visions and dreams, and has brought me, with my family, through many afflictions, and I this day thank his holy name."

This, then, is the summum bonum of the whole matter! As a humble servant, and seeing the vastness of opportunity, Father Smith feels some inadequacies. But God, the perfect judge of character, who knows all things, including the hearts of men, judges otherwise: he has *often*—not once or twice, but *often*—entrusted Father Smith with the learning of heaven through the medium of inspired dreams and visions. And then, in a reaffirmation of that trust, that same God, who works only according to the faith of men,[56] has many times honored the faith of Father Smith and delivered him from "many afflictions." If Father Smith stands approved in the presence of God, ought he not win our approval as well—in spite of his own modest self-appraisal?

But the voice of Father Smith continues: "I look round upon you before me, and I behold . . . three seats are, as it were, empty. The Lord, in his just providence, has taken from me, at an untimely birth, a son. This has been a matter of affliction, but the Lord's ways are just. My next son, Alvin, as you all are aware, was taken from us in the vigor of his life, in the bloom of youth.[57] My heart often mourns his loss, but I have not disposition to complain against the Lord." Then, adds the sainted Patriarch, "another has been taken also in his infancy. I pray that my loss may be abundantly supplied, and made up in additional blessings, and that his grace may attend me, and his Holy Spirit be shed abroad in my heart, that I may pronounce such blessings upon your heads as will be fulfilled."[58]

With these spirit-filled introductory remarks concluded, a prayer was offered, and then Father Smith laid his hands on his children, blessing Hyrum and his wife, Jerusha; Calvin Stoddard and his wife, Sophronia; Joseph and Emma; Samuel and his wife, Mary; William's wife, Caroline; Catherine Smith Salisbury; Don Carlos and his wife, Agnes; and young Lucy.

Some of what Father Smith said and promised is perhaps too personal or sacred for us to share. There are, however, portions that have a place in the minds of all the Saints, because of the instruction the declarations provide and the inspiration they offer, both about gospel law and the character of the Smith family. When blessing the Prophet Joseph, for example, Father

Smith, like Mother Smith in her writings,[59] states that from his youth the Prophet had been a particularly reflective youth and had always sought to know the will of the Lord. The Prophet is also commended for his protective care of his own father and his constant obedience to both parents. In addition, the Prophet is reminded that he was uniquely prepared and qualified for his mortal mission. There was, said Father Smith, none other like him, and his work such as "no other man would do as thyself, in all things according to the will of the Lord."

Then comes an inspired interpretation and enlarged view of the vision given to Jacob's son Joseph, who was sold by his brothers into Egypt. This vision is mentioned in the Book of Mormon,[60] but from the blessing given by Father Smith we learn a good deal that is not in the Book of Mormon account. Lehi knew that Joseph had seen the Lehites in vision; Father Smith added that that vision had also shown the ancient Joseph the Prophet Joseph Smith and the events of the restoration of the gospel in the latter days. Father Smith also emphasized that it was because of faith that Joseph in Egypt obtained the promise that, in the words of that same Joseph of old, "my seed are to inherit the choice land whereon the Zion of God shall stand in the last days," and that Joseph Smith, the agent of restoration, was to descend from Joseph, son of Jacob, as well.

The ancient Joseph described the Prophet Joseph Smith, saying, "His bowels shall be as a fountain of truth, whose loins shall be girded with the girdle of righteousness, whose hands shall be lifted with acceptance before the God of Jacob to turn away his anger from his anointed [i.e., Joseph Smith], whose heart shall meditate great wisdom, whose intelligence shall circumscribe and comprehend the deep things of God, and whose mouth shall utter the law of the just. . . . He shall feed upon the heritage of Jacob his father. The just shall desire his society, and the upright in heart shall be his companions;[61] no weapon formed against him shall prosper,[62] and though the wicked mar him for a little season,[63] he shall be like one rising up in the heat of wine—he shall roar in his strength, and the Lord shall put to flight his persecutors; he shall be blessed like the fruitful olive, and his memory shall be as sweet as the choice cluster of the first grapes. Like a sheaf fully ripe, gathered into the garner, so shall he stand before the Lord, having produced a hundredfold. Thus," said Father Smith, "spake my father Joseph."[64]

Oh, how fresh and contemporary—and how accurate!—is the prophetic word that is thirty-five hundred years old! It sees the Prophet Joseph Smith as God sees him, a seer on whom the direct rays of heaven would shine, reflecting the truths of eternity to all who would open the eyes of their understanding. More than any man in this dispensation, Joseph Smith comprehended eternity, and with contagious fervor spread that understanding among his fellows until it produced a hundredfold, and then a thousandfold, and then more.

In addition to the Prophet Joseph Smith, others were comforted by the inspiration to fall from the lips of Father Smith. Hyrum was promised that he would be the agent of bringing many souls unto salvation, that his name would be written on the ledgers of heaven, and that because of his faithfulness he would be sealed up unto eternal life. Less than three months after receiving these promises, Father Smith laid his hands on Hyrum once again, and, said Hyrum, "I was blessed with the privilege of obtaining the desires of my heart in all things."[65] Similarly, Hyrum's wife, Jerusha, whose own family had chosen not to accept the gospel, was promised that the Lord would nonetheless comfort her, and, said the inspired Patriarch, "thy name is recorded on high." Sophronia, Samuel, and Samuel's wife were all promised similar comfort, and Calvin Stoddard (Sophronia's husband), whose membership in the Church at that moment stood forfeit, was promised that if he would repent, he too would be blessed.

As a father in Israel, Father Smith was calling down the blessings of heaven upon his posterity. In the blessing conferred upon Lucy, his youngest child, he gives us some insight into how this occurred. "I have besought the Lord for blessings for thee in much fasting and prayer," he said, and in so speaking leaves for all posterity a lesson in parenting. Because of her youth, he adapts the language of the blessing to her understanding, and therein we learn yet a second lesson on parenting. We learn a third when he teaches that he exerted much faith in order to obtain the blessing.

A father's influence and a father's prerogatives are not limited by the generations. A righteous grandfather may stretch his influence down into the nest of his grandchildren as well. Thus it was that Father Smith, again a natural patriarch in Israel, gave a name and a blessing to Hyrum's son John;[66] and at a patriarchal blessing meeting convened in Samuel's home, he gave the name of Susannah to the daughter of Samuel and Mary. At the same meeting he gave patriarchal blessings to Mary's parents.[67]

Even as the hourglass of his life was dropping its final sand, Father Smith was filled with blessings that he sought to pronounce upon the heads of his children. Mother Smith provides the details: It was September 1840, and for several weeks Father Smith had been confined to bed, the enervating effects of disease and exhaustion having almost destroyed his system. He vomited blood. Still, he had a mind that could not grow torpid with old age, and as he stood on the precipice of eternity, he seemed to see with renovated eyes all the good to which his posterity was foreordained. The Prophet Joseph came to him with the happy news that for the moment he was free from the persecuting hand of the Missourians. Father Smith was cheered, then doubly cheered to learn, for the first time, of the doctrine of baptism for the dead. He requested Joseph to be baptized for Alvin.

Then commenced a meeting such as Jacob convened with his twelve sons. Father Smith asked that his family assemble. Catherine was not present, and so he sent Arthur Millikin, young Lucy's husband, to bring her. But first he blessed Arthur, fearing it might be too late by the time he returned. "My son," he said, taking Millikin by the hand, "I have given you my youngest, darling child, and will you be kind to her?" "Yes, father," he replied, "I will." Father Smith then blessed Arthur, who left to bring Catherine.

He next reached for his own dear Lucy. "Mother, do you not know," he testified, "that you are the mother of as great a family as ever lived upon the earth?" This was not the fond folly of a dying man. Rather, it was an eternal reality, for this was the family foreordained to the eternal purposes which it fulfilled. Yet because it was a family that had endured constant hardship and persecution, Hyrum leaned over the bed and asked, "Father, if you are taken away, will you not intercede for us at the throne of grace, that our enemies may not have so much power over us?" It was a just request, for there is that which the faithful can do on the other side of the veil which cannot be done here.

Then followed a word of blessing for Hyrum, and another for the Prophet Joseph, who he promised would be permitted to finish his work. Mother Smith reports that "at this Joseph cried out, weeping, 'Oh! my father, shall I?' 'Yes,' said his father, 'you shall live to lay out the plan of all the work which God has given you to do. This is my dying blessing upon your head.' "

He then commended the faithful Samuel, because the Lord had never chastised him. In what we now see as a prophetic announcement of Samuel's death, he added, "The Lord . . . has called you home to rest; and there is a crown laid up for you." On William, Don Carlos, Sophronia, Catherine, and Lucy he pronounced the blessings of the faithful, and then spoke one more time to Lucy: "Mother, do you not know, that you are one of the most singular women in the world?" Lucy replied that she did not, so Father Smith reaffirmed his conviction: "Well I do," he said, and then summarized the spirit of her calling: "you have brought up my children for me by the fireside, and when I was gone from home, you comforted them. You have brought up all my children, and could always comfort them when I could not." He then exhorted her to be comforted, and paused in his speech, overcome with exhaustion. After a few moments, he spoke again, "I can see and hear, as well as ever I could." He then paused for what Lucy calls a considerable length, and looked beyond the veil: "I see Alvin," he said. Another pause followed, and then he announced, "I shall live seven or eight minutes."[68]

Then, after eight minutes had expired, like his father Jacob before him, when he "had made an end of commanding his sons, he gathered up his feet into the bed, and yielded up the ghost, and was gathered unto his people."[69]

Such a death can only come after such a life as Father Smith lived. He received with the eagerness of youth every communication that the Lord sent him; he walked life's dusty trails in shoes of poverty, suffering hardship and persecution (on more than one occasion, for example, he was warned out of the towns where he lived); he walked thousands of miles in the gospel cause, both as a missionary and as one out to homestead in Zion; he was the father of prophets and raised many faithful posterity, to whom he taught the gospel and with whom he shared his burdened lot; he conferred hundreds of inspired blessings and left a legacy of compassion and faith; and, through it all, he was true and faithful in all things; he endured to the end in righteousness. He was, in the most exalting sense, a natural patriarch in Israel.

The Patriarch
to the Church

On December 18, 1833, the Prophet Joseph Smith—in company with Oliver Cowdery, Sidney Rigdon, and Frederick G. Williams—laid his hands upon his father's head and ordained him as the Patriarch to the Church.[1] "This ordination marked the restoration of the calling of 'evangelical ministers'[2] again on the earth," explained Elder Bruce R. McConkie, "an order of priesthood which 'was confirmed to be handed down from father to son,' one which 'rightly belongs to the literal descendants of the chosen seed, to whom the promises were made.' Adam, Seth, Enos, Cainan, Mahalaleel, Jared, Enoch, Methuselah, Lamech, and Noah all enjoyed the rights and powers of this priesthood calling. (D&C 107:38-53)"[3] Indeed, the Prophet Joseph Smith taught that whenever the Church of Jesus Christ is found upon the earth, a Patriarch is called and ordained so that patriarchal blessings might be given the Saints.[4]

This ordination of Father Smith as the Patriarch to the Church placed him at the high point of his ministry. None can gainsay the good that he did in supporting the Prophet throughout his life, nor the importance of his teachings in the home where the Prophet and his family were raised. Neither can we underestimate the important role he played in guiding, supporting, and, in some instances, protecting the Prophet

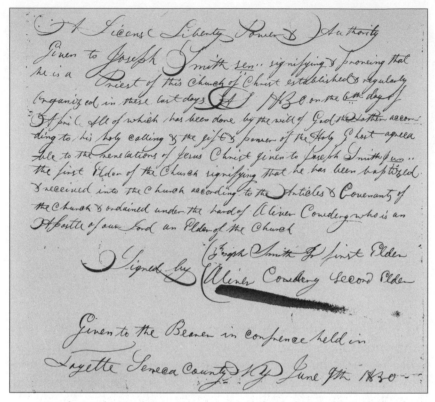

*Joseph Smith, Sr., license, given to identify Father Smith as both a
member and an authorized missionary of the Church
(signed by Joseph Smith, Jr., and Oliver Cowdery)*

during the early days of his ministry, especially following the
First Vision, the visits of Moroni, and during and after the
translation of the Book of Mormon. Father Smith will also be
long remembered for the role he played in the construction and
dedication of the Kirtland Temple. We know that he taught in
the temple and in other meetings of the Saints, and, for that
matter, tradition has it that he preached in the local churches in
the neighborhood of Tunbridge, Vermont, years before the First
Vision and the restoration of the gospel. In spite of all this,
however, he was best remembered among the early Saints as
"Father Smith, the Patriarch," and our best and most complete
records of him deal with his officiating in that office. We have
but one set of abbreviated notes of a sermon—or, better said, a
speech—he gave, but we have hundreds of recorded blessings

CHAPTER 5

he conferred, which in many instances are accompanied by the testimonies of the recipients about the fulfillment of at least parts of those blessings.

Oliver Cowdery was the scribe who recorded the ordination of Father Smith, and he testified that the Prophet Joseph Smith had his eyes opened, so that he beheld in vision the things that he conferred upon his father's head. "Thus spoke the Seer," wrote Oliver, "and these are the words which fell from his lips while the visions of the Almighty were open to his view, saying:

"Blessed of the Lord is my father, for he shall stand in the midst of his posterity and shall be comforted by their blessings when he is old and bowed down with years, and shall be called a prince over them, and shall be numbered among those who hold the right of Patriarchal Priesthood, even the keys of that ministry: for he shall assemble together his posterity like unto Adam; and the assembly which he [Adam] called shall be an example for my father, for thus it is written of him."

It appears that Father Smith holds a position unique among Patriarchs—what we might call a presidency over the Patriarchs of this dispensation. Moreover, he is compared to Father Adam, whom in patriarchal capacity Father Smith is destined, said the Prophet, to imitate. Thus, one prophet imitates another; one Patriarch repeats that which inspired Patriarchs before him have done—and Father Smith follows the example of Father Adam.

Continuing in vision, the Prophet Joseph Smith sees something which is not recorded in the Bible—or the Pearl of Great Price, for that matter—but which has since been included in the Doctrine and Covenants: "Three years previous to the death of Adam, he called Seth, Enos, Cainan, Mahalaleel, Jared, Enoch, and Methuselah, who were all high priests, with the residue of his posterity who were righteous, into the valley of Adam-ondi-Ahman, and there bestowed upon them his last blessing. And the Lord appeared unto them, and they rose up and blessed Adam, and called him Michael, the prince, the archangel. And the Lord administered comfort unto Adam, and said unto him: I have set thee to be at the head; a multitude of nations shall come of thee, and thou art a prince over them forever."

The account included in the Doctrine and Covenants adds something which Oliver did not record but which we would not be surprised to learn was a part of the blessing conferred upon

Father Smith: "And Adam stood up in the midst of the congregation; and, notwithstanding he was bowed down with age, being full of the Holy Ghost, predicted whatsoever should befall his posterity unto the latest generation. These things were all written in the book of Enoch, and are to be testified of in due time."5

In any event, after describing Adam and some of the patriarchal portions of his ministry, the Prophet Joseph continued his blessing on his father, saying that as it was with Adam, "so shall it be with my father: he shall be called a prince over his posterity, holding the keys of the patriarchal Priesthood over the kingdom of God on earth, even the Church of Jesus Christ of Latter-day Saints,6 and he shall sit in the general assembly of Patriarchs, even in council with the Ancient of Days when he shall sit and all the Patriarchs with him and shall enjoy his right and authority under the direction of the Ancient of Days."

Then, in a phrase which shows Father and Mother Smith as possessing that perfect unity and harmony which characterize any eternal union, the Prophet blessed his mother through his father: "And blessed also, is my mother, for she is a mother in Israel, and shall be a partaker with my father in all his patriarchal blessings."

In like manner, he blessed his brothers and sisters, only to return and pour out additional blessings upon his mother: "Blessed is my mother, for her soul is ever filled with benevolence and philanthropy; and notwithstanding her age, she shall yet receive strength and be comforted in the midst of her house: and thus saith the Lord, she shall have eternal life."

The Prophet then continued: "And again, blessed is my father, for the hand of the Lord shall be over him, and he shall be full of the Holy Ghost; for he shall predict whatsoever shall befall his posterity unto the latest generation, and shall see the affliction of his children pass away, and their enemies under their feet: and when his head is fully ripe he shall behold himself as an olive tree whose branches are bowed down with much fruit." Then, in what constitutes a reaffirmation, or a resealing, of blessings to which Father Smith was already heir because they had been promised Joseph the son of Jacob, the Prophet Joseph said: "Behold, the blessings of Joseph by the hand of his progenitor, shall come upon the head of my father and his seed after him, to the uttermost, even he shall be a fruitful bough; he shall be as a fruitful bough, even a fruitful bough by a well whose branches run over the wall, and his seed shall abide in strength, and the arms of their hands shall be made strong by the hands of the mighty God of Jacob, and the God of his fathers: even the God of Abraham, Isaac, and Jacob, shall help him and his seed after him: even the Almighty shall bless him with blessings of heaven above and his seed after him, and the blessings of the deep that lieth under: and his seed shall rise up and call him blessed. He shall be as the vine of the choice grape when her clusters are fully ripe: and he shall also possess a mansion on high, even in the Celestial Kingdom. His counsel shall be sought for by thousands, and he shall have place in the house of the Lord; for he shall be mighty in the council of the elders, and his days shall yet be lengthened out: and when he shall go hence he shall go in peace, and his rest shall be glorious; and his name shall be had in remembrance to the end. Amen."[7]

Thus stood Father Smith, ordained a Patriarch, likened unto Father Adam, with the promise of triumph over his enemies and the assurance of eternal life resting on his soul. Who would not have increased faith, confidence, and capacity, given such divine pronouncements?

Surely this was the reaction of Father Smith, and while our records do not tell us when he gave his first patriarchal blessings, we know that he gave blessings to the Prophet Joseph and Samuel Smith in February 1834.[8] In addition, Benjamin F. Johnson tells us that "in the summer of 1834 Father Joseph Smith, Sr., commenced to visit the families of the Saints and give patriarchal blessings, and greatly was the Spirit of the Lord manifested among the Saints in the gift of tongues, with interpretation, prophecy, and the gift of healing."[9] Again, faith begot faith, and one spiritual experience gave birth to another.

This principle of surrounding himself with the circle of faith in order to more perfectly draw upon the powers of heaven was characteristic of the entire ministry of Father Smith. With regard to the giving of patriarchal blessings, he frequently convened patriarchal blessing meetings, or what are sometimes called "blessing meetings." Orson Hyde received his patriarchal blessing at one such meeting, and noted that the meeting opened with a song and a prayer, after which fifteen blessings were given.[10] Oliver Cowdery tells us that the practice of opening these meetings with prayer was "strictly observed in all patriarchal meetings, either by the one pronouncing the bless- ings or one whom he appoints."[11]

Perhaps the most complete description of these meetings was given by Oliver B. Huntington, who tells of a "blessing meeting" at the home of his father, William Huntington. The meeting was convened sometime in 1836, and Father Smith presided. It was Father Smith's custom, says Brother Hunting- ton, "to appoint meetings of families, at which all that desired patriarchal blessings," whether members of the immediate fam- ily or relatives, were invited to attend. The Patriarch would then "spend most of the day in blessing all that had a desire to hear what the Lord had in store for them, through their faithfulness.

"At such times," continued Brother Huntington, "we would listen by spells to the wonderful rehearsals from the Patriarch of the events the [Smith] family had passed through in bringing forth and establishing the Church of Christ. Sometimes he would tell us of wonderful things that would take place in the future."

The early Saints describe these blessing meetings as mo- ments of pentecostal spiritual outpourings, and with brethren such as Oliver Cowdery, Orson Pratt, Frederick G. Williams, Thomas B. Marsh, William E. McLellin, Heber C. Kimball, Wilford Woodruff, and others serving as Father Smith's clerks and recorders, we are left to wonder what part of the spiritual education of these future Apostles and prophets these meetings played. Does not one learn of the processes of inspiration, for example, as he witnesses and records the inspiration given to others?

With reference to the particular meeting Oliver Huntington described, "the whole day was spent . . . talking and blessing at intervals," and Orson Pratt was appointed as the scribe. Brother Pratt recorded all that he could as the Patriarch spoke, but as the tongue was faster than the hand, some of what Father Smith said was not recorded by Brother Pratt, and so those present filled memory's empty spaces from that which they re- called having been spoken.[12] On other occasions the Saints were less fortunate: Wilford Woodruff and George A. Smith, in writing a short history of the Patriarchal Blessing Book, noted that "a considerable number of blessings which were given by [Father Smith] were not recorded, through the negligence of the scribes."

Martha Jane Knowlton Coray, according to her husband, Howard Coray, complained that her blessing "was taken by a very poor scribe, and that much was not taken at all," and that in addition there were mistakes among those portions recorded.[13] George Washington Johnson explained that he never received a copy of the blessing Father Smith gave him;[14] and because the blessing given Don Carlos Smith was not fully recorded, in his final words to him Father Smith instructed him that he should take the Patriarchal Blessing Book, in which Father Smith recorded the blessings he gave, and fill in those parts of his blessing that were not recorded. He was promised that he would "have the Spirit of the Lord and be able to fill up all the vacancies which were left by Oliver when he wrote it."[15] Transcription problems such as these are a caution to all in how we interpret patriarchal blessings, particularly these early ones.[16]

Father Smith knew and taught, however, that transcription problems were not the only difficulties in understanding patriarchal promises. In the first instance, the promised blessings are conditional, and their realization depends on the faithfulness of the recipients. John Murdock, for example, was promised certain blessings, in the words of Father Smith, "if thou are faithful,"[17] and Oliver Snow, the father of Lorenzo and Eliza R., also received great promises "on conditions of thy obedience."[18] Samuel Rogers, for his part, received similar comfort, instruction, and blessings, all of which were given "on conditions of keeping the commandments and the Word of Wisdom."[19]

Not all patriarchal promises are fulfilled in mortality; some blessings apply to the next world, and some promises are eternal. Father Smith told Michael Barkdull, for instance, that after he died he would "preach to spirits in prison [and] lead some from thence to . . . unspeakable joy."[20] Wilford Woodruff and Phoebe Carter, as well as Jonathan Holmes and Mary Carter, were married on April 13, 1837. The Prophet Joseph Smith was scheduled to perform the ceremonies but, being pressed by mobs, was forced out of the city. Frederick G. Williams, the Prophet's Second Counselor, performed the ceremonies in the Prophet's absence and in the Prophet's home. "President J[oseph] Smith, Sen., the Patriarch, then blessed us in the name of the Lord and pronounced great blessings upon us and our posterity," wrote Wilford, and added in a disclosure of a pure heart: "No day [was] more pleasing than April thirteenth,

1837. While all nature smiled without, friendship's purest joys were felt beneath a prophet's roof." Then, after reflecting on the regrettable absence of the Prophet Joseph, he wrote: "A Patriarch yet was left. He, possessing a holy priesthood more ancient than his gray hairs, arose upon his feet to bless in the name of God the married four. Being clothed in the Spirit, through the power of the priesthood, he pronounced upon the wedded heads and their posterity blessing[s] that never decay." Two days later, Wilford received a formal patriarchal blessing from Father Smith (Phoebe had received hers in November 1836). In his journal, after recording his and his wife's blessings, Wilford reflected on the grand, sweeping events of the last dispensation and concluded: "[The Church] will continue to be propelled by the arm of Jehovah until the kingdom fills the whole earth and Israel [is] gathered, Babylon falls and Christ reigns. Then marvel not, O ye reader, that the Patriarch Joseph pronounces blessings upon the children of Ephraim."[21]

Just as some patriarchal promises endure forever and "never decay," the meaning of some promises is unfolded over time. Mary Brown Pulsipher, for instance, tells of joining the Church and coming to Kirtland, where she received her patriarchal blessing from Father Smith. "He said I should have my friends with me in this church," she said, "and that I would be the means of saving and redeeming them. I believe[d] every word, but did not understand how it could come to pass. I never heard nor thought of being baptized for the dead. He said I had left all for the gospel, I should have a hundred fold in this world and in the world to come, life everlasting, with many more good blessings if I would be faithful." More than thirty years later, on March 2, 1879, she added an addendum to her reflections: "I left all my friends but my own family. Father Smith, the first Patriarch in the Church, laid his hands on my head and blessed me. He said I should have my friends in this church, [that I] would stand on Mt. Zion, [and] help save and redeem them. He said I had left all to obey the gospel and I should in this world have a hundred fold. That [promise] is fulfilling very fast. I have 56 grandchildren and 75 great grandchildren. So you see, there is upwards of a hundred fold now and increasing at a wonderful rate."[22]

A Patriarch can, of course, pronounce inspired predictions of things yet future simply because the blessings he gives are not of his own invention. He has no private or personal message, but like Micaiah of old, he is authorized to speak only that which the Lord puts into his mouth.[23] Illustrating this principle, Father Smith began one blessing in a prayerful plea, saying, "I ask God the Eternal Father to speak through [me] all the things which he would say were he to stand in my place."[24] On another occasion he said, "I lay my hands upon thy head in the name of the Lord Jesus Christ, not knowing at this time what I shall say unto thee," but praying that the Lord will "inspire my heart and give me knowledge of those things which shall befall thee in time, and also of those blessings which he has determined to bestow upon thee, if thou art faithful." It was not uncommon for Father Smith to pray that the Lord would put thoughts into his heart and words in his mouth, that when the Patriarch spoke his voice would be the voice of the Lord.[25]

Inspired patriarchal blessings come because of inspired Patriarchs. Inspiration, of course, comes because of the faith of those involved, which means that those Saints who exerted greater faith received greater blessings. As descendants of Abraham, they all have claim upon the blessings promised unto Abraham.[26] But just as there were many widows in Israel in the days of Elijah, and Elijah eased the famine of only one; and just as there were many lepers in the days of Elisha, and Elisha cleansed only one,[27] so also has it been in every dispensation that those who exerted greater faith called down greater blessings upon their own heads. Understanding this principle, Brigham Young quotes Father Smith as having said: "If I have not promised blessings enough on your head, and stated enough in the blessing I have given you, sit down and write every good thing you can think of, and every good thing your neighbour can think of, and put all into your blessing, and I will sign it and promise the whole to you, *if you will only live for it.*"[28]

This principle of seeing desired blessings with the eye of faith and then living worthy of them is reiterated in the life of the Prophet Joseph Smith, who, tradition holds, was asked for a blessing by his wife. At the moment of the request he was unable to respond, so the Prophet told Emma to write the best blessing she could and he would sign it upon his return from Carthage. Unfortunately, the Prophet was martyred before he could return.[29]

There is, of course, a general anxiety among the righteous

to receive all the blessings of the kingdom, and there is a similar Spirit-borne desire on the part of faithful priesthood leaders to make the blessings of the kingdom available to deserving Saints. In the spirit of his calling, Father Smith sought out opportunities to give blessings. Thus our history records that "the venerable Patriarch of our church Joseph Smith, sen. and Elder John Smith set out on a mission from [Kirtland, Ohio,] May 10th, [1836,] to visit some of the branches of the church south of [Kirtland], to regulate them and set in order the things that were wanting; they returned again on the 18th, being absent but eight days, during which time they either baptized, or witnessed the baptism of 16, and 95 received their patriarchal blessing."[30]

About a month after this experience, Father Smith and Uncle John, reported the Prophet Joseph Smith, "started on a mission to visit the branches of the Church in the Eastern States, to set them in order, and confer on the brethren their patriarchal blessings. I took my mother and Aunt Clarissa (my Uncle John's wife,) in a carriage, and accompanied them to Painsville, where we procured a bottle of wine, broke bread, ate and drank, and parted after the ancient order, with the blessings of God."[31] During this mission Father Smith and Uncle John travelled 2,400 miles[32] through the states of Ohio, Pennsylvania, New York, Vermont, and New Hampshire; gave blessings to several hundred people;[33] cheered the Saints wherever they went;[34] suffered considerable disappointment and depression in spirit because of the persecution received at the hands of their brother Jesse;[35] and returned in October, four months after their departure.

No doubt the patriarchal blessings given on this journey, as is the case with all such blessings, contained an inspired declaration of lineage, a prophetic statement of the life of the individual involved, and whatever statements of blessing, caution, admonition, and warning that the Spirit of the Lord may have inspired. The giving of patriarchal blessings is one of the great distinguishing features of the gospel of Jesus Christ and is one of the great evidences that the work restored through Joseph Smith is true.

And, again, Father Smith is our teacher and exemplar.

Of the Lineage of Abraham

Father Abraham was baptized, ordained to the priesthood, and married for eternity according to the Lord's order. Then, because of his faith and faithfulness, he secured from the Lord the promise that these same blessings—the blessings of the gospel, of the priesthood, of celestial marriage, and of eternal life—would be the natural and legal inheritance of his descendants, if they would but live worthy of them.[36] The chief and most significant reason for giving patriarchal blessings is to give the recipient an inspired declaration of Abrahamic lineage, thereby gaining the inspired assurance that he or she has, if faithful, a full and complete claim on and share in the blessings promised Abraham. To be Abraham's faithful seed is to be an heir of all the blessings promised to Abraham. Thus we have come to call Abraham the "father of the faithful," and his righteous descendants the "children of the covenant," or "the children of the promise,"[37] meaning the promises which the Lord made to Abraham.

Isaac received the promise that through his lineage the promises given Abraham would be transferred to posterity;[38] Jacob in turn received the same promise[39] and therefore blessed his sons. Jacob's eldest son, Reuben, lost the birthright because of sin, and it was given instead to Joseph and then passed on to Abraham's descendants through Joseph's son Ephraim.[40] Over time, the tribe of Ephraim proved rebellious, and the Lord mixed them among all nations.[41] Still, the Lord was, by his own oath, bound to honor the birthright claim of Ephraim and therefore of his descendants, and the gathering of Israel that takes place in our day is a gathering of Ephraim first and then of the other tribes. Most members of the Church, therefore, are of Ephraim, and as Joseph Fielding Smith notes, most of the patriarchal blessings given by Father Smith reflect Ephraimite lineage: "Brother Hyde [not Orson Hyde]," said Father Smith in a patriarchal blessing, "I seal upon thee the blessings of Joseph, for thou art a pure descendant of Joseph through the loins of Ephraim." This blessing was typical of many others.

While noting that most members of the Church are

Ephraimites, Joseph Fielding Smith gives examples from the blessings given by Father Smith of those who were of the lineage of Dan and Judah, and even of one to whom the Lord would yet reveal lineage, all to show that it is Abrahamic lineage that gives a person, if faithful, the right to the promised blessings.[42] Thus it was that Abigail Meade McBride could rejoice that Father Smith said to her, "Thou art of the lineage of Abraham,"[43] and Charles C. Rich could thrill that "Father Smith told me I was the pure blood of Joseph,"[44] while Sophronia Smith was comforted to have "the blessings of thy father Jacob"[45] conferred upon her head. We emphasize for clarity, however, that most members of the Church in this day descend from Ephraim, a truth that is reflected in the blessings that Father Smith gave.

Blessings Give Direction

Patriarchal blessings give directions, charting the course for the faithful as they traverse the waters of life. In the blessing given to Martha Jane Knowlton Coray, for example, she was promised that nothing could overthrow her if she was faithful, that she would have power to overcome life's difficulties, that she should not marry outside of the Church, "for this is contrary to the order of heaven," and that if she was faithful the Lord would "guide her through the slippery paths of youth" and direct her in finding a proper marriage partner, who would join with her in raising children. The knowledge of these promises became a guide and director for her throughout her life.[46]

Emeline Grover Rich relates that in her blessing, Father Smith promised that someday she would become a nurse and bring relief to many people. She had had the desire to become a nurse, she records, from age nine, but no doubt the effect of the patriarchal blessing was to encourage her to further prepare herself and sharpen her focus. She observed that, years after receiving the blessing, while living in Paris, Idaho, she "was called upon a great deal to go out among the sick, there being no doctors or drug stores, and," she wrote, "I had very good success; after a little I was called upon to tend the sick both temporally and spiritually and I was set apart [by Brigham Young] for that work."[47]

In the instance of Edward Stevenson, his patriarchal blessing became a standard against which he measured his progress
and worthiness in the kingdom. He recorded that Father Smith
had said (using a biblical metaphor) that he was one who was
appointed to push the Saints together. He wrote that in 1847,
thirteen years after receiving his blessing, he was "a captain of
ten under Charles C. Rich, thereby helping to push the people
together; and in 1855, I had charge of a company of Saints
from Liverpool to Philadelphia, thence to St. Louis and on to
the frontier [of] Atchison, Kansas, called by our people 'Mormon Grove'; and from there to Zion, in charge of the 'Texas
Company.'" He concludes this recitation of some of what he
considered major events in his life by saying, "I only mention
this here in connection with my patriarchal blessing, and the
words of Moses in Deuteronomy 33:17," which Father Smith
had used in his blessing.[48] For Stevenson, knowing that he was
doing things that fulfilled patriarchal promises left him with the
assurance that the Lord approved of the course he was pursuing in life.

So let it be with all of us!

Patriarchal Promises Provide Hope, Build Faith

Faith is born of hope; if there is something we hope for, or
can exercise faith in, then faith can grow and be strengthened.
Patriarchal blessings are given, in part, so that people have
things to hope for, or to believe in, and work for. As these
things unfold, and as the things people have hoped for occur,
faith is strengthened. In this sense, patriarchal promises are designed to sustain and strengthen faith. Cyrena Dustin Merrill,
for instance, endured the persecutions of Missouri and the trials of walking across the plains to the Salt Lake Valley. Because
of the promises made in her patriarchal blessing, she had the
hope in her heart that she could overcome every obstacle and
hardship: "I went forth trusting in the Lord, in full faith that he
would give me grace sufficient to overcome all obstacles and
difficulties which might be thrown in my way and that I might
endure to the end."[49]

Mary Horne reported a similar circumstance. She and her husband journeyed from Canada to join the Saints in Missouri. After they arrived, she received her patriarchal blessing from Father Smith, who told her that "the Lord will bring you through six troubles, and in the seventh he will not leave you"— a promise which helped create the hope, and thus the faith, that she could endure the trials of Missouri and elsewhere.[50]

Similarly, Abel Butterfield tells of an Indian raid that occurred at Summit Creek in 1854. One man was killed, and some, including his daughter, thought they would all be killed. Butterfield knew otherwise. He had the faith to grab his gun and run at the Indians, calling out to some others to do the same, so that it appeared as if they were part of an army. The Indians fled, for, wrote Abel, "it was predicted in Kirtland fifteen years ago, by the Patriarch Joseph Smith, Sr., and Patriarch John Smith in Great Salt Lake City three years ago that the Lamanites should try to kill me and I should have the gift of tongues and even the earth should tremble at the sound of my voice. . . . Some of the brethren said that my voice sounded like a clap of thunder."[51]

During the discouraging days in Kirtland, Benjamin F. Johnson, surrounded by what seemed to be endless trial and affliction—including his eldest sister's death by a disease that had previously taken three other family members—passed discouragement and courted despondency. "Everything now seemed to confirm the idea of a short life for myself," he said, "if not for all my father's children." During these times, "some influence like the whisper of the Evil One was always saying in my ear, 'You are doomed to die young.'" But then sometimes, Johnson recalled, "I would remember the promises made by Father Smith in my patriarchal blessing, and the blessing of the Prophet upon my head, and a desire to live and fulfill them, and to preach the Gospel would enthuse my whole being."[52]

It was during the fall of 1839 that little James Knight, the infant son of Newel and Lydia Knight, became seriously ill. Many thought he would die, and some said to Lydia, "Sister Knight, you can not keep that child; why do you cling so to him? You will displease our Father [in Heaven]. Let him go, give him up, and his sufferings will be at an end."

Sister Knight was guided by a different faith, however—a faith sustained by a patriarchal promise: "Oh I cannot think of such a thing!" she said. "Father Smith said in my blessing that my heart should not be pained because of the loss of my children." So great indeed was her confidence in that patriarchal promise that she could not let the child die, feeling that it was the Lord's will that he live. On the following Sunday, however, the child lay like a breathing skeleton, with skin drawn, his eyes glassy, and his breathing all but stopped.

Lydia pleaded with her husband to know what to do, and he said she should "give him up" and ask the Lord for the strength to bear such a loss. Still, her confidence was unabated. The following day she saw the Prophet Joseph walk past the house, and so she invited him in, asking his advice. Seeing faith radiate from her eyes, he said, "Sister Lydia, I do not think you will have to give him up." He then counseled her to send for Father George W. Harris and have him bless the child, which she did, and the baby was healed. The Prophet told her that should his health relapse again, she should again call on the elders. His health did decline, and she again called on the elders, who blessed him. His health recovered—and we note that it was faith generated by a patriarchal promise that triggered the entire healing process.[53]

In the winter of 1866, William Smith of Kaysville, Utah, became so sick that his family feared he would die. Brother Smith had the confidence that if he were blessed by Lorenzo Snow, he could be healed—but it was winter, very cold, and Brother Snow was living forty miles distant. Sister Smith, while praying about her husband's illness, remembered that years before while living in England she had read Brother Snow's patriarchal blessing, in which Father Smith had told him that the diseased would send him their handkerchiefs and that by Lorenzo's touch their owners would be made whole. Sister Smith immediately sent Brother Snow a new silk handkerchief, with a note explaining her request as well as describing her husband's condition.

Brother Snow was deeply touched. He took the handkerchief, he said, and "bowed before the Lord, and in earnest supplication besought Him to remember the promises He made through His servant, the Patriarch, whom He had now taken to Himself, and let the healing and life-inspiring virtues of His Holy Spirit be imparted to this handkerchief, and from thence to Brother Smith when it shall be placed upon him, speedily restoring him to life, health and vigor."

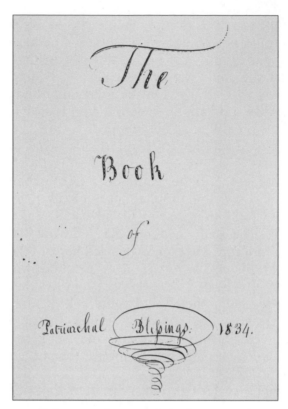

Title page of Patriarchal Blessing Book

The messenger immediately returned with the handkerchief, which was spread over the head and face of the apparently dying man. Eliza R. Snow recorded, "His immediate recovery was observed with surprise and astonishment by all around, and well might they exclaim: 'It is the Lord's doing, and it is marvelous in our eyes.' "[54]

In recalling this experience we note that it was the faith of the participants, and not the handkerchief, that wrought the miracle, just as it was the faith of Naaman, and not the washing seven times in the river Jordan, that healed him.[55] Naaman's washing and the Smiths' handkerchief were but symbols of a living faith. At the same time, it was memory of a patriarchal promise that triggered the faith of Sister Smith, and the faith of Lorenzo Snow in that same patriarchal promise that helped him to exercise his faith.

In order for faith to exist, we must have the knowledge that the course we are pursuing accords with the will of the Lord. One means of obtaining the assurance that the Lord approves of what we do is through a patriarchal blessing. We have this principle illustrated in a blessing given by Father Smith to Nancy Rigdon, the mother of Sidney Rigdon: "Sister, . . . in thy old age thou hast obeyed the Gospel. Thou hast been blessed with a family and thou hast been faithful in bringing them up."[56] These words provided her the assurance that the Lord approved of the course she had taken, which assurance undoubtedly gave her added capacity to exercise faith. In a similar vein, Abraham O. Smoot went to Father Smith to receive a patriarchal blessing prior to leaving on a journey to the South, presumably so that the directions and promises of the blessing would strengthen his faith and support him while he was away.[57]

Wilford Woodruff, for his part, constantly referred to his patriarchal blessing with the prayer that its promises might be fulfilled. His faith-filled prayer is a model for the righteous everywhere: "O Lord, if it be thy will, give me the privilege of recording in this year's journal [the] great blessing[s] pronounced upon my head from mine anointing and from under the hands of the Patriarch Joseph . . . that I may be a special witness of thee."[58]

Once again, inspired patriarchal promises inspired faith!

Encouragement, Comfort, and Reassurance

The Spirit of the Lord causes people to rejoice, filling their souls with joy. Indeed, the Lord said to Hyrum Smith, "I will impart unto you of my Spirit, which shall enlighten your mind, which shall fill your soul with joy."[59] Obviously, recipients of inspired patriarchal blessings are uplifted and encouraged, and filled with the joys and hopes of the gospel. At the same time, the Comforter comforts through the medium of patriarchal blessings, and the receiving Saints are thereby encouraged and reassured.

We turn for an illustration of this principle to Cyrena Dustin, who had lived with infirmity from her youth. She had never experienced good health and, she remembered, "was never expected to do anything around the house but all the family waited on me."

Physical infirmity could not, however, cripple her spirit. When the missionaries came, she rejoiced in their testimony and was baptized, being the only one of her father's family to join the Church. Feeling the spirit of gathering, she prepared to leave for Missouri to join with the Saints. Prior to her departure she visited her family. "My father and mother cried and begged me not to go," she said, "even until late into the night. When they found pleading was of no avail," they offered her money to stay. When money failed, they threatened her with an arrest and legal action, but her resolution was firm. So heartbroken was her father that he left the house to avoid saying farewell. To those who remained at home, she "bore a faithful testimony to the truth of the gospel; and," she adds, except for one short visit by a brother years later, "that was the last time I ever saw any of my father's family."

Wherein, we ask, does a young woman, alone and without family, find the courage to stand against comfort, tradition, and life's rigors? Cyrena answers: "In April [1838] . . . I . . . went to a blessing meeting held at the house of Bro[ther] Sears, in Randolph, Ohio, . . . and received a patriarchal blessing under the hands of Joseph Smith, Sen." With seeric insight Father Smith looked into her future and announced her divine potential. It filled her ever-enlarging soul with hope and gave her the confidence to confront trouble and trial. "My blessing has been a great comfort to me in the trials which I have had to pass through," she said, "and it also assisted to give me the necessary faith, courage and fortitude to make the sacrifice of leaving home and friends and to start out alone in the world to fight the battle of life among strangers." From the power of that patriarchal blessing, she went forth "trusting in the Lord, in full faith that he would give me grace sufficient to overcome all obstacles and difficulties which might be thrown in my way and that I might endure to the end."

And did she overcome trial and difficulty, and endure to the end? Five short months after receiving her blessing, in company with a small group of Saints she commenced her wearisome journey to Missouri. Exhausted by exposure and exertion, and the fear that her father would overtake her and force her return, she "took a severe cold, which with the long walk and worry of leaving home under such trying circumstances brought on a fever and nervous prostration."

Eventually all in her company but one—the fatherly Alexander Stanley—despaired and concluded she would die. Visitors to her travelling camp asked, "Why do you drag that sick girl with you? Can't you stop long enough to let her die in peace? It looks inhuman to take her over these rough roads." And "when told it was prophesied that she should go to Zion, they would shake their heads and say, 'She'll never live to get there anyway.'" Still, said Cyrena, "I had great faith, for my blessing said I should go to Zion and I clung to that, (and so did Bro[ther] Stanley) and I felt as if that must be true."

The weight of sickness was made heavier by bothersome mobs, but, concludes this faithful daughter of Abraham, "we finally overcame all difficulties and arrived at Far West."

(Oh, that all could have such faith!)

Summarizing the influence of the patriarchal blessing over the next six decades, Cyrena said: "I have lived to see my patriarchal blessings fulfilled: my life has been spared; many times I have been raised up as from the dead; I have had my prayers answered; my posterity is numerous, and they rise up and call me blessed; my faith has been (and still is) strong; I have lived in perfect harmony with my husband 57 years"—all according to the inspired promises pronounced by Father Smith almost sixty years earlier.

Was she not right to say, "My blessing has been a great comfort to me in the trials which I have had to pass through"?[60]

Cyrena Dustin is but one example. Benjamin F. Johnson is another. He too tells of the joys that came from patriarchal promises: "In the spring of 1835 before I was baptized, my mother and all her children met at the house of my sister, Delcena Sherman, to receive from Patriarch Joseph Smith, Sr., our patriarchal blessings. He blessed all according to age until he came to Joseph E. and myself, when he placed his hands first upon my head. My mother told him I was the youngest, but he said that mattered not—to me was the first blessing; and in blessing me, among other great and glorious things, he told me the Lord would call me to do the work of brother Seth, who had been called away by death. *In this promise there was to me more joy than ever before I had known;* my dear brother was not to be robbed of his blessings, and if I could only live faithfully his work would be done, and I should do it for him. I felt this was the greatest boon the Lord could bestow upon me."[61]

Because Lydia Knight had lost two children, she took great comfort in her patriarchal promise that she would have many children, teach them righteousness, and be enabled to keep them from the destroyer;[62] and Freeborn DeMille, who lost much of his worldly possessions in the Missouri persecutions, was similarly comforted to receive the promise that "God will make up thy losses."[63] It was George A. Smith, however, who perhaps summarized the entire issue in the obituary notice he published on Mother Smith, wherein he observed that Father Smith, "a Patriarch of the Most High over all the Church of God," poured out blessings "in the name of his Redeemer upon the heads of thousands, by virtue of his priesthood and office," and thereby caused "their hearts to beat with joy."[64]

A Voice of Warning, and the Invitation to Repent

To warn is to advise of impending danger, and the gospel message itself is a warning to the world against the desolation and destruction that are to be poured out without measure upon the wicked and ungodly.[65] "For this is a day of warning," the Lord has said, "and not a day of many words," and he has sworn that he will not be mocked in these last days.[66] And just as prophets in every dispensation have raised the warning voice, so Patriarchs, in the blessings they have given, have often felt the inspiration to warn the Saints against the dangers of disobedience. Such warnings are almost always associated with the invitation to repent, and in their very nature are spoken in the spirit of love.

To one young man whom Father Smith loved, his inspired voice spoke, saying: "Thou has[t] conducted [thyself] foolishly, and suffered the devil to toss thee about, and to sift thee many times. The Church has been grieved with thy conduct, and thy family has been sorely afflicted because of thy wickedness. The Lord has given thee a talent, and he will require an account of the same in eternity. Thou must repent and seek forgiveness, . . . and I say that inasmuch as thou shalt humble thyself and keep the commandments of the Lord thou shalt be blessed with a place and an inheritance among the Saints, . . . and thou shalt

be saved in the kingdom of God."[67] The language of the blessing is reminiscent of Alma's pleadings with his wayward son
Corianton,[68] who, we are encouraged to know, repented and
served faithfully in the gospel cause.[69]

To another Father Smith's inspired warning voice said:
"Thou must be humble and meek in heart, or Satan will seek to
raise thee up in pride unto boasting . . ." but "if thou art faithful, thou shalt know Christ more perfectly."[70] In yet another instance, the Holy Ghost spoke through Father Smith, saying,
"Thou has been rebellious against the work of the Lord, in that
thou hast buried thy talent, as it were, in the earth; but if thou
wilt stir thyself up to faithfulness before the Lord, and humble
thyself before him, thou shalt obtain forgiveness and receive the
Holy Spirit." Then Father Smith promised great blessings upon
his head, and closed the blessing by adding—in a promise that
reminds us all that an ever-compassionate Father is always willing to forgive those who repent—"If thou art faithful all these
blessings shall come upon thee, even so. Amen."[71]

Sometimes there is an almost blunt, straightforward honesty in the warning voice. "Thou must now keep the commandments of God because thou hast lived many years in sin and
vanity," said Father Smith to one man. Then he added this comforting note: "Yet the Lord hath looked on thee and brought
thee into the covenant of the people in the last days and made
thee an heir of Abraham and joint heir with Jesus Christ."[72]

We do well to remember that all blessings are conditioned
upon the faithfulness of the recipient and that therefore an implicit warning is a part of every blessing—a warning, in effect,
that if we are not faithful we will not receive the promised
blessings. The honest in heart, however, receive such inspired
warnings in the spirit in which they are given, and a warning
and invitation to repent becomes a stepping-stone to increased
righteousness. Jonathan and Caroline Crosby, for example, received their patriarchal blessings from Father Smith and
recorded them, said Caroline, "for the perusal of my posterity,
and friends." She also recorded the effect that receiving those
blessings had on them: "These blessings cheered and rejoiced
our hearts exceedingly. I truly felt humble before the Lord, and
felt to exclaim like one of old, 'Lord, what am I, or what my father's house, that thou art thus mindful of us?'" Then, in an expression that demonstrates that the effect of having experiences

with the Spirit of the Lord is to cause people to desire to repent, she said: "[Our blessings] led me to search into my own heart, to see if there was any sin concealed there, and if so, to repent, and ask God to make me clean, and pure, in very deed."[73]

An Evidence That the Work Is True

The ordinance and practice of conferring patriarchal blessings is an evidence that the gospel has been restored in its fulness. From the days of Father Adam[74] to the present, whenever there has been a dispensation of the gospel on the earth, Patriarchs have been ordained to give blessings to the faithful. Where Patriarchs exist, there the Church and kingdom of God are to be found; where there are no Patriarchs, there the Church and kingdom of God are not.

"God is the same yesterday, today, and forever, and in him there is no variableness neither shadow of changing"[75]—a truth that teaches that if he is calling Patriarchs in our day, so also did he call them anciently. In other words, the fact that we have received revelations in this day, through which the office and calling of Patriarch have been announced as essential parts of the Lord's system for helping to save his children, is an evidence and proof that he did so anciently. In short, the living, modern experience proves the credibility of the ancient testimony; inasmuch as God works with us, and since he is an unchangeable being, we know that in like manner he worked with the ancients.

There is, however, yet a second way in which patriarchal blessings are a testimony that the great latter-day work is true: they repeatedly provide illustration of inspired prophetic utterances that have come true in the lives of their recipients. This has been the case with all inspired patriarchal expressions, and nowhere is it more dramatically seen than in the blessings that Father Smith conferred. Orson Hyde[76] and Orson Pratt,[77] for instance, were both told that they would travel "to the ends of the earth" to preach the gospel; and Erastus Snow was promised that his missionary voice would "be heard in distant lands."[78] For Brother Hyde, fulfillment came in missions to England and in travelling across Europe to dedicate Palestine for the return of the Jews. Brother Pratt, for his part, filled missions in Canada and Europe and crossed the Atlantic twelve times in missionary service. Brother Snow also served in Europe, where, among other things, he opened Denmark to the preaching of the gospel in 1850.

Wilford Woodruff was promised that he would perform a great missionary service—which he did, baptizing thousands!— but he seemed to find the greatest satisfaction in the promise that if he was faithful he would be the instrument in baptizing his father's family—which he also did.[79] Echoing a similar promise, Oliver B. Huntington said: "In my blessing I was told that I should preach the Gospel before I was twenty-one years old; that I should preach to the inhabitants of the islands of the sea.

"That prediction and others, have taken place; in fact every item, but one, in that blessing has been fulfilled that can be fulfilled in this life. That one promise is, that I should live until I was satisfied with life"[80]—which he did.

The lives of Orson Hyde, Orson Pratt, Erastus Snow, and Wilford Woodruff—because of the apostolic positions they held and the valiance with which they honored their positions—are held up as examples to us. In a lesser degree the same is true of all the faithful Saints, though our illustrative purposes here are fully fulfilled without detailing additional examples. We are content to note that Father Smith gave thousands of blessings, according to Church historian George A. Smith, and that in them we see promises that men and women will preach the gospel, heal the sick and raise the dead, raise righteous posterity, overcome evil and build the kingdom, and eventually be saved in the kingdom of God. We rejoice in the fulfillment of these promises, because of the joy they brought those who experienced their fulfillment, and because they are, individually and collectively, a witness that the great latter-day work in which we are involved is true and that the hand of the Almighty guides his Patriarchs.

As we reflect on the patriarchal ministry of Father Smith, we recall the expressions of Wilford Woodruff with regard to his own father's baptism, though we apply them to the patriarchal ministry of the father of the Prophet: are not these "events worthy to be recorded upon the archives of heaven, or to be engraven with an iron pen and laid in a rock forever upon the earth"?[81]

CHAPTER 6

Preach the Word!

Would you save *your* soul?
Then preach the word![1]
Would you have your sins remitted?
Then preach the word![2]
Would you test your discipleship, to discern whether you have in fact received the gospel of Christ?[3] Or would you be protected against the judgments predicted upon the wicked,[4] cultivate the gift to recognize and receive the words of living prophets,[5] or exercise gifts of the Spirit with signs following your belief?[6] Or, for that matter, would you lay claim to the promise—such as is given to none others!—that the Lord will walk with you, and that no power on earth or in hell will stay your course?[7] Or would you treasure up for your soul everlasting salvation in the kingdom of God,[8] and be numbered with those of the first resurrection?[9]

Then preach the word!

The word is the gospel of Jesus Christ. To preach the word is to bear testimony of Christ, of his atoning sacrifice and all that flows therefrom. It is, therefore, to teach the gospel by the power of the Holy Ghost, testifying of the Father and the Son, of Joseph Smith and the Restoration, of the Book of Mormon and the revelations that have come in this dispensation, and of the apostolic and prophetic ministry of those ordained in this day. To preach the word is to bear testimony that The Church of Jesus Christ of Latter-day Saints is the kingdom of God on earth and that it holds the keys, ordinances, powers, and truths of salvation.

One of the great evidences that people have the spirit of the gospel is that they desire to share with others what they have. Father Smith, even before the Lord began to give revelations commanding men to share the gospel, felt the spirit of what was to come and desired to share what he knew with others. The Prophet Joseph Smith, of course, was the first missionary in this dispensation. The moment he returned from the grove and told his mother (or was it his parents?) that he had learned for himself "that Presbyterianism is not true"[10]—and presumably he would soon relate to her and other family members the experience of his vision—at that moment he was involved in missionary service, first to his family and then to others. Father and Mother Smith were but a step behind him, and our records show that they were soon out speaking of their son's experiences to their neighbors. This was the pattern that characterized their entire lives: the Prophet Joseph called the cadence, and his humble parents nobly marched the distance.

Early Missionary Experiences: Palmyra

Some few days after the Prophet saw the Father and the Son, he told others of his experience.[11] From the beginning, this brought antagonism from those outside his family—although there are more early historical records that show prejudice and alarm aroused by the Smiths' recounting of Moroni's visits and the coming forth of the Book of Mormon than there are that show these same reactions to anything said about the First Vision. It is certain, however, that their speaking of any or all of these newly received truths immediately quickened the hand of persecution. Local gossip, carried on the vicious tongue of rumor, disfigured much that they said. One compilation of such distortions was published by E. D. Howe,[12] in which he presents a set of confused and contradicting testimonies, uniformly provided by enemies of the Prophet and all designed to portray the Prophet and his family as lazy, indolent, dishonest, and credulous souls whose judgment was so faulty that their

Palmyra home of Joseph Smith, Sr., and Lucy Mack Smith

testimony could not be regarded by honest men. While the accounts are jumbled and the evidence distorted, one fact consistently runs through all the testimonies given: even before Joseph received the plates from the angel Moroni, he and other family members had been involved in bearing testimony to others that the age of restoration had begun and that Joseph had received a vision.

In order to resist what the Smith family was saying, with regard to the Book of Mormon, many described them as gold-digging treasure seekers, and it appears that as early as 1824 a story circulated tying the Prophet's dead brother, Alvin, to the visit of Moroni. This widely circulated story seems to have suggested that during the Prophet's first visit to the Hill Cumorah, Moroni had instructed Joseph to bring Alvin to retrieve the plates the following year, but that Alvin died before the date for obtaining the plates arrived. This raised the hostile speculation that the Prophet would take the bones of his dead brother with him when he went to obtain the plates. The refutation of this gossip occurred when, on September 25, 1824, Father Smith and "some of [his] neighbors" exhumed Alvin's remains almost one year after his death and subsequently published a notice in a local newspaper confirming that the bones had not been tampered with. This appears to have been done to disprove the slanderous gossip that portrayed the Prophet Joseph, his brother Alvin, and the Smiths in general as being in league with evil spirits.[13] The episode is important because it demonstrates, first, that Father Smith and others had been speaking publicly of the visions and revelations that the Prophet had received and that their testimony had aroused widespread public opposition—enough to warrant a response in a local newspaper. It is important, second, because it shows that Father Smith was so certain in the testimony of the truths of which he had spoken that he was willing to take the extraordinary step of unearthing his son's grave and examining his remains in order to substantiate what he had said. Had he been a deceiver, would he have wittingly sought out, in the presence of others, the very evidence that would have shown him to be a fraud?

One year after this episode the Smiths lost their farm, being unable to make their last land payment. The pressures brought by their creditors that forced foreclosure were, according to the Prophet's brother William, caused by religious prejudice resulting from what the Smiths had been saying about the Prophet Joseph's experiences,[14] thus reminding us again that they were out telling people about Joseph's experiences. This prejudice against revealed religion also reached into the larger Smith family. When Hyrum wrote his grandfather Asael about the visions and promises then unfolding, his uncle Jesse responded with vituperation, much of which was directed against Joseph Smith, Sr. "What is man when left to his own way?" asked the censuring Jesse, who responded to his own question with a mocking scorn: "He makes his own Gods: if a golden calf, he falls down and worships before it, and says, 'This is my god which brought me out of the land of Vermont'; if it be a gold book discovered by the necromancy of infidelity, and dug from the mines of atheism, he writes that the angel of the Lord has revealed to him the hidden treasures of wisdom and knowledge, even divine revelation." Jesse charged that Joseph Smith, Sr., and his family were carrying on "a work of deception," saying, "Uncle Jesse did and still does think the whole pretended discovery, not a very deep, but a very clear and foolish deception, a very great wickedness, unpardonable unless you are shielded by your ignorance." Jesse called Hyrum a "blasphemous wretch," a "miserable creature," and a "perjured villain" for his part in the "barefaced falsehood," which, he went on to say, was nothing but a "tale of nonsense" and an "abominable wickedness."

Jesse's motivations were religious, and he charged Father Smith with bearing a false witness: "Your father would not be implicated in this place, but for the message he sent by the hands of a fool to my brother Samuel. This fellow says that you and your father are in this business very deep. The fellow also believes all to be a fact; this to be sure, for no one, unless predisposed to believe a lie, would have heard a syllable from either of you on the subject."[15]

Religious prejudice was not the only obstacle to testimony bearing. Sometimes apparently honest people who lacked the spiritual depth to understand what was transpiring simply assumed that the Prophet and his family spoke nonsense when they spoke of angels and revelations, and therefore, unable to comprehend things eternal, they searched their own experiences and vocabularies to describe what they had heard. This may have been the case with people such as Fayette Lapham, who visited Palmyra and interviewed the Prophet's father and then translated what Father Smith had said into the only language that made sense to him—the language of "witchcraft and other supernatural things," such as dreams and "supernatural light." Looking back through the periscopes of history it is impossible for us to know just exactly what understanding or bias existed through which Lapham interpreted what Father Smith said to him. The larger and more important point, however, is that Father Smith was clearly telling the story of the coming forth of the Book of Mormon and bearing witness that both the Book of Mormon and the angel Moroni were sent of God.[16]

Nevertheless, while the process of bearing testimony was inevitably followed by distortion, the wheat among the worldly tares heard and rejoiced in what Father Smith and his family were saying. We know that Father Smith had spoken to Martin Harris about the Book of Mormon plates "some two or three years previous" to the time Joseph actually received them and that Martin responded warmly.[17] When the time came to retrieve the plates from Cumorah, other friends to whom the Smiths had obviously spoken about the Lord's workings with the Prophet were helpful and supportive. Father Joseph Knight, for example, felt no complaint upon learning that the Prophet, without permission, had used the Knights' horse and carriage for the journey to the Hill Cumorah.[18] After receiving the plates Joseph hid them in a log in the woods for several days until he could obtain a wooden chest in which to keep them. On the day that he retrieved them from their hiding place in the woods, the Prophet was assaulted three times, each time by a different man. Father Smith and two of his friends who were obviously friendly to things Father Smith had said about the forthcoming Book of Mormon—namely, Joseph Knight, Sr., and Josiah Stowell—then went in search of the young prophet's assailants.[19] While many rejected the testimony of the Prophet and his associates, a good many, like his assailants in the woods, thought it credible enough that they devised schemes to steal the plates for their own financial gain.[20]

The Smiths were obviously guarded in what they said and to whom they spoke, about both Moroni and the gold plates. Still, it seems clear that they did confide in a small circle of close friends. As the translation process proceeded, that circle grew, and we see a picture of Father Smith reminiscent of Paul, "not ashamed of the gospel of Christ"[21] but anxious to stand, in the words of Alma, as a witness "of God at all times and in all things, and in all places that [he was] in, even until death."[22] As early as the fall of 1828 he wrote a letter to his father, Asael Smith, telling about some of the inspired visions that had been given to the Prophet. Asael rejoiced, saying that he had long known that the Lord would raise up a prophet through some branch of his family, though some of Father Smith's brothers, as George A. Smith reported, "ridiculed Joseph's visions."[23]

Shortly thereafter (in February 1829), Father and Mother Smith left their Manchester home to visit Joseph and Emma in Harmony. En route they stopped overnight at the home of David Whitmer and, according to Mother Smith, "gave him a brief history" of the Book of Mormon.[24] While the Prophet's parents were in Harmony, the Lord spoke to Father Smith in a revelation (now section 4 of the Doctrine and Covenants) given through the Prophet Joseph Smith. With an eye on both the coming forth of the Book of Mormon and the restoration of the full powers and knowledge of the gospel, the Great Creator of all things announced that "a marvelous work is about to come forth among the children of men," and commanded, "O ye that embark in the service of God, see that ye serve him with all your heart, might, mind and strength, that"—and here is a great promise which we are left to conclude motivated the missionary efforts of Father Smith through the years—"ye may stand blameless before God at the last day."

The Lord reassured the father of the Prophet that he was justified in his desires to serve God, that the field was "white already to harvest," and that if he would thrust in his sickle with his might he would not perish, but bring "salvation to his soul." Then, in a list of virtues that over the years the Saints who knew Father Smith uniformly agreed colored his life perfectly, the Lord concluded: "And faith, hope, charity and love, with an eye single to the glory of God," qualify a person for service in the kingdom. "Remember faith, virtue, knowledge, temperance, patience, brotherly kindness, godliness, charity, humility, diligence. Ask," promised the Lord, "and ye shall receive; knock, and it shall be opened unto you."[25]

It was about this time that Oliver Cowdery stayed in the Smith home and, after gaining the confidence of Father Smith, learned from him of the visits of Moroni and of the pending translation of the Book of Mormon. Oliver obeyed Father Smith's counsel that he should seek his own personal witness that the things he had been told in the Smith home were true.[26] Then he left the Smith home and went to Harmony, Pennsylvania, where he became the Prophet's friend, scribe, and confidante.

The Smith Home:
A Center of Missionary Activity

Following the receipt of the above-mentioned revelation to Father Smith, the Smith home became even more of a center of gospel teaching than it had been before. Thus we see Father Smith, in company with Martin Harris, Oliver Cowdery, and the Prophet Joseph, bearing testimony to Stephen Harding, first in the printing office where the Book of Mormon was printed and later in the Smith home to which Harding was invited to continue their conversations.[27] Later we see Father Smith joining Mother Smith and the Prophet Joseph and frequently visiting the home of Orrin Rockwell, the father of the Prophet's lifetime friend Porter Rockwell, and relating the story of the coming forth of the Book of Mormon.[28] In the natural flow of events, Thomas B. Marsh reported being led by the Spirit of the Lord to a place where he heard of the Book of Mormon, causing him to go to Palmyra, New York, where he met Martin Harris, received as much of the Book of Mormon as had then been printed—sixteen pages—and then went to the home of Father Smith to learn more.[29] Shortly thereafter Solomon Chamberlain appeared on the Smith doorstep, testifying that he had received visions in which the Lord showed him that an apostasy had occurred, that "all churches were corrupt," that the Lord would soon raise up his own church "after the apostolic order," and that "there would a book come forth like unto the Bible, and the people would [be] guided by it, as well as the Bible." Chamberlain was guided by the Spirit of the Lord to the Smith home in Manchester, where he knocked on the door asking, "Is there anyone here that believes in visions or revelations?" Father Smith, Hyrum, and others instructed Chamberlain, who stayed in the Smith household for two days before taking sixty-four pages of printed copy—all that was then ready—of the Book of Mormon and leaving to preach in Canada.[30]

Another who sought out the Smith home to increase his understanding of the gospel was Parley P. Pratt, who, having read from and obtained a testimony of the Book of Mormon, went to Manchester, where he met Hyrum Smith, the Prophet's brother. Later—after being baptized, receiving the priesthood, and for a time spreading the restored gospel message—Parley again came to Manchester and the home of Father Smith, where for the first time he met the Prophet Joseph Smith.[31] It was, we note, not an unfamiliar practice for people to seek out the home of both the Prophet and his parents when seeking firsthand accounts of the events leading to the coming forth of the Book of Mormon and the restoration of the gospel. Like nonmembers of the Church, members felt the desire to hear what the parents of the Prophet had to say, and both Father and Mother Smith were ever ready to respond.[32]

In that spirit, throughout the duration of their mortal ministries Father and Mother Smith were forever inviting people into their home to hear the gospel preached. They established the practice of holding evening devotionals in the home, to which neighbors on occasion were invited.[33] One logical extension of such devotionals was to convene cottage meetings, which were frequent. Sidney Rigdon, for example, within a month of his own baptism in Kirtland, Ohio, brought his friend Edward Partridge to a meeting held in Father Smith's home at which the Prophet Joseph spoke. Mother Smith tells us that they arrived during Joseph's sermon "and seated themselves in the congregation. When Joseph had finished his discourse, he gave all who had any remarks to make, the privilege of speaking. Upon this, Mr. Partridge arose, and stated that he had been to Manchester, with the view of obtaining further information respecting the doctrine which we preached; but, not finding us, he had made some inquiry of our neighbors concerning our characters, which they stated had been unimpeachable, until Joseph deceived [them] relative to the Book of Mormon. He also said that he had walked over our farm, and observed the good order and industry which it exhibited; and, having seen what we had sacrificed for the sake of our faith, and having heard that our veracity was not questioned upon any other point than that of religion, he believed our testimony, and was ready to be baptized, 'if,' said he, 'Brother Joseph will baptize me.' "[34] The following day he was baptized by the Prophet in the Seneca River.[35]

When the Smiths left New York to settle in Kirtland, Mother Smith continued the family practice of holding meetings and devotionals, in this instance on the flatboat that carried them on the Erie Canal to Buffalo, New York.[36] An early convert named John Smith (not the Prophet's uncle and not a family relation) records a number of cottage meetings held, it appears, in Father Smith's home during the Kirtland years. On January 7, 1832, for example, he held a cottage meeting in Father Smith's home, as he did on the following day when he preached to "a large congregation."[37]

Bearing Witness at Every Opportunity

When not inviting people into his home to receive gospel instruction, our gray-haired eminence was determined that he would let his own light so shine that by it others too would glorify their Father in Heaven. Thus it was that when the Kirtland Temple was dedicated he took Edwin Holden through the temple, showing him the rooms and then showing him the

Egyptian mummies and the papyrus from which the Prophet translated the book of Abraham;[38] when young George A. Smith first read the Book of Mormon and was yet uncertain, it was Father Smith who answered his questions and soothed his doubts;[39] and when Lorenzo Snow attended a patriarchal blessing meeting in the Kirtland Temple and was awed at what he saw and heard, it was Father Smith who said to him, "I discover that you are trying to understand the principles of Mormonism," and counseled him to "pray to the Lord and satisfy yourself; study the matter over, compare the scriptures with what we are teaching; talk with the brethren that you are acquainted with, and after a time you will be convinced that 'Mormonism' is of God, and you will be baptized."[40]

Father Smith's prophetic insight was realized within two short weeks, when Lorenzo was baptized. Later, when Lorenzo and Abel Butterfield departed on missions to the South, it was the missionary-minded Father Smith who gave them blessings and advice, and in the case of Brother Snow, he even gave him a Bible.[41] In the same spirit of blessing, Father Smith joined Sidney Rigdon, Brigham Young, Newel K. Whitney, and others in promising Heber C. Kimball that on his mission to England he would "prosper and be blessed with power to do a glorious work."[42] We see the same thing in the life of departing missionary George A. Smith, who was fond of quoting the good missionary counsel he received from Father Smith.[43] At the same time, Father Smith blessed him and promised him that he would be restored from the ill health he then experienced, and that he would accomplish a great deal of good and return home safely.[44]

Father Smith's missionary courage grew out of his testimony of the Restoration. Even though he had established himself, as early as the period of the First Vision, as "a good deal of a smatterer in Scriptural [meaning biblical] knowledge,"[45] he made little or no endeavor to prove the truths of which he spoke by an appeal to Christian tradition or in Bible-bashing argumentation. We illustrate with an incident that occurred in November 1830. In October of that year Father Smith was imprisoned in the Canandaigua jail for his inability to pay a fourteen-dollar debt. The greater issue, however, was that those who imprisoned him hoped to induce him to renounce his testimony of the Book of Mormon. While imprisoned he labored in the jail's cooper shop to earn monies to pay off his debt. In addition, however, he preached every Sunday he was there, and at the conclusion of this thirty-day stay he baptized two.[46] During a portion of his jail tenure, he met Eli Bruce, formerly the sheriff of Niagara County, who had been imprisoned because of his Masonic beliefs and practices. Bruce maintained a diary, in which he mentioned a conversation with the father of the Prophet: "Had a long talk with the father of *the Smith,* who, according to the old man's account, is the particular favorite of Heaven! To him Heaven has vouchsafed to reveal its mysteries; he is the herald of the latter-day glory. The old man avers that he is commissioned by God to baptize and preach this new doctrine. He says that our Bible is much abridged and deficient; that soon the Divine will is to be made known to all, as written in the *new Bible,* or *Book of Mormon.*"[47]

Thus, in one short paragraph we gain solid insight into the missionary approach of Father Smith—he was teaching and testifying of the prophetic mission of his son, of the restoration of the Church, of his power to baptize, of the universal destiny of the restored gospel, and of the fact that the Book of Mormon is the divinely inspired written testimony that would enable people to understand the principles of eternity.

Opposition from the Press

This same zeal for Christ that inspired the Prophet's father to bear testimony to Eli Bruce ferried his Spirit-born convictions deep into the Palmyra community. Even though he carried half a hundred years under his belt, he spoke with the bold voice of youth, knowing, as have the righteous in every age, that it is written in the ledgers of heaven that the work of God can never be carried on the shoulders of cowards. His testimony was ever linked to that of the Prophet in a constant advance against darkness. The outpourings of one local newspaper give us some insight into how the ears of the orthodox tingled at their words. The editor—onc Abner Cole, writing under the pseudonym of Obediah Dogberry—varnished his hard script and gilded his assault under the guise of correcting the morals and improving the thought of his readership.[48]

Cole took direct aim at "that spindle shanked ignoramus Jo

Smith,"[49] who was, he informs us, a counterfeit, or simply a "pseudo prophet."[50] He also shot at Father Smith, whom he dubbed "Joseph the Elder, sir-named Malt,"[51] and then threw additional darts at Oliver Cowdery, "even Oliver, the pedagogue";[52] "St. Martin [Harris], a certain (would be) great man";[53] "the notorious Sidney Rigdon,"[54] that "man of many creeds";[55] and Parley P. Pratt, who, he said, had run "away from a constable, and numerous creditors."[56] Cole energetically attacked all who were so foolish, in his judgment, as to follow Joseph Smith and his teachings.

Cole wrote that Mormonism was a collusion with evil, spearheaded by the Prophet and his father. He emphasized that the fruit bears the stamp of the tree from which it falls, and that the Prophet's evil first had root in the mind and heart of his parents—particularly his father. He paints a picture of Father Smith as being "a man of words" who "instructed the people in 'the way they should go,' howbeit he pursued, in his own person all the bye ways and sly ways he could discover in the wilderness of sin." The father thus instructed the son in the arts of private as well as public deception.[57] This constant attack upon the Smith character gnarled on, stating, "We have never been able to learn that any of the family were ever noted for much else than ignorance and stupidity, to which might be added, so far as it may respect the elder branch [i.e., Father Smith], a propensity to superstition and fondness for every thing *marvelous*."[58]

Cole tells—but grossly distorts—the account of the Prophet retrieving the gold plates from Cumorah, and notes that the account was widely repeated by both the Prophet and his father. He wrote that after a difficult journey through the woods, the Prophet "returned to the house with his father, much fatigued and injured. This tale [of the coming forth of the Book of Mormon] in substance, was told at the time the event was *said* to have happened by both father and son, and is well recollected by many of our citizens."[59]

In a later issue of his paper, Cole claimed, "We have on hand a new edition of the prophet's vision, at the time the Gold Bible was revealed to him by the Spirit, and the subsequent transactions, as related by Jo's father and his elder brother."[60] Significantly, in an earlier issue Cole pointed out that everything unfolded according to the "predictions made by the elder Smith, a number of years before."[61]

Looking back through the century and a half that separates us from these events, we neither see nor feel the intensity of the times. But it is nonetheless clear that the Smiths—particularly the Prophet and his father, if we can believe Cole's account of things—were earnestly contending for the faith that was once delivered to the Saints and restored anew. Their testimony, by Cole's own admission, was widely known; they were consumed by a missionary spirit. Indeed, theirs was such a widely circulated story that Cole invited readers to write to him, sharing additional details beyond what he had published, for which he would award them with a free edition of the newspaper.[62] The larger point to be made, of course, is that the Smiths' testimony of the Book of Mormon and of the restoration of the gospel was not the sand pebble Cole thought it to be—it was a stone that moved a rock which pushed a boulder and started an avalanche. It was, quite literally, a stone cut out of a mountain without hands that began to roll forward to eventually consume all nations. In the years since the world has forgotten Abner Cole, we are reminded that the Prophet's goose quill was far more powerful than Abner Cole's printing press.

Taking the Gospel to the Family

In June 1830, Samuel Smith set out on the mission to which he had been set apart by his brother the Prophet Joseph. He met with early discouragements and little success. At the end of one particularly dispiriting day he was thrown out of an inn, the owner of which roughly renounced him and his message. He walked a short distance and washed his feet in a small brook as a testimony against the man.

Shortly thereafter he met John P. Greene—a brother-in-law of Brigham Young—who was a Methodist preacher. Greene was not yet ready to accept the Book of Mormon, but he did promise that in his own preaching journey he would make a list of people who showed an interest in obtaining a copy of the Book of Mormon. Samuel left a copy with Greene and agreed to return later and provide copies to those interested.

On his follow-up journey, Samuel was accompanied by his parents. Mother Smith provides the details: "It was our intention to have passed near the tavern, where Samuel was so abusively treated a fortnight previous, but just before we came to the house, a sign of small-pox intercepted us. We turned aside, and meeting a citizen of the place, we enquired of him, to what extent this disease prevailed. He answered, that the tavern keeper and two of his family had died with it not long since, but he did not know that any one else had caught the disease, and that it was brought into the neighborhood by a traveler, who stopped at the tavern over night."

With an eye that saw beyond the temporal, Mother Smith concluded: "This is a specimen of the peculiar disposition of some individuals, who would sacrifice their soul's salvation rather than give a Saint of God a meal of victuals. According to the word of God, it will be more tolerable for Sodom and Gomorrah, in the day of judgment, than for such persons."

The Smiths continued on to the home of Squire Alvah Beaman, in Livonia, from which place Samuel went to visit John P. Greene to see if he had secured the names of any interested in obtaining copies of the Book of Mormon. Finding that no names had been obtained, the Smiths returned home,[63] thus concluding the first recorded formal missionary journey of which Father Smith was a part.

Some weeks later, Father Smith took his fourteen-year-old son, Don Carlos, and left his home in Ontario County, New York. They travelled some two hundred fifty miles and arrived in St. Lawrence County, New York, where Father Smith's father and brothers resided.[64] The seeds of gospel preparation had been sown, for two years earlier Father Smith had written his father, telling of the remarkable visions vouchsafed to the young Joseph. Asael responded by saying that he had long known that the Lord was going to raise up a branch of his family whose work would revolutionize the religious world. According to George A. Smith, the Prophet Joseph Smith had joined in the testimony bearing and also written a letter "in which he declared that the sword of vengeance of the Almighty hung over this generation, and except they repented and obeyed the Gospel, . . . humbling themselves before the Lord, it would fall upon the wicked, and sweep them from the earth." Both the logic and the spirit of the letter left a deep impression on John, Father Smith's brother, who rejoiced, saying, "Why, he writes like a prophet."

Father Smith and Don Carlos arrived first at the home of

John Smith, whose wife, Clarissa, had never before seen the
father of the Prophet. As he entered John's house, however,
Clarissa eyed him and said, "There, Mr. Smith, is your brother
Joseph."

In surprise, John turned and, seeing the brother whom he
had not seen for eighteen years, gasped, "Joseph, is this you?"

"It is I," said Joseph; "Is my father yet alive? I have come to
see him once more, before he dies."

In that same evening Father Smith, it is reported, "preached
a beautiful sermon," the content of which has not been preserved for us. We are left to guess that he spoke of the restoration of the gospel, of the prophetic mission of his son, and of
the coming forth of the Book of Mormon. How could it have
been otherwise?

When the morning came the brothers, Joseph and John,
took John's horse and wagon and left for Stockholm, some
twelve miles distant. John's wife, Clarissa, and his thirteen-year-
old son George A., remained at home reading one of the copies
of the Book of Mormon that Father Smith brought. About dark
the two brothers arrived at the home of a third brother, Jesse,
who with his wife had gone to the house of a fourth brother,
Silas, "to see father [Asael] Smith die."

Death, however, had been cheated, for though Asael had
suffered a severe fit, he was reviving, as Joseph and John were
told upon their arrival at Silas's. Prudence suggested that Asael
not be bothered that night, so the two travellers went to spend
the night in the home of Jesse, unaware of the farrago that
steamed in the family cauldron. They were soon to learn of it,
however, for as they settled for the evening, the conversation
turned to sharing accounts of their respective families. Father
Smith told of the death of his son Alvin, and then began to
speak of the discovery and translation of the Book of Mormon.
At this, the censorious Jesse unleased his violent and acerbic
tongue: "If you say another word about that Book of Mormon,
you shall not stay a minute longer in my house, and if I can't
get you out any other way," he threatened, "I will hew you down
with my broadaxe."

Perhaps we are bettered by not having the fuller content of
the conversation. We do know, at least, that Jesse was a well-
educated and a religious man, and that he saw himself as protecting his own sacred thought and tradition. But had he in

truth represented that Master whom he said he represented, he would have known intuitively that the spirit of his eruption placed him outside the camp of the Lord's approval. Regrettably, some men read the Bible by the light of their own dim understanding and see but little of the divine intent. Uncle John, for his part, summarized the evening conversation by saying, "We had always been accustomed to being treated with much harshness by our brother, but he had never carried it to so great an extent before."

The following morning, with the twanging harp of Jesse's displeasure ringing in their ears, Joseph and John visited their aged parents. "They were," said John, "overjoyed to see Joseph, for he had been absent from them so long, that they had been fearful of never beholding his face again in the flesh." This was not, however, simply the reunion of a father and a son. It was more—much more! This son was a missionary, motivated by eternal longings, and he had come to announce the restoration of the gospel, with all its powers and potentials. Unavoidably, then, recorded John, "the subject of the Book of Mormon was introduced. Father [Asael] received with gladness that which Joseph communicated; and remarked, that he had always expected that something would appear to make known the true Gospel."

In a few minutes the tart-tongued Jesse came in, and, said John, "on hearing that the subject of our conversation was the Book of Mormon, his wrath rose as high as it did the night before. 'My father's mind,' said Jesse, 'is weak; and I will not have it corrupted with such blasphemous stuff, so just shut up your head.'"

Father Smith reasoned mildly with him, but, the wisdom of Solomon notwithstanding, his soft answer could not turn away Jesse's wrath. Nimble words failed to tranquilize Jesse's frenzied spirit. John's account continues, "Brother Silas then said, 'Jesse, our brother has come to make us a visit, and I am glad to see him, and am willing he should talk as he pleases in my house.'" But, it is reported, "Jesse flew in a rage and talked so abusively that Silas was under the necessity of requesting him to leave the house."

Freed from the influence of the whirlwind, Father Smith and his father continued their conversation uninterrupted, and Father Asael seemed pleased with every word he heard. These gospel conversations between the father and his missionary son continued throughout the following day, though John was required to return to his home.

It was not long, however, until Jesse went to John's house, hoping to find in the yet uncommitted John a friendly ally in his war against the Book of Mormon. Jesse's fury seemed to give him resolution; he sensed that the message of the Restoration was spreading with fluid readiness through his family. John reported "Jesse . . . informed me that all my brothers were coming to make me a visit, 'and as true as you live,' said he, 'they all believe that cursed Mormon book, every word of it, and they are setting a trap for you, to make you believe it.'"

John thanked his elder brother for telling him that his brothers were coming to visit, but insisted that in matters of religion he was quite able to make his own judgments. Still, Jesse had an itch on his soul that he could not scratch: "I know," he said, "that you are a pretty good judge of such things, but I tell you that they are as wary as the devil. And I want you to go with me and see our sister Susan and sister-in-law Fanny, and we will bar their minds against Joseph's influence."

John compromised. He went with Jesse. They conversed with the two sisters, "as [they] thought proper," and requested them to come to John's house for a meeting the following day. When the brothers arrived at John's home, Jesse policed every word to ensure nothing was said about the Book of Mormon. The power of the message, however, was already beginning to rest upon the souls of some of the brothers, and even as they were arranging to visit their sisters the following day, Asael pulled his brother John aside and told him he should converse with Joseph in spite of Jesse's obdurance. Together they arranged for John and Joseph to be alone that night, and a conversation unfolded in which the spirit of testimony so touched the heart of Uncle John that he came to know and could never thereafter deny the truths restored through his nephew the Prophet Joseph Smith.

During the early part of Father Smith's visit to the home of Uncle John, he left young George A. and his mother (John's wife, Clarissa) with a copy of the Book of Mormon. They spent the burden of that Saturday and Sunday reading and discussing it. George A. recorded his objections as he read. In recalling those events later, he said it was about five o'clock in the evening when some of the neighbors came by, wanting to know about the book of which they had heard so much—the Book of Mormon. Like so many who have followed them, they took the book and, without reading it, began to criticize its contents. As there were none there to defend it, young George A. stepped forward, answering their charges one by one, he said, "until I came off victoriously and got the compliment of being a very smart boy."

Curiously, no one raised the objections that had addled George's wits—objections dealing with the geography described in the Book of Mormon. These objections, however, were little steps for Father Smith, who walked through them with such logic and conviction that all of George A.'s concerns were banished in a short conversation of about thirty minutes with his Uncle Joseph.

Up to this point in time George A. had been the favorite of his Uncle Jesse, just as Jesse had been a favorite of young George A. Indeed, George A. thought that what the educated and pious Jesse "did not know was not worth knowing." It was natural, therefore, in a spirit of confidence, for George A. to go to Jesse and tell him that he had had a private conversation with his Uncle Joseph in which all his objections to the Book of Mormon were answered, and that therefore he was certain that it was a revelation from God. He was surprised by Jesse's surprise, and wounded by Jesse's reaction. "He abused me," said George A., "because I had become favourable, and because uncle Joseph had a private conversation with me."

Finally, in the discussion that ensued, Jesse chided George A. for holding the private conversation with Father Smith, saying, "Joe dare not talk in my presence." Continuing, Jesse added, "The Devil never shut my mouth." George A. immediately replied, "Perhaps he opened it, uncle."

In the explosion that this comment ignited, George A. saw a new side of Jesse. "I thought I should have lost my identity," he later recalled, for "he gave me to the Devil *instanter.*" When the Dutch blessing had been fully administered, George A. went and told his Uncle Asael what had occurred, "and the old gentleman laughed," reported George A.; "and I then went to see uncle Silas and told him; and he said, 'If old men begin to talk with boys, they must take boys' play.'"

Who, then, would say that the gospel cannot be taught with an occasional smile?

But men are mixtures, co-minglings of good and evil. One wit has suggested that Jesse was one of the premortal host not designated to receive a body, but that he stole one and came to earth anyway. The witticism is both unkind and untrue, but it somehow touches upon the meanness of spirit that Jesse sometimes manifested. While Jesse opposed and even feared the Book of Mormon, he still held natural affections for his brother Joseph. Thus it was that when the time came for Father Smith and young Don Carlos to return to their home, Father Smith, not expecting to see Jesse again, extended his hand in a pleasant, affectionate manner and said: "Farewell, brother Jesse." "Farewell, Joe, forever," sneered the angry Jesse, in a surly tone.

" 'I am afraid,' returned Joseph, in a kind, but solemn manner, 'it will be forever, unless you repent.' "

Uncle John recorded the moment for us, and in so doing observed: "This was too much for even Jesse's obdurate heart. He melted into tears; however, he made no reply, nor ever mentioned the circumstance afterwards," though "he wept like a child all the while we were riding," a distance of four miles.

Thus it was that the eloquence of sincerity adorned the elegance of truth with a force that pierced a wooden heart—a heart which was quick and sudden in quarrel, but which was learning by the painful schooling of mortality that love is stronger than spite, and that truths spoken in humility are a rebuke more powerful than the collective bitterness of lemon prejudice and meanness.

1834 Mission to Pontiac, Michigan

Who could blame us for lamenting the brevity of records that have come down to us from Father Smith? For a man to whom the Lord granted almost threescore and ten years, he uttered an amazing minimum of nonsense, and we are left to wish that we could rub and polish our own brains by contact with his. Yet it was not the brain but the spirit of the man that molded his greatness. The moment his eye saw into the eternities unfolded by the testimony of his son, he plunged headlong and without retreat or regret into the surging gospel tide, knowing that he could ride the crest of its power into a celestial reward. "He was," said the Prophet Joseph, "already in the wane of his life, when the light of truth broke in upon the world, and with pleasure he hailed its benign and enlightening rays, and was chosen by the Almighty to be one of the witnesses to the Book of Mormon. From that time, his only aim was the promotion of truth—his soul was taken up with the things of the Kingdom; his bowels yearned over the children of men; and it was more than his meat and his drink to do the will of his Father, who is in heaven."[65]

Do we sin in wishing for a fuller account of his ministry and the example he set? We prefer to think we simply show good gospel sensitivities.

We know little of the mission he took in 1834 to Pontiac, Michigan, though we do know that he went with the Prophet Joseph, Hyrum, and the Three Witnesses to the Book of Mormon—Oliver Cowdery, David Whitmer, and Martin Harris. We have only so much information as has been preserved by the pen and memory of Edward Stevenson, but we remain grateful for that little, for we know, as the Prophet Joseph once wrote, "that one man empowered from Jehovah has more influence with the children of the kingdom than eight hundred millions led by the precepts of men"[66] and this was a mission in which these missionaries were clothed with the power and Spirit of the Lord. "Let me as a living witness," said Stevenson, "speak of the moving, stirring sensation created in this town and surrounding country of the then Territory of Michigan."

In a meeting that lasted over two hours, the Prophet Joseph Smith lifted his hand and said, "I am a witness that there is a God, for I saw Him in open day, while praying in a silent grove, in the spring of 1820." He further testified that two personages appeared to him, and that the Eternal Father pointed to the Savior and said, "This is my Beloved Son hear ye Him." The Prophet also testified of the coming of the angel Moroni and the coming forth of the Book of Mormon, and promised those present that if they would repent of their sins and be baptized, they would receive the Holy Ghost and experience the gifts of the Spirit.[67] Stevenson reported that not long after, this promise was fulfilled as members of the Pontiac Branch indeed exercised gifts of the Spirit such as speaking in tongues.[68]

While in Pontiac, the Prophet, Hyrum, Father Smith, and the Three Witnesses all bore record that they had seen the plates from which the Book of Mormon was translated. With

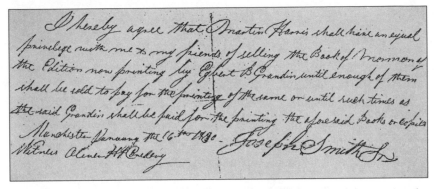

Agreement between Joseph Smith, Sr., and Martin Harris granting equal privilege to sell copies of the Book of Mormon

particular reference to the power that attended the labors of Father Smith, Stevenson testified: "The power of his priesthood rested mightily upon Father Smith. It appeared as though the veil which separated us from the eternal world became so thin that heaven itself was right in our midst. It was at one of these meetings held during this time when I received my patriarchal blessing under the hands of Father Smith. Naturally Father Smith was not a man of many words, but sober-minded, firm, mild and impressive. The exception, however, was at those blessing meetings; for truly the Holy Ghost gave utterance. Many of his words, although not written, recur to my mind as I pen these lines, for so impressive and strikingly were they sealed upon our heads."[69]

What a blessing to meet an inspired missionary! One who, like his Master, taught as one having authority, and not as the scribes of his day.

1836 Mission with Uncle John

In May 1836 the sixty-four-year-old Patriarch and father of the Prophet joined hands with his fifty-four-year-old brother, John, and left Kirtland to preach the gospel and administer patriarchal blessings. They set their course for New Portage, Ohio, about fifty miles south of Kirtland, where in a matter of eight hurried days they either baptized or witnessed the baptisms of sixteen souls, and Father Smith conferred patriarchal blessings on ninety-five of the Saints. In addition, according to a report in the *Messenger and Advocate,* an unspecified number of people, "from a thorough conviction of the error of their former ways, followed them home and were baptized" in Kirtland on the Sabbath following their return.

The *Messenger and Advocate's* homolitic summary of their labors concluded with the lesson the Saints were intended to learn: "Thus we see, that when men, (and they are but men) go forth clothed with authority from on high, and the ancient order of things is being established according to the word of God, the honest in heart see it, and know it, and prejudice and error give way before the light of truth and reason." Then, as if to observe that missionary success breeds the desire for additional success, the newspaper added its benediction: "While we are penning this article, these aged fathers are about to set out on a mission to the East. We most devoutly pray the Lord to be with them and bless them. We also entreat our brethren in the Eastern churches to receive them cordially, entertain them hospitably, and above all, to appreciate their instructions. The Lord, for his Son's sake preserve them in health and strength and return them to the bosom of their families and the church in this place in peace."[70]

The reason for the abrupt termination of the New Portage mission was that seven days after leaving Kirtland, the mother of the missionary brothers, Mary Duty Smith, arrived in Kirtland. The family immediately sent word to the travelling harvesters asking that they return, which they did, finding "the old lady in good health and excellent spirits," Mother Smith reported. Two days after their return, however, the ninety-two-year-old matriarch "was taken sick and survived but one week; at the end of which she died, firm in the faith of the gospel."[71] It had been Mary's intent to have the Prophet Joseph Smith baptize her and then have "my Joseph," as she called Father Smith, give her a patriarchal blessing.[72] Her sudden illness and subsequent death interfered with her intent, though she is clearly the kind of person the Lord had in mind when he revealed the doctrine of baptism for the dead.

Thus it was that she was freed to join her husband, Asael, who six years previous while on his deathbed, it is reported, "declared his full and firm belief in the everlasting gospel and also regretted that he was not baptized when Joseph his son was there, and acknowledged that the doctrine of Universalism which he had so long advocated was not true, for although he had lived by this religion fifty years, yet he now renounced it as insufficient to comfort him in death."[73]

With the dirt on their mother's grave not yet hardened, and with the increasing infirmities of age pressing upon them, the brothers Smith began a walk and wagon ride that would take them over twenty-four hundred miles and last more than three months. Before the brothers returned home, their feet would carry the roadway dust of Ohio, New York, Pennsylvania, Vermont, and New Hampshire. They were destined to baptize many, confer "blessings upon many hundreds," and preach the gospel "to many thousands."[74] Both would celebrate birthdays while away from home. The wagon that carried them was powered by one horse.

Intending to take the gospel to members of their family, they also bore the Prophet's charge that they visit "the branches of the Church in the Eastern States, to set them in order, and confer on the brethren their patriarchal blessings." Anxious that they know of their support, the Prophet Joseph, Mother Smith, and John's wife, Clarissa, accompanied them in a carriage as far as Painesville, Ohio, where, recorded the Prophet, "we procured a bottle of wine, broke bread, ate and drank, and parted after the ancient order, with the blessings of God."[75]

They headed first for New Hampshire, visiting on the way Father Smith's brother-in-law Daniel Mack. But alas, "they are not all Israel, which are of Israel,"[76] and though Mack treated them very kindly, he was unwilling to hear the gospel message. Saddened by his disinterest, the travellers pressed on, moving to Grafton, where they met their sister Mary, whom neither had seen for twenty years. Uncle John recorded their double lament: "The prejudice of her husband had become so strong against Mormonism, that she was unwilling to treat us even decently."

From Mary's, the two missionaries walked and rode to Vermont, through communities where both had once lived in Windsor and Orange counties, and, said John, "found many of our relatives, who treated us kindly, but would not receive the gospel." The disappointments of these rejections carried them across the Green Mountains to Middlebury, where they found their oldest sister, Priscilla, who was very pleased to greet her two brothers and who received their testimony. They spent the night with her before proceeding on the next day for St. Lawrence County, New York, to visit the gloomy and irritably tempered Jesse and their one remaining sister, Susannah, who was also called Susan, and who was but two years younger than John.

Arriving in Stockholm, the two missionaries spent a day in the home of their brother Jesse. Uncle John said succinctly: "He treated us very ill."[77] Preferring not to enlarge existing antagonisms, but being, in the words of George A. Smith, "very much grieved in consequence of the persecution they had received from their eldest brother, Jesse,"[78] Father Smith and Uncle John departed, heading toward Potsdam and the home of their sister Susan.

Uncle John, having some personal business to attend to, temporarily parted company with Father Smith to go about ten miles to one side of Potsdam. Meanwhile, riding a wave of anger that was years long, the shrill and incessant Jesse still imagined that he could destroy his brother with his mouth. He therefore followed Father Smith to Potsdam, where he sued Father Smith on a pretended twelve-dollar claim that he said was thirty years old. Stunned, a weary Father Smith insisted that the debt had long since been paid but was nonetheless compelled to return to Stockholm, where, in John's words, the still seething Jesse "abused him most shamefully, in the presence of strangers."[79] George A. Smith provides us with the remaining details: "As the Patriarch had no money, Jesse attacked his horse. The circumstances were the more aggravating as he was too old and feeble to proceed on his mission on foot. Fortunately, in the midst of this dilemma, Silas, another brother, arrived, having come from Kirtland to settle some business in St. Lawrence. He paid fifty dollars for the release of his brother Joseph from the obligation."[80]

Father Smith, for his part, presented an honorable contrast. His was the example of Christlike patience and meekness. "The meekness manifested by brother Joseph upon this occasion," said John, "won upon the feelings of many, who said that Jesse had disgraced himself so much that he would never be able to redeem his character."[81] And we, for our part, are left to mourn over how little profit is to be gained in the treasures of wickedness.

Looking back on these events, George A. said he could not

"easily express the grief manifested by these venerable fathers in Israel at the unkind treatment they received from their elder brother, who possessed a small farm and other comfortable property in Stockholm." Nonetheless, as soon as the two missionary brothers were united once again in Stockholm, they went with young George A. into the woods to pray for comfort, guidance, and assistance. Because they prayed with faith, the Lord heard their pleas, and, said George A., "their hearts were comforted, and the Spirit of the Lord rested upon them." They certified to their sympathetic nephew that they had treated Jesse with only kindness and respect, and that Jesse had no occasion against them "except for the ministry of the gospel, and the priesthood which had been conferred upon them. He despised them for the gospel's sake, and for its sake only."

As is ever the case, Jesse's bitterness bought its own reward. He had hated Mormonism with a rancor that incapacitated his reason and blinded his sight, and in offending the Lord's agents he offended the Lord who commissioned them. George A. reported that Father Smith and John "prophesied that [Jesse] should become a pauper, that he should die penniless, and that his children should be estranged from him and be scattered."

Seven years after Jesse's death, George A. Smith, by then a member of the Quorum of the Twelve Apostles, recorded the fulfillment of this sad prophesy: "My uncle, Jesse Smith, died in 1852, in his eighty-fifth year. His numerous family were scattered, and his property wasted away, so that when he died he had no friends able to bury him, and his funeral expenses were defrayed, out of the poor fund, by the township of Stockholm, where he died."[82]

Such an unfriendly death. And all for fifty pieces of silver!

While the encounters with Jesse represented some of the least pleasant portions of the entire missionary journey, and while there is a certain sadness associated with every rejection of true testimony, there were great blessings that gave encouragement to the two missionary brothers as well. Leaving the area of Stockholm and Potsdam, the two superannuated elders went to Ogdensburg, New York, where Heber C. Kimball had been laboring and had raised up a branch of some twenty members. When they arrived, they were, in the Prophet Joseph's words, "very much depressed in spirits"[83] because of the troubles they had experienced with Jesse.

Brother Kimball and the Ogdensburg Saints, however, were lifted in spirits by the arrival of the two travelling ministers. Two days after they arrived, Brother Kimball gathered the Saints together, and Father Smith pronounced patriarchal blessings upon those assembled. The following day, being the Sabbath, the Saints convened their Sunday services, at which Uncle John spoke, and, said Heber, "four of us bore testimony to the Book of Mormon and the truth of the work."[84] The following day Father Smith and Uncle John left Ogdensburg, arriving in Kirtland in the early part of October 1836.

In Retrospect

How do we summarize in a paragraph the missionary spirit and labor of the father of the Prophet? No more could we capture the ministry of Abraham in a chapter, or that of Adam in a single book. Looking back, it is clear that in the early days, when there were no other missionaries, he was one; later, when converts came, he assumed other roles, particularly that of Patriarch. He was one of the first missionaries in this dispensation, but in the larger view, who was first and who was last is of no eternal consequence. Let every man and every woman serve in his or her time—as did Father and Mother Smith.

The endeavor to bring people to a knowledge of the gospel was the constant thought and effort of both Father and Mother Smith. They were forever bearing testimony to member and nonmember alike. Their first efforts were directed at members of their families, as both their correspondence and their actual missionary visits demonstrate. Later, when Father Smith was serving as the Patriarch and the giving of patriarchal blessings had first claim upon his ministerial attentions, he still joined the giving of patriarchal blessings to the preaching of the gospel to nonmembers. His missions to Pontiac, Michigan, in 1834 and to the eastern states in 1836, for example, occurred during his tenure as Patriarch.

When he was not out preaching himself, he was blessing and encouraging others who were—or he was housing them, or inviting them into his home to preach to nonmember neighbors, or tending to things at home so that Mother Smith could be engaged in missionary activities.

There was an order, however, to all that he did. He never got ahead of the Prophet but was always his humble follower. What the Prophet sowed, Father Smith watered—but God gave the increase.

As we look back now, through the unerring judgments of time, it becomes clear that one of the great evidences of the divinity of the work is the giant missionary success that has accompanied the message of the Restoration. That so powerful and so appealing a personality as Joseph Smith, divinely called and commissioned, would come on the latter-day scene; that a few simple men would preach so lofty and so inspiring a vision as to suggest that men could become gods and that angels and revelations would instruct them so to become; that revelations and visions and priesthood powers such as the ancients experienced would be not only restored but also shared by all the righteous; that these early missionaries' simple but powerful testimonies would be magnified a million times over by the voice and energies of their converts; that this simple work that they began would roll forth and consume the earth, and that through them and their agents the voice of the Lord would be to all nations and that none would escape; that there would be no eye that should not see, nor ear that should not hear, nor heart that should not be penetrated—that this great accumulation of promise and prophecy should even occur, boldly announced by a people scorned and impoverished by the trials of life, is a miracle far more incredible than anything recorded in the Old or New Testaments, with but two exceptions: the creation of the earth; and the death, burial, and resurrection of Jesus Christ. And Father Smith, with a vigor almost unquenched by the flow of time, was one of the first, one of the most enduring, and one of the doughtiest of the early voices of the Restoration. Truth was in the air, and he breathed it in large doses; then, with enlarged lungs and an invigorated tongue, he shared it with all who would listen.

So finally, we are driven to ask: If we announce that he was not a man for an age, but for all time, do we overstate the case? Do we then make of him more than he was?

Bound by the eternal law of witnesses, we hear the resounding, thundering, and crashing response: No, no, ten thousand times no! We do not overstate the case. Father Smith was appointed to be one of the Eight Witnesses who handled the plates from which the Book of Mormon was translated, and it is the destiny of the Book of Mormon to bring more people to Christ than has any other book; it is the destiny of the Book of Mormon to lead the missionary endeavors of the pre-millennial millions who are to prepare the world for the coming Lord; and then, in addition, it is the destiny of the Book of Mormon to open millennial doors and lead more people in the millennial era to accept Christ and his gospel than have accepted him in all previous dispensations combined. We are foolish to specu-late at the numbers such a conversion process will embrace, but surely it reaches into the billions and more. And on these, all of whom will be readers of the Book of Mormon, the testimony of the Eight Witnesses is eternally binding. As a part of their testi-mony, the testimony of the missionary Joseph Smith, Sr., is also eternally binding.

No, in truth, we do not overstate the case.

CHAPTER 7

Against the World

On the one hand, the voice of the Lord speaks softly, for it is a "still small voice,"[1] even "a still voice of perfect mildness"[2]—"a pleasant voice, as if it were a whisper";[3] it is "not a harsh voice," neither is it a loud voice, but rather a voice that pierces to the very soul of man, causing the heart to burn.[4] On the other hand, the voice of the world speaks loudly, imitating thunder, or some great and strong wind, the crashing earthquake, or the raging fire.[5] The voice of the Lord says, "Peace, peace be unto you, because of your faith in my Well Beloved."[6] Indeed, it is the voice of the Lord that says to the righteous of every age: "I will not leave you comfortless," for "peace I leave with you, my peace I give unto you."[7] The finger-pointing voice of the world, in contrast, is but the echo of the voice of Satan—the slanderer, that "accuser of [the] brethren"[8]—and it is the voice of accusation, of naysaying, of character assassination, gossip, and falsehood; it is the voice of ridicule and scorn, always speaking against the cause of Christ, promoting vice in the name of some virtue, and, like Korihor, speaking with missionary zeal.

But wait! The voice of the world is many voices: the voice of skepticism, the voice of doubt, the voice of anger, the voice of prejudice and disbelief. Often it is the voice of intellectuality and reason. Frequently it is the voice of piety, the voice of worldly worship and man-made religion. Thus it was that Paul said, "There are . . . so many kinds of voices in the world, and none of them is without signification."9

We—all of us, every son and daughter of Adam!—are, then, the multitudes that stand in the valley of decision, left to choose what voices we will hear and what voices we will follow. As is to be expected, we hear voices that speak of prophets and prophesy, of saints and sinners, of new Bibles and old scriptures, of golden books and secret writings. We hear voices speak of angels and spirits, of revelation and necromancy, money digging and witchcraft, of night-writings and rituals, and even of astrological signs and sight-conferring "peeping stones."

What shall we believe? Which voices shall we hear and follow? Whom shall we trust, and how shall we know? And in the instance of the Prophet Joseph Smith, and in that of his father, which voices speak the truth? Which rightly describe the two men, accurately describing their conduct and character, their motive and instinct, their design and dealings with their fellowmen?

We take as our measuring rod the testimony of Jesus, who warned that both true and false prophets are judged by the same standard. "Wherefore," he said, "by their fruits ye shall know them." For, "not every one that saith unto me, Lord, Lord, shall enter into the kingdom of heaven; but he that doeth the will of my Father which is in heaven."10

Let us, then, hear the voices that speak of Father Smith, and weigh what they say against the fruits that he bore. Then, by the Savior's own standard, we can judge whether these voices give a life-giving sound or whether they speak a lie.

One Clamorous Voice: "Old Joe . . . Entirely Destitute of Moral Character"

Had the press, gazeteers, and pamphleteers of the day shot musket balls instead of words, the entire Smith family would have been dead shortly after the publication of the Book of Mormon, and perhaps before. Salvo after salvo was directed against the family. The voice of Parley Chase, for example, announced that "not one of the male members of the Smith family were entitled to any credit, whatsoever. They were lazy, intemperate and worthless men, very much addicted to lying. In

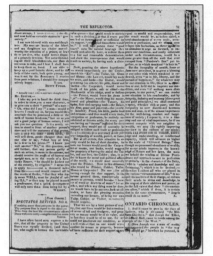

Palmyra newspaper, The Reflector, *containing a column entitled "Ontario Chronicles" that attacked the character of the Smith family*

this they frequently boasted of their skill."[11] David Stafford voiced the same sentiment, claiming, "I have been acquainted with the family of Joseph Smith Sen. for several years, and I know him to be a drunkard and a liar, and to be much in the habit of gambling. He and his boys were truly a lazy set of fellows."[12] Barton Stafford agreed, though his voice spoke not just of the male members but of the entire family: "Joseph Smith, Sen. was a noted drunkard and most of the family followed his example, and Joseph, Jr. especially, who was very much addicted to intemperance. In short, not one of the family had the least claims to respectability."[13]

Indeed, E. D. Howe, in a united chorus of insinuating voices, collected the testimonials of scores of Palmyra citizens, all certifying that the very family that put Palmyra in history books and on the historical map consisted of people schooled by their parents in deception, reared on an appetite for the fabulous, and addicted to lying, deceit, falsehood of every color, and a congenital delight in chicanery. For years to follow, these testimonials became the footnotes and evidence quoted by scores of others in painting word pictures of the Smiths as a group with larceny and mendacity in their blood.

One to quote the Howe testimonials, and then to add a number of his own, was Dr. W. Wyl, who concluded the

following about Father and Mother Smith: "Lying was as natural to them as drinking water, and they do it in a delightful
way; it's a prestidigitation with the truth, you see; artistic skill,
acquired by a life's practice." Moreover, wrote Wyl, "Old 'Mr.
Smith'" had a graphic imagination, filled with "delightful absur-
dities" that infiltrated the entire family. Wyl later claims that the
Smiths' family physician assured the world that "Joseph Smith,
Senior, was a drunkard, a liar and a thief, and his house a perfect brothel."[14]

Joel K. Noble voiced his memory, saying that during the
Vermont years Father Smith ran around with a band of coun-
terfeiters and at one point "eloped (seduced a married woman)
to Canada"—accusations that Noble apparently thought should
not be ignored, for it was clearly a case of "like father like
son."[15] Indeed, the father of the Prophet was frequently de-
picted only by the sour epithets his critics threw at him, and he
was variously called the "indulgent father,"[16] "the old man," "old
Joe," "old Mr. Smith,"[17] "the old gentleman,"[18] and even "the
old blesser."[19] The point of such name-calling was to underscore
the belief that Father Smith, a man with "a constitutional aver-
sion to labor," was "the last person in the world who would have
been suspected by those who knew him of being the father of a
prophet."[20]

Surely, the voices of the world warned, no good thing could
come of Palmyra's most celebrated son, for he was born of
"poor and vicious parents, whose influence was, in his early
years, constantly exerted to suppress the development of any of
the higher qualities of the human soul to the exercise of which
his disposition might incline him."[21]

In short, the voice of the world was gruff and blunt, and
spoke as an erupting volcano, announcing its collective resent-
ment with a constant flow of molten words and fiery images all
designed to burn to stubble the growing testimony of the
Smiths in general and of the Prophet in particular. It was a
voice that accused the Smiths of almost every imaginable deceit
and of a willingness to double-cross even the devil himself, if
they could. This voice attacked their character, damned and
double-damned them as scurvied, leprous spirits, maimed and
lacking in every element of decency that a just God would de-
mand of one through whom he could work.

The United Voice of the Saints

There is an eternal law, however, which stipulates that truth will ultimately prevail and that falsehood will ultimately be buried under the weight of her own self-contradicting excess. Such is the case in the testimonies dealing with the Prophet, his parents, and his family. The testimony of those who knew them well stands as a jewel in the crown of truth, reflecting good at every angle and inspiring millions to live more Christlike lives. Meanwhile, the doleful voices of detraction are generally forgotten. When recalled, they are never carried by a good spirit, never uplift nor inspire, never motivate toward good works or righteous conduct, and never invite the companionship of the Holy Spirit into the lives of those involved.

And that is one of the first fruits of which Jesus spoke—the spirit associated with what men say and do. The Spirit of the Lord can no more carry an untrue testimony than a man can resurrect himself or remit the sins of another. These are the prerogatives of God. So also is the granting of the ratifying seal that the Holy Spirit places on words of truth spoken in a spirit of humility.

Then let the reader judge for himself if there is not a different spirit—a diviner spirit!—which accompanies the testimony of those who truly knew both the Prophet and his father and spoke of them. They speak with a different voice than does the world, and they announce that Father Smith is a fresh and vibrant soul, filled with that spirit and those gifts that make men prophets. Edward Stevenson, for example, tells of "the venerable and venerated father of the Prophet,"[22] who, when seeking the inspiration to give blessings, so parted the veil that it seemed as if those present stood in the midst of heaven itself; and this "sober-minded, firm, mild and impressive" Patriarch spoke with such power on such occasions that Stevenson could remember his words sixty years after the event.[23] Wilford Woodruff also testified that when Father Smith gave a blessing, the heavens seemed to open, and "he could reveal the whole life of that person."[24]

Joseph Holbrook recorded that he "gained much strength, faith and hope" in visiting with Father Smith and others of the brethren; less than two months later, while out preaching the gospel, he encountered a man who did not believe in the divinity of the Book of Mormon but who said he knew the Smith family and willingly certified that "the Smith family were honest, industrious farmers."[25] Joseph Fielding, for his part, considered his visit to the parents of the Prophet as one of the highlights of his visit to Kirtland.[26] His sister Mary, after visiting the Kirtland Temple and seeing Father Smith, two of his brothers, and Sidney Rigdon on the stand, wrote to Mercy Thompson and testified that they were all "faithful servants of the living God."[27] Mother Smith, looking back over decades of marriage, called her husband "an affectionate companion and tender father as ever blessed the confidence of a family."[28]

When for the first time Lorenzo Snow met the father of the Prophet, the silver-haired Patriarch made the staggering promise that young Lorenzo would one day become even as great as God himself. The promise made such a penetrating impression on the young truth-seeker that he could not shake it from his thinking. He asked himself the obvious question: "Can that man be a deceiver?" His honest, soul-searching reflection concluded in favor of the guileless Patriarch: "His every appearance answered in the negative. At first sight, his presence impressed me with feelings of love and reverence. I had never seen age so prepossessing. Father Joseph Smith, the Patriarch, was indeed a noble specimen of aged manhood."[29] Indeed, Lorenzo also noted, "anyone seeing Father Smith as he then appeared and having read of old Father Abraham in the scriptures, would be apt to think that Father Smith looked a good deal like Abraham must have looked; at least, that is what I thought. I do not know that any man among the Saints was more loved than Father Smith; and," he added, in a retrospective that showed how widespread was the esteem in which the Patriarch was held by the Saints, "when any one was seriously sick Father Smith would be called for, whether it was night or day. He was as noble and generous a man as I have ever known."[30]

In August 1837 several apostates, brandishing bowie knives and flashing pistols in the air, broke up a Sabbath worship service held in the Kirtland Temple. The following day the apostate party issued formal charges against Father Smith and sixteen others, who then were bound over to the court to answer charges of assault, battery, and riot.[31] Eliza R. Snow, who was present during the temple disturbance, was called as a witness.

She had known Father Smith well for a number of years, and said she "found the court scene as amusing as the Temple scene was appalling. The idea of such a man as Father Smith—so patriarchal in appearance—so circumspect in deportment and dignified in his manners, being guilty of riot, was at once ludicrous and farcical to all sane-minded persons."[32]

Father Smith and his associates were all acquitted, but the spirit of apostasy seething in the streets of Kirtland needed but a few months to falsely accuse him a second time. In this instance he was placed in the charge of the local constable, Luke Johnson, an apostate who nevertheless knew of the character of the father of the Prophet, as well as the disingenuity of the charges brought against him. Johnson, rather than bring a good and innocent man before the court on trumped-up charges, helped him escape through a window in a room adjoining the courtroom. When the other officers of the court came to escort their prisoner into the courtroom, he was gone, and the officers, not knowing Johnson had locked the window from the inside after the escape, could not account for Father Smith's disappearance. Johnson told them it was "another Mormon miracle." Thus it was that even a man enveloped in the spirit of apostasy went out of his way to help Father Smith—simply because he knew he was both honest and innocent, and that he was being charged before a prejudiced court.[33]

Fleeing the injustice of his persecutors, Father Smith found refuge in the home of Oliver Snow, father of Lorenzo and Eliza, where he lodged for two weeks. "We were proud of our guest," said Eliza, "and all of the family took pleasure in anticipating and supplying his wants."[34] Eliza also said that Father Smith possessed a "kind, affable, dignified and unassuming manner" that "naturally inspired strangers with feelings of love and reverence. To me he was the veritable personification of my idea of the ancient Father Abraham." Moreover, she said, he had an acute sense of justice unhampered by personal ambition or prejudice.[35]

The kind regard extended to Father Smith was but the reflection of the love he had shown the Saints and others over the years. We illustrate by returning to the day the Kirtland Temple was dedicated. The brethren had ruled that children in arms should not be admitted to the dedicatory services, but one mother, carrying her babe in her arms, travelled a long distance to attend the dedication before she heard of the ruling. With her babe of six weeks she went to Father Smith, pleading, for the prospect of being denied admission to the dedication seemed more than she could endure. Yet she knew of no one with whom she could leave her infant. Eliza R. Snow reported: "The ever generous and kind-hearted father volunteered to take the responsibility on himself, and told her to take her child, at the same time giving the mother a promise that her babe should make no disturbance; and the promise was verified. But when the congregation shouted hosanna, that babe joined in the shout. As marvelous as that incident may appear to many, it is not more so than other occurrences on that occasion,"[36] where the Spirit of the Lord worked wonders beyond the comprehension of fallen man.

This is but a simple illustration of the way in which the Spirit of the Lord worked with this particular friend of heaven, but it is the kind of quiet and reassuring example that refutes the character assassinations directed against him which both vilify his character and accuse him of that double knavery that alienates the Spirit of truth.

But the Spirit of truth operates on the souls of those who "hunger and thirst after righteousness," and they are sensitive to injustice wherever it raises its vicious voice. Thus it was that Oliver Cowdery wrote in defense of the Prophet and his family. "I feel myself bound," he said, "to defend the innocent always when opportunity offers. Had not those who are notorious for lies and dishonesty, also assailed the character of the [Smith] family I should pass over them here in silence; but now I shall not forbear. It has been industriously circulated that they were dishonest, deceitful and vile. On this I have the testimony of responsible persons, who have said and will say, that this is basely false; and besides, a personal acquaintance for seven years, has demonstrated that all the difficulty is, they were once poor, (yet industrious,) and have now, by the help of God, arisen to note, and their names are like to, (indeed they will,) be handed down to posterity, and had among the righteous.—They are industrious, honest, virtuous and liberal to all. This is their character; and though many take advantage of their liberality, God will reward *them;* but this is the fact, and this testimony shall shine upon the records of the saints, and be recorded on the archives of heaven to be read in the day of eternity, when the wicked and perverse, who have viley slandered them without cause or provocation, reap their reward with the unjust, where there is weeping, wailing and gnashing of teeth!—if they do not repent."[37]

Oliver knew the Smiths well; he had lived in their home, eaten at their table, and shared in their day's labor. His is the voice of personal acquaintance and of experience. Some may claim Oliver's friendship with the Smiths creates a bias that overrides good judgment and perception. But if friendship and family ties or sharing in the same gospel commitments disqualify one from testifying about the deeds and character of others, we would lose the Bible itself, which is nothing more than the record of friends and family writing about the deeds and character of friends and family; the life story of Jesus was written, for example, by his own friends, associates, and disciples.

Thus we comfortably call upon Joseph Smith and listen to the voice of the son in speaking of the father. "He was the first person who received my testimony after I had seen the angel," said the Prophet, and he "exhorted me to be faithful and diligent to the message I had received." This, then, is a father humble enough to follow a son, and sensitive enough to enjoin that son to follow angelic instruction.

"He was one of the most benevolent of men," the Prophet further said; "opening his house to all who were destitute. While at Quincy, Illinois, he fed hundreds of the poor Saints who were flying from the Missouri persecutions, although he had arrived there penniless himself."[38] The Prophet also observed, in an expression that might tempt the rest of us to the sin of envy, "His soul soared above all those mean and groveling principles that are so subsequent to the human heart. I now say, that he never did a mean act that might be said was ungenerous, in his life, to my knowledge."[39]

Now—note it well—these are deeds we speak of here, not the empty words of those claiming from a distance to know the man of whom we speak. And it was of the deeds of Father Smith that Robert Thompson spoke in the funeral eulogy of the aged Patriarch. The father of the Prophet had done so much for the Saints—given so much counsel and so many blessings, that through the voice of Brother Thompson, all Israel joined in a collective shout: "If ever there was a man who had claims on the affections of the community, it was our beloved but now deceased Patriarch. . . . A man faithful to his God and to the Church in every situation and under all circumstances through which he was called to pass." He was driven from New England to New York by the cold hand of uncaring circumstance; then from New York he uprooted his family and moved to Kirtland, where the persecutions of the ungodly pounded on his shoulders; from Kirtland he moved again, this time to Missouri, where the angry hand of hatred hit him with such a blow that his system never fully recovered, though he was left with sufficient strength to walk the wintry path to Nauvoo before lying down to die. Through it all, he whimpered not a word, but rather, Brother Thompson tells us, "like the Apostle Paul he could exclaim, . . . 'None of these things move me; neither count I my life dear, so that I may finish my course with joy.' "

Even from before the day of the publication of the Book of Mormon, "his only aim," Thompson declared, "was the promotion of truth—his soul was taken up with the things of the Kingdom; his bowels yearned over the children of men; and it was more than his meat and his drink to do the will of his Father, who is in heaven." In that same spirit, when the Kirtland Temple was constructed he sedulously committed his energies to worshipping there, for "to dwell in the house of the Lord, and to inquire in his temple, was his daily delight, and in it he . . . spent many hours in sweet communion with his heavenly Father. He has trod its sacred aisles, solitary and alone from mankind, long before the king of day has gilded the eastern horizon; and he has uttered his aspirations within its walls, when nature has been asleep. In its holy enclosures have the visions of heaven been opened to his mind, and his soul has feasted on the riches of eternity; and there under his teachings have the meek and humble been instructed, while the widow and the orphan have received his patriarchal blessings."

From his Kirtland home, said Thompson, Father Smith "saw the work spreading far and wide; saw the Elders of Israel go forth under his blessing—bore them up by the prayer of faith."

Such was the quality of his life, Thompson concluded, that in him "there were no reflections of a misspent life—no fearful forebodings of a gloomy nature in relation to the future," but rather only that peace which a pure conscience permits.[40]

The Voice of the Smiths

What say the Smiths of all this? Dare we permit them to say a word in their own defense? What, perchance, were their feelings with regard to honesty? And is not what Jesus said of all men true of them, that "every tree is known by his own fruit"[41] and that men do not gather figs of thorns or grapes of a bramble bush?

Is not the voice and testimony of the Smiths one of their many fruits?

Jesus said: "A good man out of the good treasure of his heart bringeth forth that which is good; and an evil man out of the evil treasure of his heart bringeth forth that which is evil: for of the abundance of the heart his mouth speaketh."[42]

Will not this same test apply to Father Smith—and, for that matter, to the whole Smith family?

Both reason and revelation cry out in their defense. Justice requires that they too be heard. An eternal law, spoken by the Savior, says "that every idle word that men shall speak, they shall give account thereof in the day of judgment," for, said Jesus, "by thy words thou shalt be justified, and by thy words thou shalt be condemned."[43] Truly "the tongue is a fire,"[44] which, when unruly, will burn and consume the man and the reputation to which it is attached. If Father Smith and his family were good or evil, their tongues will tell.

Is there anything more reasonable than to conclude that the Smiths themselves are the world's foremost authorities on what *they* thought? Who could be more familiar with the mind of a man than the man in question?

Moreover, should we not, with Nicodemus, ask the question he asked of the chief priests and Pharisees: "Doth our law judge any man, before it hear him, and know what he doeth?"[45]

Nicodemus's question is right-spirited, and it drives to the heart of the matter, for any honest and accurate review of the writings, speeches, and doings of the Prophet Joseph Smith testify that he was as honest a man as ever lived. "I believe," he said, "in living a virtuous, upright, and holy life before God, and feel it my duty to persuade all men in my power to do the same, that they may cease to do evil and learn to do well and break off their sins by righteousness."[46] When asked what the Latter-day

Saints believed, he wrote, in part: "We believe in being honest, true, chaste, benevolent, virtuous, and in doing good to *all men.*"[47] Indeed, Joseph Smith seemed to sum up his view of life by saying, "It is the delight of my soul to be honest";[48] and one Church member reported that the Prophet "once said that he would rather have every man on earth against him than to have his conscience accuse him."[49]

The Prophet constantly taught the gospel of honesty: "Truth is 'Mormonism,'"[50] he once said, underscoring the importance of individual as well as doctrinal integrity. Indeed, he set honesty as one of the central standards against which participation in the privileges of Church membership was judged. When Sidney Rigdon faltered, for example, Joseph "expressed entire willingness to have Elder Sidney Rigdon retain his station, provided he would magnify his office, and walk and conduct himself in all honesty, righteousness, and integrity."[51] On an earlier occasion, writing to the Church from the confines of Liberty Jail, the Prophet pleaded, "Brethren . . . let truth and righteousness prevail and abound in you. . . . Be honest one with another."[52] And he told an assembled group of General Authorities, "Act honest before God and man. . . . Be honest, open, and frank in all your intercourse with mankind."[53]

Joseph Smith taught that God rejoices in an honest heart,[54] and that when the gospel was taught, "the hearers should have good and honest hearts as well as the speaker,"[55] lest the Spirit of the Lord be offended and withhold approval of what is said. Throughout his ministry he exhorted the Saints to be honest ("I proclaim in the name of the Lord God that I will have nothing but virtue and integrity and uprightness,"[56] he said) and thanked the Lord for the privilege of leading an honest people,[57] even though he knew that their very honesty was a cause of the persecutions against them.[58] Toward the end of his ministry he was, in good conscience, able to testify, "I never stole the value of a pinhead or a picayune in my life."[59]

Which of us could say the same?

Or of which of us could a brother or sister say, as Don Carlos Smith said of his brother Samuel, "He is as faithful as the sun," and "the Lord will not forsake him, and angels will bear him up, and bear him off triumphant and victorious"?[60] Similarly, are there many in the world today of whom it might be said, as Joseph said of his brother Hyrum, "Blessed of the Lord is my brother Hyrum, for the integrity of his heart; he shall be girt about with truth, and faithfulness shall be the strength of his loins"?[61] Or, for that matter, are there not far too few in the world today who have adopted that maxim which Hyrum Smith adopted as his own: "A man is safe as long as he says what he knows to be true?"[62] And would not the world be a far more celestial sphere if more grandchildren could say of their parents and grandparents what one grandson of Father Smith said of both the Prophet and the first Patriarch, "Though poor, his [i.e., the Prophet Joseph Smith's] parents were honest and good; they delighted in the truth, and it was their honest desire to live according to the best light within them," and "their children were imbued with like sentiments"?[63]

Thus it was that even in the early days of the Restoration, when doubt-casters and critics wondered if the Prophet's own family might not consider his claims too fantastic to be believed, Joseph's family accepted his testimony, as his brother William later recalled: "We all had the most implicit confidence in what he said. He was a truthful boy. Father and mother believed him, why should not the children? I suppose if he had told crooked stories about other things we might have doubted his word about the plates, but Joseph was a truthful boy. That father and mother believed his report and suffered persecution for that belief shows that he was truthful. No sir, we never doubted his word for one minute."[64] In describing the family councils in which Joseph told of Moroni's coming and the history of the Book of Mormon peoples, William said: "The whole family were melted to tears, and believed all he said. Knowing that he was very young, that he had not enjoyed the advantages of common education; and knowing too, his whole character and disposition, they were convinced that he was totally incapable of arising before his aged parents, his brothers and sisters, and so solemnly giving utterance to anything but the truth. All of us, therefore, believed him, and anxiously awaited the results of his visit to the hill Cumorah, in search of the plates."[65]

Critics of the Prophet sought to implicate the family as dishonest in thought and deed, hoping thereby to show that Joseph was but the slime that stuck to a rotted and rotting tree. The fact, however, is that the parents were honest and their children inherited from them a legacy of integrity, and the children knew it. "My father's religious habits were strictly pious and moral," said William, as he recalled daily family prayer and devotional services. "My father's favorite evening hymn runs thus:

> "The day is past and gone
> The evening shades appear
> O may we all remember well
> The night of death draws near."

William continued: "Again and again was this hymn sung while upon the bending knees. My parents, father and mother, poured out their souls to God, the donor of all blessings, to keep and guard their children and keep them from sin and from all evil works.

"Such was the strict piety of my parents."[66]

This piety was, with the Smith's, a devotion to duty, and it stayed with them until death. At the October conference of 1845, with her husband and four of her sons in the grave, Mother Smith was called upon by Brigham Young to address the Saints. In the course of her remarks, she said, "[I] want the young men to remember that I love children, young folks and everybody. [I] want them to be obedient to their parents and do everything just right." Then, in a piece of counsel that perfectly defines integrity—doing and being the same in public as in private—Mother Smith continued: "[I want them to] be good and kind and do in secret as you would do in the presence of millions."

Then, in continuing her theme of honesty, Mother Smith addressed the then pressing concern of the Saints about going west, or, as they often said with reference to the entire western portion of the country, "to California." She told first of the struggles that the Smith family endured in order for the Book of Mormon to be obtained, translated, and published; and she said, "This was the way it commenced, and now see what a congregation is here." Then, applying the lesson to the circumstance of these soon-to-be pioneers, Mother Smith said: "You talk about going to California. . . . You need not be discouraged [because] you can't get wagons and everything else. As Brigham says, you must be honest. But if you are not honest you won't get there, and if you feel cross you will have trouble."[67]

In short, Lucy preached that honesty was one of the keys to obtaining the Book of Mormon, just as it was to be one of the keys to successfully crossing the plains. In so speaking, she was true to the traditions that the family had lived, as well as to the teachings that they had taught. We have no recorded instance of Father Smith or any of his sons or daughters, during the entire lifetime of the Prophet, ever encouraging or inducing another person to be dishonest in any way—we have only the so-called testimony of false or prejudiced witnesses, or of witnesses who never met and did not know the Smiths but were willing to quote others who had falsified information before them.[68] The lives of Father and Mother Smith, the Prophet Joseph, and his brothers Hyrum, Samuel, and Don Carlos are living sermons on honesty. What little information we have on Alvin suggests that the same is true of him. And where the daughters are concerned, we have no reason to question their integrity either, though in truth we admit there is less available historical data telling of their lives.

The most eloquent statements of Father Smith regarding honesty, however, are his deeds. Thus, having heard the unified voice of the Smith family speaking in favor of honest and upright behavior, we look now to the voice of action, or the voice of experience. No fruit from the Smith tree tastes sweeter than the fruit of their good works. The Prophet Joseph stands as the most prized of the family offerings, but when the character of the family is considered, there is no surprise that the Great God of Heaven foreordained this faithful family to nurture the seedling of the Restoration so that the great gospel tree of life could spread its branches over the whole earth, giving life to all who will but eat of its fruits. What the Smiths did in general, and what Father Smith did in particular, speaks so loudly that the discordant and condemning voices of criticism, were they honest, would be embarrassed and frozen into silence.

The Voice of Accomplishment: The Fruits of Integrity

It is one of the curiosities of history that Father Smith should be accused of dishonesty, for integrity was the keystone in the arch of his character. Moreover, it was his natural, familial inheritance, and we see it as the distinguishing feature in the lives of his ancestors as far back as we are able to trace the stories of their lives.[69] When the barter economy of New England caught Samuel Smith, Father Smith's grandfather, by surprise and he died insolvent, Father Smith's father, Asael, said, "I am not willing that my father, who has done so much business, should have it said of him that he died insolvent." Thus Asael, who had been too sick to do any but small clerical tasks for three years, and while burdened with the responsibilities of a large and growing family, concluded, in his own words, "Notwithstanding all my embarrassments, I will undertake to settle my father's estate and save his name from going down to posterity as an insolvent debtor."[70]

This decision cost Asael five years of hard labor during which time he paid off in a depressed economy the debts his father had incurred in an inflationed economy. The surge and thunder of illness, growing family needs, caring for his father's widow, and the press of unrelenting and hungering creditors left him, in the words of John Smith, "almost destitute of means to support his family,"[71] but nobly enriched in character. Thus Asael personified honesty for the betterment and instruction of both his children and his larger posterity.

The integrity that flowed in the veins of Asael coursed just as deeply in those of his son Joseph. When the young Joseph Smith and Lucy Mack were married, Lucy's brother Stephen Mack joined with his business partner and gave the newlyweds a thousand dollars as a wedding gift. With dowry in hand, they set out for the farm Jospeh owned in Tunbridge, Vermont. After six years of farming, Mother Smith says that they opened a "mercantile establishment." Some time later, upon learning "that crystalized ginseng root sold very high in China, being used as a remedy for the plague which was then raging there," Father Smith invested his all in the crystalizing and exporting of ginseng. He acquired enough ginseng that one greed-inspired merchant named Stevens offered him three thousand dollars for his cache. Father Smith refused, as his payload was worth about forty-five hundred dollars. Instead of selling, he went to New York and hired a ship and its captain to carry his ginseng to China, sell it, and return with the profits. Mr. Stevens followed Father Smith to New York, sought out the ship, and contracted with the captain to couple his own ginseng produce to

Tunbridge Gore, Vermont, the first home of
Joseph Smith, Sr., and Lucy Mack Smith

that of Father Smith, and then carry and sell it in China. To ensure the reliability of the business arrangement, Stevens left his son on the ship for the China trip and sale.

In China, the ginseng sold for a high price. Young Stevens returned to the United States but chose to lie to Father Smith about the sale. He told what Lucy called "a plausible tale" and said that the deal was a failure, and that the only earnings the Smiths would realize was a chest of tea. The young Mr. Stevens, inspired as we suppose by his newly won but nonetheless perfidious largesse, returned to Vermont to continue the ginseng business. He rented a house from Stephen Mack, Lucy's older brother, and commenced his production.

Liars, it seems, frequently come endowed with multiple vices. Such was the case with young Stevens. With liquor lubricating his lips, he one night fell into an intoxicated mindlessness during which he boasted to Stephen Mack of his swindling from the Smiths their honest ginseng proceeds; he even ventured so far as to show Mack "a large amount of silver and gold," which he had stashed in a trunk. Mack immediately went to report to Father Smith, but in his absence, Stevens sobered sufficiently to recognize his folly, whereupon he released his hired hands and fled to Canada. Father Smith pursued him, but to no avail.

This business fraud left the Smiths nearly penniless. Their burden was compounded by the accummulated weight of two thousand dollars in unpaid debts owed them, and by the fact that Father Smith was in debt yet another eighteen hundred dollars for goods purchased in Boston in connection with his ginseng venture. Resolving that a good name was more to be desired than a warm house, Father and Mother Smith decided to sell their farm "in order to make a speedy payment on the Boston debt." The real-estate market, however, was unkind, and they were able to obtain only eight hundred dollars for a farm valued at fifteen hundred dollars. Thus, after selling their farm at nearly half its value, they added the one thousand dollars of dowry money to the monies from the farm sale so that they could free themselves from their financial imprisonment in Boston.[72]

Having so acted, they were left with almost no earthly holdings, but like Father Asael before them, they had increased a thousandfold the value of their name in the eyes of heaven and honest men. In reviewing these events, we are reminded that the winnings of more than six years of hard labor were stolen from them; that they might have manufactured myriad excuses for choosing to default their creditors just as they had been defaulted; and that the poverty these circumstances created added hardship and social cruelty to life's lot, for, unable to purchase property of their own, they were forced to move from rented holding to rented holding: they moved seven times in the next fourteen years. Indeed, we have record of their having been "warned out of town"—a legal procedure whereby the town selectmen, in order to avoid responsibility for the poor, "warn" them to leave—on at least one occasion,[73] and we know that they did not own property again until after their move to Palmyra. Through all the incidental discomfort, much of it triggered by circumstances they neither created nor controlled, they remained honest and were gratified by having made right and honorable choices.

Nonetheless, the years between 1802 and 1816 were hardship years, and, said Mother Smith, "we were compelled to strain every energy to provide for our present necessities, instead of making arrangements for the future, as we had previously contemplated."[74] Enervated by typhus and pushed to the ends of their means by three successive years of crop failure, the Smiths found the advertisements of fertile lands in New York all the more inviting, and they decided to move. Two constraints, however, prevented their immediate departure: the impoverished condition of the family and the fact that Father Smith "was owing some money that must first be paid."[75]

Accordingly, the Smiths called together both their creditors and their debtors and settled their accounts. "There were, however, some who, in the time of settlement, neglected to bring forward their books," reported Mother Smith, "consequently they were not balanced, or there were no entries made in them to show the settlement; but in cases of this kind, [Father Smith] called witnesses, that there might be evidence of the fact."[76] Father Smith then left for Palmyra and shortly thereafter called for his family to follow. Just as the family was ready to leave, however, several of the men who had previously withheld their books at the time of settlement brought them forth, claiming accounts which had in fact been previously settled "and which they had," said Mother Smith, "in the presence of witnesses, agreed to erase."[77] Caught between the press of dishonest claims on the one hand, and the time, expense, and hazards of a lawsuit as well as the additional expenses associated with moving the family on the other, Mother Smith decided it better to pay the false claims and retain an honorable name rather than to contest her falsifiers. Thus it was that the Smiths, who have constantly been accused of dishonesty even while living in Vermont (but who, while there, never faulted on a note or a loan[78]), made the conscious effort to attend to the issues of integrity before leaving and, when confronted by deceit, weighed the most honorable course and followed it.

This pattern of honesty adorned their character throughout their lives. The circumstances that directed them to leave Palmyra, for instance, were somewhat different, but the groundwork of integrity was the same. Palmyra neighbor Orlando Saunders said: "They [the Smiths] have all worked for me many a day; they were very good people; Young Joe, (as we called him then), has worked for me, and he was a good worker; they all were. . . . I always thought them honest; they were owing me some money when they left here; that is, the old man and Hyrum did, and Martin Harris. One of them came back in about a year and paid me."[79] Another Palmyra resident, Abel Chase, complimented the Smiths, for, though he thought them "poorly educated, ignorant and superstitious," he knew they "would do a good day's work."[80]

The account books of Palmyra storekeeper Lemuel Durfee show a consistent pattern of the Smiths laboring to pay off debts incurred by purchases.[81] We even have an instance in which Hyrum was called to account before the court for a debt of $20.07, and of Father Smith going to testify that the charge was true—an episode that Richard Lloyd Anderson interprets to illustrate that the Smiths sought "to be honest in their financial obligations."[82]

Thus it is that when we judge the Smiths by what they did, we can only judge them to be honest. With respect to the varied voices speaking of Father Smith, however, we note in addition that in many instances, fair and accurate assessments can be made only by those who have ears to hear. The world holds in scorn the doctrine that he could see visions, yet he was a visionary man who learned more of eternal truth in his night dreams than many men learn in a lifetime of plodding study. In the early years of Joseph and Lucy's marriage, the Lord prepared Father Smith by dreams and visions to receive the dreams and visions of his son the Prophet. The Lord taught him by vision of the Apostasy and of the opposition that the restored work would encounter,[83] and not long before the Prophet Joseph saw the Father and the Son in the spring of 1820, Father Smith had an inspired dream in which he was commended for having maintained strict honesty in all his dealings.[84] This practice of seeing inspired dreams and visions continued until his death. During one of the prayers at the dedication of the Kirtland Temple, an angel seated himself next to Father Smith,[85] and in subsequent worship services the Lord opened to his view the visions of eternity.[86] We have multiple accounts of his giving patriarchal blessings in which he saw through the veil and made pronouncements according to what he was seeing; and on his deathbed the veil was so thin that he saw into the spirit world, seeing his deceased son, Alvin.[87]

Such experiences come not but to those whom the Lord trusts and who are honest before him in all things. As we consider the many prophetic blessings he bestowed, and remember that the Spirit of the Lord will not inspire a dishonest man, we seem to hear the voice of heaven itself crying from the ends of eternity that this is not only a man whom God loved but also one whom He trusted. Then, as we reflect on the visions he beheld and upon the angels he entertained, that same voice reminds us that if men are judged by the company they keep, then Father Smith was one of the greatest of all the sons of Adam.

Sifting Through the Discordant Voices

How, then, do we reconcile these discordant voices, some calling Father Smith a dishonest and doleful wretch who never did an honest day's labor in his entire life, and others speaking of him with the same regard given Fathers Abraham, Isaac, and Jacob?

Many causes conspire to create the voices of criticism and disbelief. In some instances, simply put, they are as united in falsehood as was Lord Melbourne's cabinet, and we witness one falsifier quoted by a second, then by a third, and a fourth, through numberless iterations.[88] In some instances the Smiths' detractors are so filled with insinuation, prejudice, and distortion of fact that those very detractors condemn themselves by their contradicting testimonies.[89] In many cases, what we are hearing is the voice of offended piety, angered or annoyed that the Prophet and his family would sustain a system that called into question the very piety that these detracting voices nurtured. In the instance of other voices—and here we judge generously—we are simply hearing the voices of men and women who do not and cannot understand the things that they seek to describe: angels, visions, revelations, new scriptures, Apostles and prophets, gifts of the Spirit, and such things as the natural man cannot comprehend.

It is fair to note, in this regard, that those who knew the Smiths well judged them differently, and that when we call into account the credible witness of their deeds, we see that they lived the gospel they preached. Could the nobility of sentiment contained in the Book of Mormon have come from a perverse mind? Or would a man filled with a vile or loathsome spiritual cancer proclaim Book of Mormon truths wherever he went? Would so many honest and good people have flocked to Father Smith for blessings and counsel if his character was infected? Could he have pronounced so many prophetic blessings if the God of Heaven did not trust and inspire him?

Joseph Smith restored a kingdom that has grown to millions; it will yet grow to billions and cover the earth as the waters cover the sea. Father Smith, for his part, was true to every principle that is a part of that kingdom. The Prophet Joseph Smith lighted a lamp by which those millions and soon-to-be billions see more clearly the light and life of the world, even Jesus Christ.

Of the Prophet's critics, and of the critics of his father, we ask: What lamp have they lit?

When the high court of heaven sits in judgment of us all, let us pray that we may sit down to an eternal rest in that same kingdom where the Prophet and his father dwell.

CHAPTER 8

Measuring Greatness

It is the lot and reward of the faithful to dwell eternally in the kingdom of Heaven, where all that God has is given unto them.[1] There they share in all his might, power, and dominion.[2] After death, and yet prior to their entrance into that celestial kingdom, the spirits of all men enter what is called the world of the spirits, where they await the resurrection and final judgment. In that spirit sphere, the gospel is taught, sermons are preached, meetings convened, hymns sung, testimonies borne, gifts of the Spirit exercised, converts made, and souls still come unto Christ. Repentance and forgiveness operate there even as they do here in this mortal state.

God is eternal; so also is his work. He is no less organized to save the souls of men in one sphere than in another. In the spirit world, priesthood officers operate under the stewardship of those called to preside over them, and no man is called to preach there save he first is empowered by testimony, authorized by those who preside, and worthy to carry the divine message. Thus it is that the righteous are commissioned and empowered to take the message of salvation to those in the world of the spirits who had not the opportunity to receive it while in the flesh. And so it is that we are not surprised—could we expect anything less?—to find Father Smith, the old lion of the faith, vigorously involved in building up the kingdom in the spirit world. In mortality, after gaining testimony, he devoted his every energy to the upbuilding of the kingdom wherever he went. Why should anyone anticipate that he might act differently simply because death reassigned him to labor in a different realm of existence?

Shortly before his own death, Jedediah M. Grant, who served in the First Presidency as a Counselor to Brigham Young, spent two nights in the spirit world and returned and reported to Heber C. Kimball about his experiences. While there, Brother Grant saw and conversed with his wife, Caroline, of whom he asked about the Prophet Joseph, Hyrum, and Father Smith. She replied: "They have gone away ahead, to perform and transact business for us."[3]

Wilford Woodruff, a prophet with a spiritual gift for dreaming inspired dreams and seeing inspired visions, somewhat enlarges our understanding of the business Father Smith and others were involved in. "Joseph Smith," said President Woodruff, "continued visiting myself and others up to a certain time and then it stopped. The last time I saw him was in heaven. In the night vision I saw him at the door of the temple in heaven. He came and spoke to me. He said he could not stop to talk with me because he was in a hurry. The next man I met was Father Smith; he could not talk with me because he was in a hurry"— hurrying, President Woodruff adds, to make preparations for the second coming of the Lord.[4] Just exactly what those preparations consisted of he does not tell us, but it is perfectly consistent with everything we know about the father of the Prophet that he would be just as vigorously involved in the work of the kingdom in the spirit world as he had been in the flesh.

We do know, however, that the affections born in mortality extend into the eternal world, and that those whom we love here we will also love there. Indeed, interest in the well-being of mortal family and loved ones appears to be even greater among the dead than among the living.[5] The Prophet Joseph Smith taught that "the spirits of the just are exalted to a greater and more glorious work; hence they are blessed in their departure to the world of spirits. Enveloped in flaming fire, they are not far from us, and know and understand our thoughts, feelings, and motions, and are often pained therewith."[6] Thus it is that the veil between the two worlds is often very thin and often penetrated by the faithful from either side. Benjamin F. Johnson quoted the Prophet Joseph Smith as teaching that there is an influence for good which can be exerted on behalf of the righteous by those in the spirit world which they could not exert while yet mortal.[7] Mother Smith expressed a similar thought.[8] We are not surprised, therefore, that even generations after the death of Father Smith, President Harold B. Lee would speak to those with ears to hear and say that those noble Smiths who had gone before President Joseph Fielding Smith would be "permitted to draw near to their descendant," even perhaps attending the solemn assembly in which Joseph Fielding Smith was sustained as the President of the Church.[9] It was very clear, said President Lee elsewhere, that Father Smith, his sons, and his grandsons had a marked influence on the life and character of Joseph Fielding Smith, and through him and others like him, upon the whole Church.[10]

Foreshadowing events future as if they were things present, in 1836 the Prophet Joseph Smith saw his father sitting in the celestial kingdom.[11] Five years later the Prophet received yet another revelation in which the Lord told him that his father had entered into that celestial realm, and that he sits "with Abraham at his right hand, and blessed and holy is he, for he is mine."[12]

As we look back through the telescope of time, it becomes ever clearer that Father Smith, true to his own foreordination, obtained his eternal reward in compliance with the divine law of the harvest: he reaped even as he had sown. Thus, as we review in a few simple paragraphs the life of this man whom the early Saints looked upon as a model after whom they and their descendants should pattern their lives,[13] several hallmark characteristics stand out.

First, he was a man of faith, the first to accept the testimony of the Prophet Joseph Smith regarding the angel Moroni and the coming forth of the Book of Mormon.[14] He was ever true to the testimony of the Prophet and that of the Book of Mormon, and from the moment of Moroni's visit to the moment of his own death, he stood erect against the multiplied ignorance of the ages and confronted the magnified prejudice of both religious and irreligious bigotry. He was slandered and libelled in print and at the pulpit, and warned by critics at every turn that he followed a carefully devised fable. From the moment the heaven's opened and poured forth their confidence on

*Granite memorial (right) to Joseph Smith, Jr., and Memorial Cottage (center),
completed in 1905 at the site of the Prophet's birth in Sharon, Vermont*

the youthful prophet, his father and family were persecuted
with him. Still, the angry stone throwers and worldly Jeremiahs
struck no fear in Father Smith's heart; his course was set and
his pace unslowed. Indeed, like a champion who enters the race
late, he seemed to increase in pace as the race continued, at
least until the enervating effects of age and persecution slowed
and then curtailed his life.

Where many men would lack the humility to follow a son,
Father Smith never sought prominence over the Prophet.
Rather, he humbly followed the Prophet's lead in all things pertaining to the kingdom of God, and made every effort to bring
others to the same testimony and the same spirit of obeying the
Lord's anointed that had always characterized his own life.
Theirs was a father-son relationship in which the son was
greater than the father, yet the father was, in every sense, a worthy sire to such a noble son.

He was foreordained to be called Joseph, and perhaps it is
no accident that he was also called Smith, for a smith is one
who fashions and forges untrained iron into a useful shape for a
useful purpose, much as he helped shape and form the character of his namesake son, particularly in his early years. His conviction that an apostasy had occurred was but a seed that grew
in the mind and spirit of his son; the visions that he beheld

were also preparations in the mind and soul of the young prophet, teaching him not only some of the doctrines of the kingdom but also that those doctrines might be obtained by revelation. His practice of reading the scriptures and of approaching the Lord for resolution to his problems and concerns set the pattern which led the Prophet into the Sacred Grove in the spring of 1820. Truly, the son grew in the image of the father.

The father, like the son after him, learned submission to the promptings of the Holy Spirit and became a cleansing example of simple, and therefore powerful, faith. He recognized truth intuitively, clung to it tenaciously, and hungered for it rapaciously. Scarcely has the gospel ever clothed a form more perfectly fitted to the work of the kingdom than was the case with Father Smith. He loved and was loved by the Saints, and was ever the leaven in the loaf.

Greatness lies in doing well that which is the common lot of all mankind, and by this standard Father Smith stands among the greats of all time. He married nobly and lived worthy of his noble wife. Together they raised honest and faithful children whose meat and drink it was to serve the Lord through service to their fellowmen. He eagerly submitted to the ordinances of salvation and was one of the first to be baptized in this dispensation. He was ordained to the priesthood, honored its calling, and used its power to bless the lives of others. He sought out every available temple blessing and frequently retired to its sacred chambers for prayer and meditation. He walked thousands of miles bearing testimony of the Restoration, and, in harmony with the pattern to which he adhered throughout his life, "while at Quincy, Illinois, he fed hundreds of the poor Saints who were flying from the Missouri persecutions, although he had arrived there penniless himself."[15] Through it all, he had a certain nostalgia for the future, a longing for those celestial realms ahead, free from the grinding persecutions and oppressions of mortality. He confessed himself a stranger and a pilgrim seeking for a better world, but through it all, we have no record of his ever whimpering or complaining about life's burdens.

His counsel was rich and ripe, and the Saints eagerly came to lean upon the experience of his years as well as the wisdom of his experience. His expressions, such as we have, were direct and to the point, and seemed to acknowledge the hand of the

Lord in all things. When asked if the elders should cast out un-believers before administering to the sick, for example, he replied that "if they are a company of unbelievers, cast them out. But an elder, if humble, shall know what is to be done." When asked if it was "the duty of an elder to lay hands on a sick person without solicitation," Father Smith "answered in the negative."[16] When asked about the proper course to pursue in casting out an evil spirit, Father Smith simply taught his ques-tioners how to obtain the guidance of the Holy Spirit, knowing that divine guidance was superior to anything he might sug-gest.[17]

While he was one of the Lord's favored sons, and while he was possessed of greater faith than is had among the generality of men, he did not receive all the blessings that he desired. Life is a school, and we learn from that which we do not receive as well as from that which we do. He was never long freed from the hand of persecution, for example, and he felt the pangs of sorrow when those whom he loved—even those of his own fam-ily—fell under the necessary censure of Church discipline. But through it all, he was true and faithful; and through it all, he en-dured to the end in righteousness.

This majestic mountain of a man looms as a towering pres-ence that reached into the lives of the most notable figures of the Restoration. He knew and was known by all the original members of the Quorum of the Twelve in this dispensation; he influenced, as they admit, the first five Presidents of the Church and was the grandfather of the sixth. He was the model after whom later Patriarchs patterned their ministries, and the deep impress that he left on both the Prophet and his brother Hyrum is beyond our capacity to calculate. We are certain, however, that by honoring God he honored himself, and that he left an impress upon the people and events of the Restoration that is excelled by only a handful of men or women.

He is the one whom the Lord trained and prepared in the premortal aeons to be the father of the prophet of the greatest of all gospel dispensations. To peer into his life is to be assured that he was molded according to the Lord's expectations and fitted in every regard to be the father of the Prophet.

Seldom shall we see a father so worthy of his son!

Notes

In the notes and sources that follow, "LDS Church Archives" stands for either the Church Library or the Archives Division, Church Historical Department, The Church of Jesus Christ of Latter-day Saints, Salt Lake City, Utah.

Chapter 1. "After the Name of His Father"

1. See D&C 135:3.
2. See Acts 3:19–21.
3. See JST, Ps. 14:1–4; 2 Ne. 27:24–26.
4. See JST, Matt. 17:10–14.
5. See Mal. 3:1–5 (3 Ne. 24:1–5); JST, John 1:26. The passages in Malachi deserve a brief explanation, for they are subject to dual fulfillment. Malachi quotes the Lord as saying he will send his messenger to prepare the way before his coming. Jesus quotes these verses and announces their fulfillment in the ministry of John the Baptist (see Matt. 11:7–15; 17:10–13). Later, Jesus quotes these same verses to the Nephites (see 3 Ne. 24 and 25), describing their fulfillment as yet future. Still later, when Moroni appears to the Prophet Joseph Smith he quotes these same passages and applies them to Joseph Smith, placing them in the context of passages that are "about to be fulfilled" (see JS–H 1:36–41).
6. Moses 1:41.
7. Isa. 11:10–12; see also D&C 113:5–6.
8. See Isa. 29:1–12. The fulfillment of these verses is detailed in JS–H 1:63–65, which is the account of Martin Harris taking characters copied from the Book of Mormon to Professor Charles Anthon.
9. See Morm. 8:23–25.
10. See Morm. 8:14–16.
11. Ether 5:1–4; see also 2 Ne. 27:12–14.
12. 3 Ne. 21:5–11.
13. See, for example, 2 Ne. 33:10–11; Moro. 10:27–29.
14. See 2 Ne. 3; JST, Gen. 50.

15. 2 Ne. 3:15.

16. Joseph Smith, *Teachings of the Prophet Joseph Smith,* sel. Joseph Fielding Smith (Salt Lake City: Deseret Book Co., 1938), p. 365.

17. 1 Cor. 14:33.

18. In Lucy Mack Smith, *History of Joseph Smith by His Mother,* ed. Preston Nibley (Salt Lake City: Bookcraft, 1958), p. 79.

19. Reported by Orson Pratt, in *Journal of Discourses* 15:184.

20. *History of the Church* 4:196.

21. See 2 Ne. 31:10; 3 Ne. 27:21.

22. The phrase "imitators of God" belongs to Mathetes, one of the ante-Nicene Fathers, who used it to define *Christians* in the early church. It is an apt description of what every Saint ought to aspire to be, for emulation of Deity is the purest form of worship. For the Methetes quote, see "The Epistle of Mathetes to Diognetus," in Alexander Roberts and James Donaldson, eds., *The Ante-Nicene Fathers* (Grand Rapids, Mich.: Eerdmans, 1979), 1:29.

23. See 1 Jn. 3:1–3.

Chapter 2. "Mine Aged Servant, Joseph Smith, Sen."

1. *History of the Church* 4:191.

2. Joseph Smith III, "Family Association Remarks," *Journal of History* (Lamoni, Iowa: Reorganized Church of Jesus Christ of Latter Day Saints) 1 (January 1908): 41; cited in Earnest M. Skinner, "Joseph Smith Sr., First Patriarch to the Church" (Master's thesis, Brigham Young University, 1958), p. 6.

3. Cited in Richard Lloyd Anderson, " 'Of Goodly Parents,' " *New Era* 3 (December 1973): 37.

4. Cited in Edward W. Tullidge, *The Women of Mormondom* (New York: Tullidge and Crandall, 1877; reprint, Salt Lake City, 1975), p. 97.

5. Eliza R. Snow Smith, *Biography and Family Record of Lorenzo Snow* (Salt Lake City: Deseret News Co., 1884), p. 21.

6. Edward Stevenson, *Reminiscences of Joseph, the Prophet, and the Coming Forth of the Book of Mormon* (Salt Lake City: Edward Stevenson, 1893), p. 5.

7. LeRoi C. Snow, "How Lorenzo Snow Found God," *Improvement Era* 40 (February 1937): 84.

8. *Journal of History* 1 (October 1908): 407; cited in Skinner, "Joseph Smith Sr.," p. 32.

9. Lucy Mack Smith, *History of Joseph Smith by His Mother,* ed. Preston Nibley (Salt Lake City: Bookcraft, 1958), p. 182.

10. *History of the Church* 5:125–26.

11. The words of what William calls "my father's favorite evening hymn" reveal the heart of a man very sensitive to the closeness of eternity: "The day is past and gone / The evening shades appear / O may we all remember well / The night of death draws near." (See William Smith, "Notes Written on 'Chamber's Life of Joseph Smith,'" LDS Church Archives, p. 18.)

12. Cited in J. W. Peterson, "Wm. B. Smith's Last Statement," *Zion's Ensign* 5 (January 13, 1894): 6; also in "Another Testimony: Statement of William Smith, Concerning Joseph, the Prophet," *Deseret Evening News,* January 20, 1894.

13. Mosiah Hancock, journal, Harold B. Lee Library, Brigham Young University, Provo, Utah, pp. 14–15.

14. See interview with Dr. John Stafford in William H. Kelley, "The Hill Cumorah, and the Book of Mormon . . . from Late Interviews," *Saints' Herald* 28 (June 1, 1881): 167.

15. See Richard Lloyd Anderson, "Heritage of a Prophet," *Ensign* 1 (February 1971): 15–16.

16. Joseph Smith, 1832 autobiographical sketch, in Scott H. Faulring, ed., *An American Prophet's Record: The Diaries and Journals of Joseph Smith* (Salt Lake City: Signature Books, 1989), p. 4.

17. For a consideration of Father Smith's broad-shouldered integrity, see LaMar E. Garrard, "Traditions of Honesty and Integrity in the Smith Family," in Robert L. Millet, ed., *"To Be Learned Is Good If . . ."* (Salt Lake City: Bookcraft, 1987), pp. 9–19.

18. See JS–H; see also Lucy Mack Smith, *History of Joseph Smith,* p. 90, and Peterson, "Wm. B. Smith's Last Statement," p. 6.

19. Lucy Mack Smith, *History of Joseph Smith,* pp. 43–45.

20. See *History of the Church* 2:474.

21. See Eliza R. Snow Smith, *Biography and Family Record,* p. 12.

22. Cited in Tullidge, *The Women of Mormondom,* p. 101; see also "The Kirtland Temple," *Historical Record* (Andrew Jenson) 5 (June 1886): 80.

23. Cited in Eliza R. Snow Smith, *Biography and Family Record,* p. 11.

24. *History of the Church* 4:194.

25. See Lucy Mack Smith, *History of Joseph Smith,* pp. 37–42.

26. Lucy Mack Smith, *History of Joseph Smith,* p. 63; see pp. 59–64.

27. Pomeroy Tucker, *Origin, Rise, and Progress of Mormonism* (New York: D. Appleton and Co., 1867), p. 12.

28. Tucker, *Origin,* p. 24.

29. W. D. Purple, "Joseph Smith, the Originator of Mormonism," *Chenango Union,* Norwich, New York, May 2, 1877.

30. Cited in Kelley, "The Hill Cumorah," p. 163.

31. Letter of William W. Phelps to E. D. Howe, January 15, 1831,

quoted in E. D. Howe, *History of Mormonism* (Painesville, Ohio: E. D. Howe, 1840), p. 273.

32. See Lucy Mack Smith, *History of Joseph Smith*, pp. 94–99.

33. See Lucy Mack Smith, *History of Joseph Smith*, p. 102.

34. Lucy Mack Smith, *History of Joseph Smith*, p. 104.

35. See Lucy Mack Smith, *Biographical Sketches of Joseph Smith, the Prophet, and His Progenitors for Many Generations* (London and Liverpool: Published for Orson Pratt by S. W. Richards, 1853), pp. 160–65.

36. See Kirtland, Ohio, Township Record: Livestock Ear-marks Record, 1817–1846, Family History Library, The Church of Jesus Christ of Latter-day Saints, Salt Lake City, Utah, pp. 86, 98. The warnings referred to in the text were issued on October 29, 1831, and October 21, 1833.

37. In Donald Q. Cannon and Lyndon W. Cook, eds., *Far West Record* (Salt Lake City: Deseret Book Co., 1983), p. 22. The date of the conference in Orange, Ohio, was October 25, 1831; the writ ordering Father Smith out of town was issued October 29, 1831.

38. Joseph Smith, letter to the Saints in Caldwell County, December 16, 1838, in *Times and Seasons* 1 (April 1840): 35.

39. Lucy Mack Smith, *History of Joseph Smith*, pp. 231–32.

40. Ruby K. Smith, *Mary Bailey* (Salt Lake City: Deseret Book Co., 1954), p. 32.

41. D&C 90:20.

42. D&C 90:25–27; see also *History of the Church* 1:322–31.

43. D&C 24:9; see also 2 Ne. 3:8.

44. Commenting on Father Smith's desire to care for so many of the needy, Joseph Fielding Smith said "that it was not his [i.e., Father Smith's] duty to care for those who were not of his family. Evidently he had assumed the responsibility of caring for others." (See *Church History and Modern Revelation*, Melchizedek Priesthood Quorum Study Guide [Salt Lake City: Deseret News Press, 1953], 1:391.)

45. Susa Young Gates (under the pseudonym "Homespun"), *Lydia Knight's History* (Salt Lake City: Juvenile Instructor Office, 1883), pp. 29–32.

46. Cited in Tullidge, *The Women of Mormondom*, pp. 94–95; see also "The Kirtland Temple," pp. 78–79.

47. Cyrena Dustin Merrill, "Sketch of the Life of Cyrena Dustin Merrill As Given by Herself," p. 4. Copies in private, family possession.

48. Edward Stevenson, autobiography, unpublished, 1893, LDS Church Archives, pp. 54–57.

49. See Joseph Smith, 1835–36 diary and journal, in Faulring, ed., *An American Prophet's Record*, p. 52. Though William Smith confuses events somewhat as he retells the episode, he is quite believable when

he says that upon hearing Joseph tell of Moroni's visit "the whole family were melted to tears, and believed all he said" (*William Smith on Mormonism* [Lamoni, Iowa: Herald Steam Book and Job Office, 1883], p. 9).

50. Parley P. Pratt, *Autobiography of Parley P. Pratt*, ed. Parley P. Pratt, Jr. (Salt Lake City: Deseret Book Co., 1938), p. 190.

51. Pratt, *Autobiography*, p. 293.

52. In Kenneth W. Godfrey, Audrey M. Godfrey, and Jill Mulvay Derr, *Women's Voices: An Untold History of the Latter-day Saints, 1830–1900* (Salt Lake City: Deseret Book Co., 1982), p. 48.

53. In Eliza R. Snow Smith, *Biography and Family Record*, p. 10.

54. In Thomas C. Romney, *The Life of Lorenzo Snow* (Salt Lake City: S. U. P. Memorial Foundation, 1955), pp. 12–13.

55. See *History of the Church* 4:190.

56. See Lucy Mack Smith, *History of Joseph Smith*, pp. 81–82.

57. See, for example, George A. Smith, "Sketch of the Autobiography of George A. Smith," *Millennial Star* 27 (July 1, 1865): 407, in which George A. tells of his Grandfather Asael, who was Father Smith's father, receiving a letter from Father Smith in the fall of 1828 in which Father Smith told "that his son Joseph had received several remarkable visions." On June 17, 1829, Father Smith's brother Jesse penned a letter to Hyrum Smith in which he objected to both the doctrines of the Restoration and the fact that his brother Joseph Smith, Sr., had sent a messenger to Samuel Smith, another brother, telling of the Restoration (see letter of Jesse Smith to Hyrum Smith, 17 June 1829, LDS Church Archives).

58. Among the friends to learn of the Book of Mormon from the Smiths, the list must obviously include Joseph Knight and family (see Dean C. Jessee, "Joseph Knight's Recollection of Early Mormon History," *BYU Studies* 17 [Autumn 1976]: 29–39); an unidentified "confidential friend" (see Lucy Mack Smith, *Biographical Sketches*, p. 102); Willard Chase (see Howe, *History of Mormonism* pp. 242–43); and Martin Harris, who "had been informed by Joseph Smith, Sr., two or three days before Joseph secured the plates, that the time for their removal had come" (see Larry C. Porter, "A Study of the Origins of the Church of Jesus Christ of Latter Day Saints in the States of New York and Pennsylvania, 1816–1831" [Ph.D. diss., Brigham Young University, 1971], p. 82). The Reverend John A. Clark says that Martin Harris came to him in 1827 seeking support in Harris's conviction, gained through his association with the Smiths, that Joseph was a prophet and the forthcoming Book of Mormon divine (see John A. Clark, *Gleanings by the Way* [Philadelphia: W. J. & J. K. Simon, 1842], pp. 222–25).

59. These would include such men as Stephen Harding (see

Thomas Gregg, *The Prophet of Palmyra* [New York: John B. Alden, Publisher, 1890], pp. 40–44) and Solomon Chamberlain (see Larry C. Porter, "Solomon Chamberlain—Early Missionary," *BYU Studies* 12 [Spring 1972]: 314–17; see also "Short Sketch of the Life of Solomon Chamberlain, Written 11 July 1858," LDS Church Archives). Eli Bruce told of a conversation about the Book of Mormon that he had with one of his fellow prisoners, Joseph Smith, Sr., on November 5, 1830, while confined in the Canandaigua jail (see Rob Morris, *The Biography of Eli Bruce* [Louisville, Ky.: Morris and Monsarrat, 1861], pp. 266–67).

60. See Lucy Mack Smith, *Biographical Sketches,* p. 153.

61. See *Historical Record* 5 (December 1886): 98–99; Lucy Mack Smith, *Biographical Sketches,* pp. 172–73; George A. Smith, in *Journal of Discourses* 5:101–11; George A. Smith, "My Journal," *Instructor* 81 (January 1946): 7–14.

62. See Lucy Mack Smith, *History of Joseph Smith,* p. 211; John Murdock, diary, 1832, LDS Church Archives.

63. See John Smith, diary, 1831–1832, LDS Church Archives, under dates of September 9–19, 1831 (note that this John Smith is *not* the John Smith who was Father Smith's brother and the Prophet's uncle).

64. See Edward Stevenson, "Incidents of My Early Days in the Church," *Juvenile Instructor* 29 (1894): 443; Stevenson, *Reminiscences,* pp. 1–5.

65. See Lucy Mack Smith, *History of Joseph Smith,* p. 244; *Messenger and Advocate* 2 (June 1836): 331; *History of the Church* 2:442–43.

66. See *History of the Church* 4:191.

67. George A. Smith, "My Journal," *Juvenile Instructor* 81 (November 1946): 517.

68. See Mosiah 18:8–10.

69. Acts 20:20.

70. Acts 28:23, 30.

71. See Lucy Mack Smith, *History of Joseph Smith,* pp. 191–92.

72. John Smith, diary, under dates of January 7 and 8, 1832.

73. See, for example, the account of Lorenzo Snow and Abel Butterfield in Eliza R. Snow Smith, *Biography and Family Record,* pp. 30–31.

74. In Orson F. Whitney, *Life of Heber C. Kimball* (1888; reprint, Collector's Edition, Salt Lake City: Bookcraft, 1992), pp. 103–5.

75. George A. Smith, "History of George A. Smith," unpublished September 21, 1839, LDS Church Archives; also in George A. Smith, "My Journal," *Instructor* 82 (April 1947): 168.

76. D&C 64:33.

77. George A. Smith, "My Journal," *Instructor* 81 (August 1946): 369.

78. Matt. 23:12; see also Luke 14:11; D&C 101:42; 112:3.

79. See Lucy Mack Smith, *Biographical Sketches*, p. 165.

80. This phrase comes from D&C 4:2, a revelation given to Father Smith and detailing the characteristics of the valiant missionary.

81. See William Smith, "Notes," p. 20.

82. Tucker, *Origin*, p. 12.

83. See Kelley, "The Hill Cumorah," p. 166.

84. See, for example, Lucy Mack Smith, *History of Joseph Smith*, p. 298.

85. See Journal of Wandle Mace, Mormon file, Huntington Library, San Marino, California. In what must have been about March 1839, Mace describes "frequently" visiting Father and Mother Smith and of listening "with intense interest" as they related their experiences dealing with the restoration of the gospel and the growth of the Church.

86. Heber C. Kimball, in *Journal of Discourses* 8:351. This strain of cheerfulness ran through the Smith family. George A. Smith remembered that his grandfather (i.e., Father Smith's father, Asael Smith) was "an exceedingly intelligent and cheerful old gentleman" (see letter of George A. Smith to Dr. H. Gould, Salt Lake City, May 31, 1870, cited in Richard Lloyd Anderson, "Heritage of a Prophet," *Ensign* 1 [February 1971]: 15–16).

87. In Godfrey, Godfrey, and Derr, *Women's Voices*, p. 48.

88. Patriarchal Blessing Book 1, LDS Church Archives, p. 138.

89. The phrase "used us civilly" comes from Lucy Mack Smith, though she is likely quoting either her husband or her husband's brother John; the statement that "the subject of the Book of Mormon was aggitated" comes from Father Smith's brother John, describing one of their missionary experiences. The point, of course, is that the language of Lucy and Uncle John was also the language of Father Smith. The quotations come from Lucy Mack Smith, "Joseph Smith, Sr., Family Biography," Harold B. Lee Library, Brigham Young University, Provo, Utah, pp. 13, 17.

90. See Carol Reed, *Dialects of American English* (University of Massachusetts Press, 1967), p. 11.

91. See H. L. Mencken, *The American Language* (New York: Alfred M. Knopf, 1967), pp. 151–89.

92. The phrase "a monkey without a monkey's wit," as quoted in the text, was used by the Prophet Joseph Smith but again is typical of the kind of expressions used by Father Smith as well. For this particular quote, see Faulring, ed., *An American Prophet's Record*, p. 268.

93. See Lucy Mack Smith, *History of Joseph Smith*, pp. 100–101.

94. Wilford Woodruff, *Leaves from My Journal* (Salt Lake City: Juvenile Instructor Office, 1881), p. 57.

95. See Lucy Mack Smith, *History of Joseph Smith*, pp. 289–90.

96. Acts 3:21.

97. See William Smith, "The Old Soldier's Testimony," *Saints' Herald* 31 (October 4, 1884): 643.

98. See "Interview with Martin Harris," *Tiffany's Monthly* 5 (January 1859): 163–70, cited in Porter, "A Study of the Origins of the Church," p. 81.

99. See Gregg, *The Prophet of Palmyra*, pp. 40–48.

100. See Lucy Mack Smith, *History of Joseph Smith*, pp. 165–67.

101. See Journal History, LDS Church Archives, April 6, 1830; "Interview with W. B. Saunders," Reorganized Church of Jesus Christ of Latter Day Saints, B 14, Box 2, fd 44; Brigham Young, diary, 1843, LDS Church Archives.

102. See Cannon and Cook, eds., *Far West Record*, p. 1.

103. See Lucy Mack Smith, *History of Joseph Smith*, p. 224.

104. See D&C 23:5; 90:20, 25; 102:3, 34; 124:19; and 137:5.

105. See D&C 4.

106. He was present when D&C 21 and 117 were given, and perhaps when section 20 was given.

Chapter 3. Seeing with the Eye of Faith

1. See Moro. 10:11; 1 Cor. 12:9.

2. Rom. 1:17; see also Hab. 2:4; Gal. 3:11; Heb. 10:38.

3. Alma 33:22–23.

4. See, for example, Enos 1:8; Alma 14:26; 15:10; Hel. 5:44; Moro. 10:4.

5. See, for example, 1 Ne. 12:10.

6. See, for example, 2 Ne. 9:23.

7. See, for example, Hel. 5:47.

8. See, for example, Mosiah 25:15.

9. Mark 11:22.

10. Gal. 3:26.

11. Cited in Joseph Fielding Smith, *Life of Joseph F. Smith* (Salt Lake City: Deseret Book Co., 1938), pp. 24–28; also in Richard Lloyd Anderson, *Joseph Smith's New England Heritage* (Salt Lake City: Deseret Book Co., 1971), pp. 124–29.

12. 2 Tim. 1:5.

13. *Lectures on Faith* 2:53.

14. Mosiah 10:12. For additional examples, see also Jacob 3:7; Mosiah 1:5; Alma 3:8; 9:16–17; Hel. 5:51; 15:4.

15. See D&C 74:4.

16. See D&C 93:39.

17. See D&C 123:7.

18. Anderson, *Joseph Smith's New England Heritage,* p. 89.

19. Cited in Anderson, *Joseph Smith's New England Heritage,* p. 91.

20. D&C 59:21.

21. Cited in Anderson, *Joseph Smith's New England Heritage,* p. 92.

22. See Anderson, *Joseph Smith's New England Heritage,* pp. 91–92.

23. Anderson, *Joseph Smith's New England Heritage,* p. 107.

24. Both these quotes are from George A. Smith and are cited in Anderson, *Joseph Smith's New England Heritage,* p. 112. The Prophet Joseph Smith was also aware of Asael's spiritual premonitions and noted that both Asael and his wife, Mary Duty Smith, were fully satisfied that those promptings were entirely fulfilled in the life and mission of the Prophet himself (see *History of the Church* 2:443).

25. Letter of George A. Smith to Dr. H. Gould, Salt Lake City, May 31, 1870, p. 4, cited in Richard Lloyd Anderson, "Heritage of a Prophet," *Ensign* 1 (February 1971): 16.

26. John Smith, journal, cited in Lucy Mack Smith, *Biographical Sketches of Joseph Smith, the Prophet, and His Progenitors for Many Generations* (London and Liverpool: Published for Orson Pratt by S. W. Richards, 1853), p. 155.

27. See William Smith, "Notes on 'Chamber's Life of Joseph Smith,'" LDS Church Archives, p. 18.

28. Lucy Mack Smith, cited in Anderson, *Joseph Smith's New England Heritage,* p. 207.

29. Thomas Paine, *Age of Reason,* pp. 240, 241, in *Basic Writings of Thomas Paine* (New York: Willey Book Co., 1942).

30. See *History of the Church* 2:442–43.

31. In the subtle operations of the Spirit, sometimes people are unaware of what has transpired. Jesus reminded the Nephites, for example, of some Lamanites who "were baptized with fire and with the Holy Ghost, *and they knew it not*" (3 Ne. 9:20, emphasis added). Similarly, the two disciples on the Emmaus road walked for some distance with the resurrected Christ, "but their eyes were holden that they should not know him." After the Savior left them, they reflected on their experience and realized that they had in fact felt the Holy Spirit. They said: "Did not our heart burn within us, while he talked with us by the way?" (Luke 24:16, 32.)

32. Letter of Asael Smith to Jacob Towne, Tunbridge, Vermont, January 14, 1796, originally printed in *Deseret Evening News,* July 16, 1872; also in *History of the Church* 1:285–87; Joseph Fielding Smith, *Life of Joseph F. Smith,* pp. 22–23; and Anderson, *Joseph Smith's New England Heritage,* pp. 118–19.

33. Dan. 2:44.

34. See 2 Ne. 3:14–15.

35. Lucy Mack Smith, *History of Joseph Smith by His Mother,* ed. Preston Nibley (Salt Lake City: Bookcraft, 1958), p. 46. William Smith also speaks of Father Smith as having "faith in the universal restoration doctrine," a fact which often "brought down upon my father the aprobiem [opprobrium] or slur of Old Joe Smith" (see William Smith, "Notes," p. 18).

36. Lucy Mack Smith, *History of Joseph Smith,* pp. 43–45.

37. Lucy Mack Smith, *History of Joseph Smith,* p. 47.

38. Lucy Mack Smith, *History of Joseph Smith,* p. 48.

39. See Lucy Mack Smith, *History of Joseph Smith,* pp. 48–50.

40. See "Wm. B. Smith's Last Statement," *Zion's Ensign* 5 (January 13, 1894): 6. We are left to wonder if the fact that the condemnation came from the lips of a Presbyterian minister did not intensify already existent feelings about Presbyterianism, not simply because of the vision Joseph Smith, Sr., had received about the universal apostasy but also because after the First Vision the Prophet Joseph returned to the Smith home with a testimony that both Father and Mother Smith recognized, saying: "I have learned for myself that Presbyterianism is not true" (JS–H 1:20). The Prophet's statement was made in answer to a question posed by his mother, but there is no reason to suppose that his father was not there also. Moreover, at this time Mother Smith, Hyrum, Samuel Harrison, and Sophronia had all joined the Presbyterian church, and, says Mother Smith, "to gratify me, my husband attended some two or three meetings, but peremptorily refused going any more, either for my gratification, or any other person's" (Lucy Mack Smith, *History of Joseph Smith,* p. 90).

41. See D&C 137, 138.

42. See *Lectures on Faith* 6.

43. Alma 32:21, emphasis added.

44. Orasmus Turner, *History of the Pioneer Settlement of Phelps and Gorham's Purchase, and Morris' Reserve* (Rochester, New York: William Alling, 1852), p. 213.

45. See William Smith, "The Old Soldier's Testimony," *Saints' Herald* 31 (October 4, 1884): 643.

46. See *Lectures on Faith* 1.

47. See, for example, Ether 3:19; Moses 7:50–52.

48. Lucy Mack Smith, *History of Joseph Smith,* pp. 51–53.

49. Lucy Mack Smith, *History of Joseph Smith,* p. 232.

50. See, for example, Lucy Mack Smith, *History of Joseph Smith,* pp. 257–58.

51. Wilford Woodruff, *Leaves from My Journal* (Salt Lake City: Juvenile Instructor Office, 1881), p. 94.

52. Edward Stevenson, "Incidents of My Early Days in the Church," *Juvenile Instructor* 29 (September 1, 1894): 552.

53. Edward Stevenson, *Reminiscences of Joseph, the Prophet, and the Coming Forth of the Book of Mormon* (Salt Lake City: Edward Stevenson, 1893), p. 5.

54. Cited in LeRoi C. Snow, "How Lorenzo Snow Found God," *Improvement Era* 40 (February 1937): 83–84.

55. Cited in Eliza R. Snow Smith, *Biography and Family Record of Lorenzo Snow* (Salt Lake City: Deseret News Co., 1884), p. 10.

56. See Joseph Smith, *Teachings of the Prophet Joseph Smith*, sel. Joseph Fielding Smith (Salt Lake City: Deseret Book Co., 1938), pp. 342–60.

57. See Matt. 20:1–16.

58. In LeRoi C. Snow, "Devotion to a Divine Inspiration," *Improvement Era* 22 (June 1919): 656.

59. Cited in Edward W. Tullidge, *The Women of Mormondom* (New York: Tullidge and Crandall, 1877; reprint, Salt Lake City, 1975), pp. 99–100.

60. Eliza R. Snow Smith, *Biography and Family Record*, pp. 13–14.

61. Cited in Edward W. Tullidge, *The Women of Mormondom*, pp. 207–8.

62. *History of the Church* 3:175.

63. Joseph F. Smith, "Boyhood Recollections of President Joseph F. Smith," *Utah Genealogical and Historical Magazine* 7 (April 1916): 54–55. See also *History of the Church* 3:163; 4:32–33.

64. Cited in Ruby K. Smith, *Mary Bailey* (Salt Lake City: Deseret Book Co., 1954), p. 70.

65. See Hyrum Smith, "To the Saints Scattered Abroad," *Times and Seasons* 1 (December 1839): 22–23.

66. See Lucy Mack Smith, *Biographical Sketches*, p. 254.

67. This quotation comes from N. B. Lundwall, *Assorted Gems of Priceless Value* (Salt Lake City: Bookcraft, 1944), pp. 316–17. The original account is in Hannah Sessions Burningham, "The Life of Perrigrine Sessions, Taken from His Diary," typescript of his diaries, LDS Church Archives. The quotation here inserted includes portions from both accounts.

68. See Moses 7:45, 47.

69. See D&C 1:31.

70. D&C 121:36.

71. See 1 Ne. 3:12.

72. See 1 Ne. 3:16–25.

73. 1 Ne. 4:6.

74. See *Lectures on Faith* 1.

75. Alma 5:15; see the entire chapter. See also Ether 12:19.

76. Cited in "The Kirtland Temple," *Historical Record* 5 (June 1886): 80.

77. In Kenneth W. Godfrey, Audrey M. Godfrey, and Jill Mulvay Derr, *Women's Voices: An Untold History of the Latter-day Saints, 1830–1900* (Salt Lake City: Deseret Book Co., 1982), pp. 54–55.

78. Edward Stevenson, autobiography, unpublished, 1893, LDS Church Archives, p. 17; also cited in Earnest M. Skinner, "Joseph Smith, Sr., First Patriarch to the Church" (Master's thesis, Brigham Young University, 1958), pp. 116–17.

79. In Godfrey, Godfrey, and Derr, *Women's Voices,* pp. 84–96.

80. Alma 7:13.

81. Jacob 4:13, emphasis added.

82. Sarah D. Pea Rich, journal, Huntington Library, San Marino, California, pp. 30–31.

83. See, for example, 3 Ne. 26:11.

84. In the retelling of this story, quotations from three sources have been interspersed: Ruth W. Tyler, "A Manifestation of God's Power Through Fasting and Prayer," *Juvenile Instructor* 19 (1884): 91; Terry and Nora Lund, *Pulsipher Family History Book* (1953; reprinted, 1963, copies in private, family possession), pp. 18–19; and William Smith, *William Smith on Mormonism* (Lamoni, Iowa: Herald Steam Book and Job Office, 1883), pp. 25–26. The story presents one problematic feature: Tyler refers to the sick man as Joseph Hunting, while the Pulsipher account, compiled from the records of Zera Pulsipher, identifies him as Samuel Newcomb. William Smith seems to clarify these differences, specifying that Newcomb was a new member of the Church who moved to Kirtland "and brought with him a brother that was said to be crazy; a person bereft of his reason, a raving maniac; and from all appearance possessed of evil spirits." By combining these accounts it seems that Hunting was the sick man who lived under the care of Newcomb. (While history is often made of such unresolved confusions, it is clear from reading the three accounts that both are describing the same incidents.)

85. See Brigham Young, in *Journal of Discourses* 7:289–90.

86. Patriarchal Blessing Book 1, LDS Church Archives, p. 1.

Chapter 4. In the Family Unit

1. Lucy Mack Smith, *History of Joseph Smith by His Mother,* ed. Preston Nibley (Salt Lake City: Bookcraft, 1958), pp. 43–45.

2. In Lucy Mack Smith, *History of Joseph Smith,* pp. 47–50. The account of Lehi's vision is in 1 Ne. 8.

3. See Lucy Mack Smith, *History of Joseph Smith,* p. 290; see also pp. 300–302.

4. See Lucy Mack Smith, *History of Joseph Smith,* p. 155.

5. *History of the Church* 2:387–88.

6. Blessing to Asahel Smith, 17 June 1836, LDS Church Archives.

7. Letter of Joseph Smith to Emma Smith, June 6, 1832, reproduced in LaMar C. Berrett, "An Impressive Letter from the Pen of Joseph Smith," *BYU Studies* 11 (Summer 1971): 522.

8. John Smith, journal, LDS Church Archives, March 1, 1840.

9. In Journal History, LDS Church Archives, June 17, 1840.

10. John Smith, journal, August 27, 1840; also in Journal History, August 27, 1840.

11. Lucy Mack Smith, *History of Joseph Smith,* pp. 224–25.

12. Sometimes used as a purgative, calomel is described in a local Palmyra newspaper of the day, the Palmyra *Reflector* of February 1, 1831, in the following terms: "CALOMEL—In forming this article it is only necessary to rub together equal parts of corrosive sublimate and pure mercury until the mercury entirely loses its metallic appearance. In this case the mercury abstracts a part of the oxygen from the corrosive sublimate, and lessens its activity, and converts it into calomel or muriate of mercury. This preparation is quite insoluble in water. It is used to excite salivation in small doses; and in doses from 10 to 20 grains as a cathartic."

13. In Lucy Mack Smith, *History of Joseph Smith,* pp. 86–88.

14. *History of the Church* 5:127.

15. See Luke 16:19–31.

16. Joseph Smith III, "Family Association Remarks," *Journal of History* 1 (January 1908): 41; cited in Richard Lloyd Anderson, "'Of Goodly Parents,'" *New Era* 3 (December 1973): 35.

17. JS–H 1:61.

18. Lucy Mack Smith, *History of Joseph Smith,* p. 327. Mother Smith's list of Smith family martyrs, however, is perhaps too short. It seems clear that the deaths of Father Smith, both Samuel and his wife, Don Carlos, and William's wife were all hurried by the effects of persecution and the exposure it brought. The Prophet and Hyrum, of course, were murdered by a mob, bringing to seven the number of Smiths whose lives were either directly or indirectly forfeit to mob violence and persecution.

19. "The Mormons, or Latter Day Saints," *United States Catholic Magazine* 4 (n.d.): 355.

20. See 2 Ne. 3:11–15.

21. On one occasion Mother Smith reported a vision in which she was told, "Thou art a mother in Israel. Thy spirit arose and said in eternity, that it would take a body to be a mother to [the] Prophet who should be raised up to save the last dispensation." (See Dean C. Jessee, ed., "The John Taylor Nauvoo Journal," *BYU Studies* 23 [Summer 1983]: 64.)

22. *History of the Church* 5:126.

23. See, for example, Lucy Mack Smith, *History of Joseph Smith,* pp. 151, 189.

24. See William Smith, "Notes Written on 'Chamber's Life of Joseph Smith,'" LDS Church Archives, p. 18.

25. See J. W. Peterson, "Wm. B. Smith's Last Statement," *Zion's Ensign* 5 (January 13, 1894): 6.

26. See Lucy Mack Smith, *History of Joseph Smith,* p. 154.

27. Joseph Smith, 1832 autobiographical sketch, in Scott H. Faulring, ed., *An American Prophet's Record: The Diaries and Journals of Joseph Smith* (Salt Lake City: Signature Books, 1989), p. 4.

28. William Smith, *William Smith on Mormonism* (Lamoni, Iowa: Herald Steam Book and Job Office, 1883), p. 9.

29. Lucy Mack Smith, *History of Joseph Smith,* p. 83.

30. See Lucy Mack Smith, *History of Joseph Smith,* pp. 152–53.

31. See Lucy Mack Smith, *History of Joseph Smith,* p. 155.

32. See, for example, Lucy Mack Smith, *History of Joseph Smith,* p. 191.

33. See Lucy Mack Smith, *History of Joseph Smith,* pp. 191, 196–99.

34. Reynolds Cahoon, diaries, LDS Church Archives, November 16, 1831.

35. Recollections of Mary E. Rollins Lightner in "Joseph Smith, the Prophet," *Young Woman's Journal* 16 (December 1905): 556–57.

36. See Lucy Mack Smith, *History of Joseph Smith,* pp. 221–23; see also Leonard J. Arrington, *Charles C. Rich: Mormon General and Western Frontiersman* (Provo, Utah: Brigham Young University Press, 1974), p. 21.

37. See Joseph Smith, *The Papers of Joseph Smith,* ed. Dean C. Jessee, vol. 2, *Journal, 1832–1842* (Salt Lake City: Deseret Book Co., 1992), p. 86; Joseph Smith, 1835–36 diary and journal, in Faulring, ed., *An American Prophet's Record,* pp. 65–66; Leland R. Nelson, comp., *The Journal of Joseph* (Provo, Utah: Council Press, 1979), pp. 91–92; and *History of the Church* 2:317–18.

38. Ether 3:2.

39. See Rom. 7:14–25, especially v. 23.

40. See *History of the Church* 2:293–95; see also Joseph Smith, 1835–36 diary and journal, in Faulring, ed., *An American Prophet's Record,* pp. 41–43.

41. *History of the Church* 2:342, 343; see the entire letter, pp. 340–43.

42. *History of the Church* 2:353–54.

43. *History of the Church* 2:355.

44. See *History of the Church* 2:354.

45. Cited in S. W. Richards, "Duty of Marriage," *Contributor* 13 (February 1892): 167.

46. Lucy Mack Smith, *History of Joseph Smith,* pp. 144–45.

47. See Lucy Mack Smith, *History of Joseph Smith,* pp. 290–91.

48. Lucy Mack Smith, *History of Joseph Smith,* 1985 ed., p. 306.

49. D&C 107:39.

50. See *History of the Church* 4:190.

51. See Mark 1:7; Luke 3:16.

52. See, for example, 1 Cor. 15:9; Eph. 3:8.

53. See, for example, 2 Ne. 4:17–19, 26–27.

54. See Heber C. Kimball, in *Journal of Discourses* 8:351.

55. See Jacob 5, especially v. 41.

56. See, for example, 2 Ne. 27:23 and JST, Isa. 29:25.

57. This expression of confidence in the justice of God is the more remarkable given the fact that Father Smith is speaking almost two years before the Prophet Joseph received what we now refer to as D&C 137, which outlines the doctrine of salvation for the dead, including little children who die before arriving at the years of accountability.

58. Patriarchal Blessing Book 1, LDS Church Archives, p. 1.

59. See Lucy Mack Smith, *History of Joseph Smith,* p. 82.

60. See 2 Ne. 3; see also JST, Gen. 50.

61. The Lord made this same promise to Joseph Smith (see D&C 122:2).

62. See Isa. 54:17, the interpretation of which has added meaning in light of what Joseph, the son of Jacob, here says.

63. See 3 Ne. 21:10, wherein the Savior describes Joseph Smith in language very similar to that used by the ancient Joseph.

64. Patriarchal Blessing Book 1, p. 3. See also *Utah Genealogical and Historical Magazine* 23 (October 1932): 175.

65. Hyrum Smith, diary, 1835–1844, LDS Church Archives, under the date of February 21, 1835. Salt Lake City, Ut.: LDS Church Historian's Library.

66. See Hyrum Smith, diary, 1831–1832, Harold B. Lee Library, Brigham Young University, Provo, Utah, under the date of September 30, 1832.

67. See Joseph Smith, *The Papers of Joseph Smith* 2:65; see also Joseph Smith, 1835–36 diary and journal, in Faulring, ed., *An American Prophet's Record,* pp. 47–48; Ruby K. Smith, *Mary Bailey* (Salt Lake City: Deseret Book Co., 1954), p. 46.

68. Lucy Mack Smith, *History of Joseph Smith,* pp. 307–13.

69. Gen. 49:33.

Chapter 5. The Patriarch to the Church

1. See *History of the Church* 4:190.

2. The term *evangelical minister* seems to suggest that the office of the Patriarch includes a responsibility to teach the gospel as well as to give patriarchal blessings. In explaining the meaning of D&C 107:39, where the term is used, Orson Pratt said: "When this was first given, the word 'evangelical' was not there. But Joseph was wrought upon by the Spirit to erase the word patriarchs and substitute the words 'evangelical ministers.' " (In *Journal of Discourses* 19:114.)

3. Bruce R. McConkie, *Mormon Doctrine,* 2d ed. (Salt Lake City: Bookcraft, 1966), pp. 560–61.

4. See *History of the Church* 3:381; also Joseph Smith *Teachings of the Prophet Joseph Smith,* sel. Joseph Fielding Smith (Salt Lake City: Deseret Book Co., 1938), p. 151.

5. D&C 107:53–57. The account in the Doctrine and Covenants enlarges our view of the vision that the Prophet received, for surely even as he saw Adam gather with his righteous posterity and bless them, he would have seen him predict what would befall them "unto the latest generation."

6. In the Patriarchal Blessing Book, Oliver Cowdery records the name of the Church as "the Church of Jesus Christ of Latter day Saints." If Oliver is recording verbatim that which the Prophet said in this blessing, then this is one of the first times, if not the first time, that the Church is called by its current name. Oliver notes, however, that he recorded the blessings of December 18, 1833, including this one to Father Smith, in September 1835. In either event, D&C 115:4, wherein the full name of the Church as currently used is given, was received April 26, 1838. Prior to that time the Church was called "The Church of the Latter-day Saints" (see article entitled "Communicated" in *Evening and Morning Star* 2 [May 3, 1834]: 160). When Joseph Fielding Smith included Father Smith's blessing in *Teachings of the Prophet Joseph Smith,* for historical accuracy he appears to have included the name of the Church as "the Church of the Latter-day Saints," for such it was called in September 1835 when Oliver was recording the blessings. Whether Oliver quoted verbatim the words spoken in 1833 or inserted them in September 1835, we cannot be certain. In either event, he was using the term "the Church of Jesus Christ of Latter-day Saints" in September 1835, about two and a half years prior to the receipt of D&C 115.

7. Patriarchal Blessing Book 2, LDS Church Archives, pp. 14–15; cited in Joseph Smith, *Teachings of the Prophet Joseph Smith,* sel. Joseph Fielding Smith, pp. 38–40, and in Joseph Fielding Smith, *Life of Joseph F. Smith* (Salt Lake City: Deseret Book Co., 1938), pp. 34–36.

8. See *History of the Church* 2:32.

9. Benjamin F. Johnson, *My Life's Review* (Independence, Mo.: Zion's Printing and Publishing Co., 1947), p. 17.

10. See Howard H. Barron, *Orson Hyde* (Bountiful, Ut.: Horizon Publishers, 1977), pp. 70–71.

11. Patriarchal Blessing Book 1, p. 16.

12. Oliver B. Huntington, "Resurrection of My Mother," *Young Woman's Journal* 5 (April 1894): 345–46.

13. Howard Coray, journal, Huntington Library, San Marino, California, p. 16.

14. See George Washington Johnson, diary, 1823–1893, typescript copy in Harold B. Lee Library, Brigham Young University, Provo, Utah.

15. Cited in Lucy Mack Smith, *History of Joseph Smith by His Mother*, ed. Preston Nibley (Salt Lake City: Bookcraft, 1958), p. 311.

16. Similar problems occurred in the transcription of the revelations recorded in the Doctrine and Covenants (see, for example, Earl E. Olson, "The Chronology of the Ohio Revelations," *BYU Studies* 11 [Summer 1971]: 336, 344.

17. John Murdock, diary, LDS Church Archives, May 31, 1836.

18. Patriarchal Blessing Book 1.

19. Samuel Holister Rogers, journal, Harold B. Lee Library, Brigham Young University, Provo, Utah.

20. Father Smith gave a patriarchal blessing to Michael Barkdull in Kirtland, Ohio, on March 23, 1836. Copies of the blessing are in private, family possession.

21. In Dean C. Jessee, "The Kirtland Diary of Wilford Woodruff," *BYU Studies* 12 (Summer 1972): 395–96.

22. "Autobiography of Mary Brown Pulsipher," in Terry and Nora Lund, *Pulsipher Family History Book* (1953; reprinted, 1963, copies in private, family possession), pp. 29–30.

23. See 2 Chr. 18:13. The principle is clearly stated in 2 Pet. 1:20–21.

24. In Samuel Holister Rogers, journal.

25. See, for example, Patriarchal Blessing Book 1, pp. 18–19, 26, 32. The principle herein described is illustrated in D&C 18:31–36.

26. See Abr. 2:9–11.

27. See Luke 4:25–27. The principle is also nicely stated in Jer. 17:10 but more perfectly stated in 2 Ne. 27:23.

28. In *Journal of Discourses* 8:197, emphasis added.

29. See Gracia N. Jones, *Emma's Glory and Sacrifice: A Testimony* (Hurricane, Utah: Homestead Publishers and Distributors, 1987), p. 153.

30. *Latter Day Saints' Messenger and Advocate* 2 (June 1836): 331.

31. *History of the Church* 2:446–47.

32. See *History of the Church* 4:191.

33. See *Historical Record* 5 (August 1886): 90.

34. Heber C. Kimball, serving a mission at the time in Ogdensburg, New York, illustrates the cheering spirit which accompanied Father Smith and Uncle John. He said: "On the 25th of August while assembled for a meeting our hearts were filled with joy by the arrival of Joseph Smith, sen., the Patriarch, and his brother John Smith, who were on a mission to bless the church. On the 27th the church came together and received patriarchal blessings under the hands of President Joseph Smith, sen. I wrote for him." (*Deseret News*, vol. 8, p. 33; see also Journal History, LDS Church Archives, May 10, 1836.)

35. See *History of the Church* 2:441–42; see also Lucy Mack Smith, *History of Joseph Smith,* pp. 244–46.

36. See Abr. 2:6–11; D&C 132:29–50; Gen. 17; 22:15–18; Rom. 9:3–8; Gal. 3:6–9, 29.

37. See Rom. 9:8; Gal. 3:7; 4:28.

38. See Gen. 17:19.

39. See Gen. 28:1–4, 12–22 (especially v. 14).

40. See Gen. 48:5–22; 1 Chr. 5:1–2; Jer. 31:9.

41. See Hosea 7:8.

42. See Joseph Fielding Smith, *Doctrines of Salvation,* comp. Bruce R. McConkie, 3 vols. (Salt Lake City: Bookcraft, 1954–56), 3:248–49.

43. "Biographies of Vinson Knight and Abigale Meade McBride and Copies of Letters Obtained from a Descendant of Rispah Lee Knight," Harold B. Lee Library, Brigham Young University, Provo, Utah.

44. Charles C. Rich Papers, MSS. 1052, Harold B. Lee Library, Brigham Young University, Provo, Utah.

45. Patriarchal Blessing Book 1, p. 3.

46. In Howard Coray, journal, p. 16.

47. Cited in Leonard J. Arrington, *Charles C. Rich: Mormon General and Western Frontiersman* (Provo, Utah: Brigham Young University Press, 1974), p. 303.

48. Edward Stevenson Collection, MS. 1054, LDS Church Archives.

49. Cyrena Dustin Merrill, "Sketch of the Life of Cyrena Dustin Merrill, As Given by Herself," p. 2. Copies in private, family possession.

50. In Edward W. Tullidge, *The Women of Mormondom* (New York: Tullidge and Crandall, 1877; reprint, Salt Lake City, 1975), p. 236.

51. In Journal History, LDS Church Archives, October 13, 1854.

52. Johnson, *My Life's Review,* pp. 26–27.

53. In Susa Young Gates (under the pseudonym "Homespun"),

Lydia Knight's History (Salt Lake City: Juvenile Instructor Office, 1883), pp. 55–58.

54. Eliza R. Snow Smith, *Biography and Family Record of Lorenzo Snow* (Salt Lake City: Deseret News Co., 1884), pp. 263–65.

55. See 2 Kgs. 5.

56. Cited in "Records of Early Church Families," *Utah Genealogical and Historical Magazine* 27 (October 1936): 157.

57. See Jessee, "The Kirtland Diary of Wilford Woodruff," p. 383.

58. In Jessee, "The Kirtland Diary of Wilford Woodruff," p. 378.

59. D&C 11:13.

60. Merrill, "Sketch," pp. 1–3, 11.

61. Johnson, *My Life's Review,* p. 19, emphasis added.

62. See William G. Hartley, *"They Are My Friends": A History of the Joseph Knight Family, 1825–1850* (Provo, Ut.: Grandin Book Co., 1986) p. 115.

63. In Hartley, *"They Are My Friends,"* p. 131.

64. In Journal History, July 5, 1856.

65. See D&C 1:4; 63:37, 57–58; 84:114; 109:41; 112:5; 124:106; 134:12.

66. D&C 63:58.

67. Patriarchal Blessing Book 1, p. 2.

68. See Alma 39.

69. See Alma 42:31; 43:1–2.

70. Patriarchal Blessing Book 1, p. 8.

71. Patriarchal Blessing Book 1, p. 21.

72. In Oliver Norton Harmon, reminiscences and diary, July 1857–February 1885, LDS Church Archives.

73. In Kenneth W. Godfrey, Audrey M. Godfrey, and Jill Mulvay Derr, *Women's Voices: An Untold History of the Latter-day Saints, 1830–1900* (Salt Lake City: Deseret Book Co., 1982), p. 48.

74. See D&C 107:39–57.

75. Morm. 9:9; see also 1 Ne. 10:18–19; Alma 7:20; Moro. 8:18; D&C 20:12; James 1:17; Heb. 13:8.

76. See Marinda Nancy Johnson Hyde, papers, LDS Church Archives.

77. See E. J. Watson, *Journals of Orson Pratt* (Salt Lake City: Elden Jay Watson, 1975), pp. 507–8.

78. Cited in Andrew Karl Larson, *Erastus Snow: The Life of a Missionary and Pioneer for the Early Mormon Church* (Salt Lake City: University of Utah Press, 1971), p. 25.

79. See Wilford Woodruff, *Leaves from My Journal* (Salt Lake City: Juvenile Instructor Office, 1881), pp. 48–49; see also Wilford Woodruff, in *Journal of Discourses* 12:277.

80. Huntington, "Resurrection of My Mother," p. 346.

81. Wilford Woodruff, *Wilford Woodruff's Journal, 1833–1898, Typescript*, ed. Scott G. Kenney, 9 vols. (Midvale, Ut.: Signature Books, 1983–85), 1:263–66.

Chapter 6. Preach the Word!

1. See D&C 4:2–4.
2. See D&C 84:61.
3. See D&C 35:5–7.
4. See D&C 88:81.
5. See D&C 21:9.
6. See Morm. 9:22–25.
7. See D&C 1:2–5.
8. See D&C 14:3–4.
9. See Mosiah 18:8–10.
10. JS–H 1:20.
11. See JS–H 1:21–22.
12. E. D. Howe, *History of Mormonism* (Painesville, Ohio: E. D. Howe, 1840). Of particular interest are the affidavits and testimonies of Peter Ingersoll (pp. 232–34), William Stafford (p. 240), Willard Chase (pp. 242–43), Abigail Harris (p. 253), Roswell Nichols (pp. 257–58), and Joshua Stafford (p. 258).
13. History has not preserved for us a full account detailing exactly what rumor and what prejudice impelled Father Smith to exhume Alvin's remains. Two things, however, stand out: the rumors were widespread, and the singular feature distinguishing the Smiths from others in the community was their religious experience, which formed the focus of the prejudice directed against them. The notice published in the local *Wayne Sentinel* is found in *The Papers of Joseph Smith*, ed. Dean C. Jessee, vol. 1, *Autobiographical and Historical Writings* (Salt Lake City: Deseret Book Co., 1989), p. 7. One effort to create the larger context for understanding this public notice is found in Richard Lloyd Anderson, "The Alvin Smith Story: Fact and Fiction," *Ensign* 17 (August 1987): 58–72.
14. See William Smith, *William Smith on Mormonism* (Lamoni, Iowa: Herald Steam Book and Job Office, 1883), pp. 12–15. For a more complete account of the loss of the farm, see Lucy Mack Smith, *History of Joseph Smith by His Mother*, ed. Preston Nibley (Salt Lake City: Bookcraft, 1958), pp. 94–99.
15. Letter of Jesse Smith to Hyrum Smith, June 17, 1829, LDS Church Archives.
16. Fayette Lapham, "Interview with the Father of Joseph Smith, The Mormon Prophet. . . ." *Historical Magazine* 17 (May 1870): 305–9.

17. See Lucy Mack Smith, *History of Joseph Smith,* p. 105.

18. See Lucy Mack Smith, *History of Joseph Smith,* pp. 102–3.

19. See Lucy Mack Smith, *History of Joseph Smith,* pp. 106–9.

20. See Lucy Mack Smith, *History of Joseph Smith,* pp. 105–6, for an illustrative account in which the Smiths' Palmyra neighbors hired a conjuror to help them discover where Joseph had hidden the plates.

21. Rom. 1:16.

22. Mosiah 18:9.

23. George A. Smith, "Sketch of the Autobiography of George Albert Smith," *Millennial Star* 27 (July 1, 1865): 407. See *History of the Church* 2:443 for the Prophet's statement, "My grandfather, Asael Smith, long ago predicted that there would be a prophet raised up in his family."

24. Lucy Mack Smith, *History of Joseph Smith,* p. 149.

25. D&C 4:1–7.

26. See Lucy Mack Smith, *History of Joseph Smith,* pp. 138–39.

27. See letter of Stephen S. Harding in Thomas Gregg, *The Prophet of Palmyra* (New York: John B. Alden, 1890), pp. 34–56.

28. See "Records of Early Church Families," *Utah Genealogical and Historical Magazine* 26 (October 1935): 153.

29. See Thomas B. Marsh, "History of Thos. Baldwin Marsh," *Deseret News,* March 24, 1858, p. 18.

30. Solomon Chamberlain, "Short Sketch of the Life of Solomon Chamberlain, Written 11 July 1858," LDS Church Archives; see also Larry C. Porter, "Solomon Chamberlain—Early Missionary," *BYU Studies* 12 (Spring 1972): 314–18.

31. See Parley P. Pratt, *Autobiography of Parley P. Pratt,* ed. Parley P. Pratt, Jr. (Salt Lake City: Deseret Book Co., 1938), pp. 37–38, 41–45.

32. See, for example, Wandle Mace, journal, Harold B. Lee Library, Brigham Young University, Provo, Utah. Mace tells of conversations with Father and Mother Smith in Illinois, shortly after their exodus from Missouri, occurring in about June 1839.

33. See, for example, Lucy Mack Smith, *History of Joseph Smith,* p. 189, where Mother Smith tells of the young boys in the neighborhood attending one such devotional, asking Samuel to pray for them, and she adds, "after this, they were never absent during our evening devotions."

34. Lucy Mack Smith, *History of Joseph Smith,* pp. 191–92.

35. See "Edward Partridge," *Utah Genealogical and Historical Magazine* 7 (July 1916): 106.

36. See Lucy Mack Smith, *History of Joseph Smith,* pp. 195–96.

37. John Smith, diary, 1831–1832, LDS Church Archives, under dates of January 7 and 8, 1832.

38. See Edwin Holden, "Recollections of the Prophet Joseph Smith," *Juvenile Instructor* 27 (March 1, 1892): 153. While the language is uncertain, it appears that Father Smith was also present when Emma showed those same mummies to Horace Barnes (see "Caroline Barnes Crosby," in Kenneth W. Godfrey, Audrey M. Godfrey, and Jill Mulvay Derr, *Women's Voices: An Untold History of the Latter-day Saints, 1830–1900* [Salt Lake City: Deseret Book Co., 1982], p. 52).

39. See George A. Smith, in *Journal of Discourses* 5:103.

40. In LeRoi C. Snow, "How Lorenzo Snow Found God," *Improvement Era* 40 (February 1937): 84.

41. See Thomas C. Romney, *The Life of Lorenzo Snow* (Salt Lake City: S.U.P. Memorial Foundation, 1955), pp. 28–29; see also Eliza R. Snow Smith, *Biography and Family Record of Lorenzo Snow* (Salt Lake City: Deseret News Co., 1884), pp. 31, 37–38.

42. In Orson F. Whitney, *Life of Heber C. Kimball* (1888; reprint, Collector's Edition, Salt Lake City: Bookcraft, 1992), p. 105.

43. See George A. Smith, "My Journal," *Instructor* 81 (August 1946): 369.

44. See "Memoirs of George A. Smith," typescript copy, Harold B. Lee Library, Brigham Young University, Provo, Utah, p. 59.

45. Orasmus Turner, *History of the Pioneer Settlement of Phelps and Gorham's Purchase, and Morris' Reserve* (Rochester, New York: William Alling, 1852), p. 213.

46. See Lucy Mack Smith, *History of Joseph Smith*, pp. 179–86.

47. Cited in Rob Morris, *The Biography of Eli Bruce* (Louisville, Ky.: Morris and Monsarrat, 1861), pp. 266–67.

48. In announcing the purpose of his newspaper, Cole said it was to "correct the morals and improve the mind" of the readership. See the Palmyra *Reflector*, New Series, no. 4, p. 29.

49. *Reflector*, June 30, 1830, p. 53. In a later issue Cole repeats his insinuation against Joseph Smith by saying he had "been surnamed the ignoramus" (see *Reflector*, July 7, 1830, p. 60).

50. *Reflector*, January 18, 1831, p. 84.

51. *Reflector*, January 1, 1831, p. 72.

52. *Reflector*, July 7, 1830, p. 60.

53. *Reflector*, July 27, 1830, p. 79.

54. *Reflector*, February 14, 1831, p. 102.

55. *Reflector*, February 1, 1831, p. 95.

56. *Reflector*, February 14, 1831, p. 103.

57. *Reflector*, January 1, 1831, p. 72.

58. *Reflector*, February 1, 1831, p. 92.

59. *Reflector*, February 14, 1831, p. 100.

60. *Reflector,* March 19, 1831, p. 126.

61. *Reflector,* February 14, 1831, p. 100.

62. See *Reflector,* January 6, 1831, p. 76.

63. Lucy Mack Smith, *History of Joseph Smith,* pp. 168–71.

64. The events described in this missionary journey constitute a synthesis of materials gathered from several sources, including Lucy Mack Smith, *History of Joseph Smith,* pp. 172–76; Lucy Mack Smith, "Joseph Smith, Sr., Family Biography," Harold B. Lee Library, Brigham Young University, Provo, Utah; George A. Smith, "Memoirs of George A. Smith," typescript copy, Harold B. Lee Library, Brigham Young University, Provo, Utah; George A. Smith, "Sketch of the Autobiography of George Albert Smith," *Millennial Star* 27 (July 1, 1865): 406–8; George A. Smith, "My Journal," *Instructor* 81 (January 1946): 7–10; George A. Smith, in *Journal of Discourses* 5:101–4.

65. *History of the Church* 4:193.

66. *History of the Church* 6:74.

67. Edward Stevenson, "In Early Days," *Juvenile Instructor* 29 (July 15, 1894): 443–45.

68. See Edward Stevenson, "Incidents of My Early Days in the Church," *Juvenile Instructor* 29 (August 15, 1894): 523–24.

69. Edward Stevenson, "Incidents of My Early Days in the Church," *Juvenile Instructor* 29 (September 1, 1894): 551–52.

70. *Messenger and Advocate* 2 (June 1836): 331.

71. Lucy Mack Smith, *History of Joseph Smith,* p. 244.

72. In Lucy Mack Smith, "Joseph Smith, Sr., Family Biography," p. 44.

73. Lucy Mack Smith, "Joseph Smith, Sr., Family Biography," pp. 43–44.

74. *History of the Church* 2:467.

75. *History of the Church* 2:446–47.

76. Rom. 9:6.

77. The quotations from the journal of John Smith are found in Lucy Mack Smith, *History of Joseph Smith,* p. 245.

78. George A. Smith to Thomas Bullock, February 15, 1859, LDS Church Archives.

79. Cited in Lucy Mack Smith, *History of Joseph Smith,* p. 245.

80. George A. Smith to Thomas Bullock, February 15, 1859.

81. Cited in Lucy Mack Smith, *History of Joseph Smith,* p. 245.

82. George A. Smith to Thomas Bullock, February 15, 1859.

83. *History of the Church* 2:441.

84. In Whitney, *Life of Heber C. Kimball,* pp. 96–97.

Chapter 7. Against the World

1. 1 Kgs. 19:12.
2. Hel. 5:30.
3. Hel. 5:46.
4. 3 Ne. 11:3.
5. See 1 Kgs. 19:9–12; Hel. 5:30.
6. Hel. 5:47.
7. John 14:18, 27.
8. See Rev. 12:10.
9. 1 Cor. 14:10.
10. Matt. 7:20–21.
11. "The Testimony of Parley Chase," in E. D. Howe, *History of Mormonism* (Painesville, Ohio: E. D. Howe, 1840), p. 248.
12. "The Testimony of David Stafford," in Howe, *History of Mormonism*, p. 249.
13. "The Testimony of Barton Stafford," in Howe, *History of Mormonism*, p. 250.
14. W. Wyl, *Mormon Portraits, or The Truth About the Mormon Leaders from 1830 to 1886* (Salt Lake City: Tribune Printing and Publishing Co., 1886), pp. 17, 276.
15. Letter of Joel K. Noble to Professor Jonathan B. Turner, March 8, 1842, cited in Wesley P. Walters, "From Occult to Cult With Joseph Smith, Jr.," *Journal of Pastoral Practice* 1 (Summer 1977): 133.
16. Pomeroy Tucker, *Origin, Rise, and Progress of Mormonism* (New York: D. Appleton and Co., 1867), p. 17.
17. See, for example, William H. Kelly, "The Hill Cumorah, and the Book of Mormon . . . from Late Interviews," *Saints' Herald* 28 (June 1, 1881): 163, 165, 167.
18. Affidavit of William S. Smith, sworn on March 15, 1884, and recorded in *The Braden and Kelley Debate* (St. Louis, Mo.: The Christian Publishing Co., 1884), pp. 388–91.
19. Clark Braden, "Mr. Braden's Seventh Speech on the Third Proposition," in *The Braden and Kelley Debate*, p. 369.
20. E. W. Vanderhoof, *Historical Sketches of Western New York* (Buffalo, New York: The Matthews–Northrup Works, 1907), pp. 135, 134.
21. "The Yankee Mahomet," *American Whig Review* 7 (June 1851): 555.
22. Edward Stevenson, *Reminiscences of Joseph, the Prophet, and the Coming Forth of the Book of Mormon* (Salt Lake City: Edward Stevenson, 1893), p. 5.
23. Edward Stevenson, "Incidents of My Early Days in the Church," *Juvenile Instructor* 29 (September 1, 1894): 552.

24. Wilford Woodruff, *Leaves from My Journal* (Salt Lake City: Juvenile Instructor Office, 1881), p. 94.

25. "The Life of Joseph Holbrook, Written by His Own Hand," copies in private, family possession, pp. 12, 13.

26. "Letter From Joseph Fielding," dated June 20, 1841, in *Millennial Star* 2 (August 1841): 54.

27. In Kenneth W. Godfrey, Audrey M. Godfrey, and Jill Mulvay Derr, *Women's Voices: An Untold History of the Latter-day Saints, 1830–1900* (Salt Lake City: Deseret Book Co., 1982), p. 60.

28. Lucy Mack Smith, *History of Joseph Smith by His Mother*, ed. Preston Nibley (Salt Lake City: Bookcraft, 1958), p. 182.

29. Eliza R. Snow Smith, *Biography and Family Record of Lorenzo Snow* (Salt Lake City: Deseret News Co., 1884), p. 10.

30. LeRoi C. Snow, "How Lorenzo Snow Found God," *Improvement Era* 40 (February 1937): p. 84.

31. See "Oliver Cowdery Docket," August 14, 25, and 26, 1937, Huntington Library, San Marino, California.

32. Eliza R. Snow Smith, *Biography and Family Record*, pp. 21–22.

33. See Eliza R. Snow Smith, *Biography and Family Record*, pp. 22–24; and Eliza R. Snow's recollections in Edward W. Tullidge, *The Women of Mormondom* (New York: Tullidge and Crandall, 1877; reprint, Salt Lake City, 1975), pp. 102–3.

34. In Tullidge, *The Women of Mormondom*, p. 103.

35. In Tullidge, *The Women of Mormondom*, p. 97.

36. In Tullidge, *The Women of Mormondom*, p. 95.

37. Oliver Cowdery, "Rise of the Church, Letter VIII," *Times and Seasons* 2 (May 1, 1841): 396.

38. *History of the Church* 4:190, 191.

39. Joseph Smith, journal, ca. 1841–43, in Scott H. Faulring, ed., *An American Prophet's Record: The Diaries and Journals of Joseph Smith* (Salt Lake City: Signature Books, 1989), pp. 249–50.

40. See *History of the Church* 4:191–97; also in *Times and Seasons* 1 (September 1840): 170–73.

41. Luke 6:44.

42. Luke 6:45.

43. Matt. 12:36–37.

44. James 3:6.

45. John 7:51.

46. Joseph Smith, *The Personal Writings of Joseph Smith*, ed. Dean C. Jessee (Salt Lake City: Deseret Book Co., 1984), p. 458.

47. *History of the Church* 4:541, italics in the original.

48. *History of the Church* 2:281.

49. From diary entry (November 22, 1870) of John D. Lee, in Robert Glass Cleland and Juanita Brooks, eds., *A Mormon Chronicle:*

The Diaries of John D. Lee, 1848–1876, 2 vols. (Salt Lake City: University of Utah Press, 1983), 2:147.

50. Joseph Smith, *Teachings of the Prophet Joseph Smith,* sel. Joseph Fielding Smith (Salt Lake City: Deseret Book Co., 1938), p. 139.

51. Reported in Joseph Smith, *The Words of Joseph Smith,* ed. Andrew F. Ehat and Lyndon W. Cook (Provo, Utah: Religious Studies Center, Brigham Young University, 1980), p. 252.

52. Joseph Smith, *Teachings of the Prophet Joseph Smith,* p. 129.

53. Joseph Smith, *The Words of Joseph Smith,* p. 7.

54. See *History of the Church* 1:317.

55. Joseph Smith, *The Words of Joseph Smith,* p. 160.

56. Joseph Smith, *The Words of Joseph Smith,* p. 257.

57. See Joseph Smith, *The Words of Joseph Smith,* p. 221.

58. See Joseph Smith, *Teachings of the Prophet Joseph Smith,* p. 123.

59. Joseph Smith, *The Words of Joseph Smith,* p. 257.

60. Cited in Ruby K. Smith, *Mary Bailey* (Salt Lake City: Deseret Book Co., 1954), p. 56; also in Dean Jarmen, "Life and Contributions of Samuel H. Smith," master's thesis, Brigham Young University, 1961, p. 63.

61. *History of the Church* 1:466. See also D&C 124:15, wherein the Lord announces that he loves Hyrum Smith "because of the integrity of his heart, and because he loveth that which is right before me."

62. In Osborne J. P. Widtsoe, "Hyrum Smith, Patriarch," *Utah Genealogical and Historical Magazine* 2 (April 1911): 61.

63. Joseph F. Smith, "Joseph Smith as a Boy," *Improvement Era* 9 (December 1905): 108–9.

64. Cited in J. W. Peterson, "W. B. Smith's Last Statement," *Zion's Ensign* 5 (January 13, 1894): 6; also in: "Another Testimony: Statement of William Smith, Concerning Joseph, the Prophet," *Deseret Evening News,* January 20, 1894.

65. William Smith, *William Smith on Mormonism* (Lamoni, Iowa: Herald Steam Book and Job Office, 1883), pp. 9–10.

66. William Smith, "Notes Written on 'Chamber's Life of Joseph Smith,'" LDS Church Archives, p. 18.

67. In Ronald W. Walker, "Lucy Mack Smith Speaks to the Nauvoo Saints," *BYU Studies* 32 (Winter and Spring 1992): 279.

68. To better comprehend the spirit of what is involved, and for illustrations of false witnesses repeatedly borne against the Prophet and his family, see Hugh Nibley, *The Myth Makers* (Salt Lake City: Bookcraft, 1961; reprinted in *Tinkling Cymbals and Sounding Brass,* vol. 11 of *The Collected Works of Hugh Nibley* [Salt Lake City: Deseret Book Co., and Foundation for Ancient Research and Mormon Studies, 1991], pp. 103–406).

69. Much of the available evidence has been summarized in

Richard Lloyd Anderson, *Joseph Smith's New England Heritage* (Salt Lake City: Deseret Book Co., 1971). See also LaMar E. Garrard, "Traditions of Honesty and Integrity in the Smith Family," in Robert L. Millet, ed., *"To Be Learned Is Good If . . ."* (Salt Lake City: Bookcraft, 1987), pp. 9–19.

70. From John Smith, journal, cited in Anderson, *Joseph Smith's New England Heritage*, pp. 95–97.

71. John Smith, journal, cited in Anderson, *Joseph Smith's New England Heritage*, p. 98.

72. Lucy Mack Smith, *History of Joseph Smith*, pp. 32–40.

73. Norwich Town Record (1813–17), p. 53.

74. Lucy Mack Smith, *History of Joseph Smith*, p. 59.

75. Lucy Mack Smith, *History of Joseph Smith*, p. 60.

76. Lucy Mack Smith, *History of Joseph Smith*, p. 60.

77. Lucy Mack Smith, *History of Joseph Smith*, p. 61.

78. See Garrard, "Traditions of Honesty," p. 18.

79. Cited in Kelley, "The Hill Cumorah," p. 165.

80. Cited in Kelley, "The Hill Cumorah," p. 165.

81. Lemuel Durfee, account book, 1825–1829.

82. See Richard Lloyd Anderson, "Joseph Smith's New York Reputation Reappraised," *BYU Studies* 10 (Spring 1970): 292–93.

83. See Lucy Mack Smith, *History of Joseph Smith*, p. 47.

84. See Lucy Mack Smith, *History of Joseph Smith*, p. 68.

85. See *History of the Church* 2:427. Our historical records differ somewhat as to the identity of the angel. Lydia Knight quoted the Prophet as saying it was the Savior (see Susa Young Gates [under the pseudonym "Homespun"], *Lydia Knight's History* [Salt Lake City: Juvenile Instructor Office, 1883], p. 33), while Truman O. Angell, also quoting the Prophet, recorded that it was the Apostle Peter (see Lyndon Cook, "The Apostle Peter and the Kirtland Temple," *BYU Studies* 15 [Summer 1975]: 550–52).

86. See *History of the Church* 4:194.

87. See Lucy Mack Smith, *History of Joseph Smith*, p. 313.

88. One treatment that shows how the enemies of the Prophet and his family established the practice of repeating falsehoods previously introduced by earlier enemies of the Prophet and his family is Nibley's *The Myth Makers*.

89. See, again, Nibley's *The Myth Makers*.

Chapter 8. Measuring Greatness

1. See D&C 84:33–39.

2. See D&C 76:92–95.

3. See "Vision of the Spirit World," *Utah Genealogical and Historical Magazine* 19 (October 1928): 147.

4. *Deseret Weekly News,* November 7, 1896, cited in N. B. Lundwall, comp., *Temples of the Most High* (reprint, Collector's Edition, Salt Lake City: Bookcraft, 1993), pp. 321–22.

5. See Joseph F. Smith, in Conference Report, April 1916, p. 3.

6. Joseph Smith, *Teachings of the Prophet Joseph Smith,* sel. Joseph Fielding Smith (Salt Lake City: Deseret Book Co., 1938), p. 326.

7. See Benjamin F. Johnson, *My Life's Review* (Independence, Mo.: Zion's Printing and Publishing, 1947), p. 97.; see also Benjamin F. Johnson to George S. Gibbs, 1903, LDS Church Archives.

8. See Ronald W. Walker, "Lucy Mack Smith Speaks to the Nauvoo Saints," *BYU Studies* 32 (Winter and Spring 1992): 281.

9. Harold B. Lee, in Conference Report, April 1970, p. 6.

10. Harold B. Lee to Joseph Fielding Smith Family, July 14, 1972.

11. See D&C 137:5.

12. D&C 124:19; also in *History of the Church* 4:276.

13. See *History of the Church* 4:196.

14. See *History of the Church* 4:190.

15. *History of the Church* 4:191.

16. In Lyndon W. Cook and Milton V. Backman, Jr., eds., *Kirtland Elder's Quorum Record, 1836–1841* (Provo, Utah: Grandin Book Co., 1985), pp. 22–23.

17. See Terry and Nora Lund, *Pulsipher Family History Book* (1953; reprinted, 1963, copies in private, family possession), pp. 18–19.

Index